T0305437

The DVD no longer

accompanies this book.

DVD files can be found at

www.booksupport.wiley.com

where you enter the ISBN

9780787986322

Discussing the Undiscussable

JB JOSSEY-BASS

Discussing the Undiscussable

A GUIDE TO OVERCOMING DEFENSIVE ROUTINES IN THE WORKPLACE

William R. Noonan

Foreword by Chris Argyris

John Wiley & Sons, Inc.

Published by Jossey-Bass
A Wiley Imprint
989 Market Street, San Francisco, CA 94103-1741-www.josseybass.com

Wiley Bicentennial logo: Richard J. Pacifico

The DVD-ROM is copyright (c) by William R. Noonan and Shell Oil Company. The materials contained on this DVD-ROM, including any software and all content, are protected by United States and international copyright laws. Your rights to use them are governed by terms of this license agreement. BY PLAYING THE DVD-ROM, YOU ARE AGREEING TO ALL OF THE TERMS BELOW. If you do not agree to these conditions, contact Jossey-Bass, An Imprint of Wiley, to arrange for return before any use.

THE MATERIAL ON THIS DISK IS PROVIDED "AS IS." NEITHER THE AUTHORS OF THE MATERIAL NOR JOSSEY-BASS MAKE ANY WARRANTIES OF ANY KIND, EXPRESS OR IMPLIED, REGARDING EITHER THE FUNCTIONALITY OR THE CONTENTS. NEITHER THE AUTHORS NOR JOSSEY-BASS ASSUME ANY RESPONSIBILTIY FOR ERRORS OR OMISSIONS, OR DAMAGES, INCLUDING ANY INCIDENTAL, SPECIAL OR CONSEQUENTIAL DAMAGES. TO THE FULLEST EXTENT PERMISSIBLE BY LAW, JOSSEY-BASS DISCLAIMS ALL WARRANTIES OF MERCHANTABILITY AND FITNESS FOR A PARTICULAR PURPOSE.

Readers should be aware that Internet Web sites offered as citations and/or sources for further information may have changed or disappeared between the time this was written and when it is read.

Limit of Liability/Disclaimer of Warranty: While the publisher and author have used their best efforts in preparing this book, they make no representations or warranties with respect to the accuracy or completeness of the contents of this book and specifically disclaim any implied warranties of merchantability or fitness for a particular purpose. No warranty may be created or extended by sales representatives or written sales materials. The advice and strategies contained herein may not be suitable for your situation. You should consult with a professional where appropriate. Neither the publisher nor author shall be liable for any loss of profit or any other commercial damages, including but not limited to special, incidental, consequential, or other damages.

Jossey-Bass books and products are available through most bookstores. To contact Jossey-Bass directly call our Customer Care Department within the U.S. at 800-956-7739, outside the U.S. at 317-572-3986, or fax 317-572-4002.

Jossey-Bass also publishes its books in a variety of electronic formats. Some content that appears in print may not be available in electronic books.

Library of Congress Cataloging-in-Publication Data

Noonan, William R.
    Discussing the undiscussable: a guide to overcoming defensive routines in the workplace/
William R. Noonan; foreword by Chris Argyris.—1st ed.
        p.   cm.—(Jossey-Bass business & management series)
    Includes bibliographical references and index.
    ISBN 978-0-7879-8632-2 (pbk.)
  1. Conflict management. I. Title.
    HD42.N66   2007
    650.1'3—dc22

                                                                                    2007013596

Printed in the United States of America
FIRST EDITION
PB Printing   10 9 8 7 6 5 4 3 2 1

THE JOSSEY-BASS
BUSINESS & MANAGEMENT SERIES

CONTENTS

Much research has been done on the negative impact of organizational defensive routines. Many change programs have been and continue to be executed to reduce them, and the dominant focus has been to change the culture of the organization. Yet the effectiveness of cultural change programs as documented by evaluations of the participants varies from very effective to quite ineffective. And even when participants report that the programs produced positive changes, the changes have not persisted. Why?

Most individuals answer this question by saying that

- Organizations are too rigid and bureaucratic. They contain organizational defensive routines that inhibit learning and change.
- There is a lack of appropriate rewards.
- There is a lukewarm commitment to change from those at the top.

I often hear additional explanations for why successful change is not sustainable. The following are the three main explanations I've heard:

- Most busy executives do not have the time that is required to generate lasting commitment by others.
- It is frustrating getting people to realize that they are responsible for the problem and to stop blaming others or the system.
- Many executives express concern about harming their reputation if they take initiatives that are too risky.

The implication is that if we can reduce or eliminate these problems, culture change will flow more easily and be more persistent.

I have tested the implications of removing these obstacles to sustainable change, and my findings suggest several conclusions. First, it is true that organizational cultural factors do inhibit effective change. To implement a new culture, we require the support of the type of culture that we have been able to specify but have so far been unable to create. A new culture would have to include reward systems and champions necessary to support the change. On the level of interpersonal interactions, fears associated with the loss of reputation and career can inhibit change. Resistance to changing behavior and overcoming blindness is always difficult to overcome. And the constraints of everyday pressures will inhibit the effectiveness of any change initiative.

A key criterion for effective cultural change is to change behavior. But if the changes are to persist, we must identify the most fundamental causes of the behavior. They are (1) the theories-in-use human beings hold about effective learning, (2) the defensive reasoning mind-sets that they use to design and execute their actions, (3) the organizational defensive routines that reward anti-learning, self-sealing processes, (4) the ways in which we are all causally responsible for creating these counterproductive features, and (5) our skilled unawareness and skilled incompetence, which prevent us from producing the changes that we can identify but cannot produce in sustainable ways.

This is a nontrivial challenge often acknowledged and rarely engaged. William Noonan's book provides one of the most complete and detailed answers as to how to achieve change. He engages the puzzles head-on. He provides rich, warm, and thoughtful insights into his trials and tribulations while learning to become more effective. He connects this personal learning to recommendations as to how to design and implement changes in organizational defensive routines—changes that are both effective and sustainable. I recommend *Discussing the Undiscussable* as a first-rate example of how effective individual and organizational change can happen.

Cambridge, Massachusetts   Chris Argyris
July 2007

ACKNOWLEDGMENTS

First and foremost, I would like to acknowledge Chris Argyris, whose work inspired this book and whose personal encouragement set me on the path of transforming a workshop into a book. Throughout this book, I share my reflections on how I have put into practice the skills and concepts found in his research. The "how" could not have happened without the help of Diana Smith, Bob Putnam, and Phil McArthur, the partners of Action Design. They have been mentors, colleagues, and friends on this learning pathway, and their influence is evident throughout the book. Many of the concepts and templates used in this book are from Action Design.

There were many early supporters dedicated to a deeper understanding for how we all participate in defensive routines. The inception of the workshop took place during my tenure at Shell Oil Company in 1998. The company's Learning and Transformation Services provided me a forum in which to design, experiment, and conduct workshops. I am grateful to Jerome Adams, the director at that time, and in particular staff members Bill McQuillan and Madu Prasad for their help. Paul Menzel was the creative writer with whom I collaborated to write the DVD case study, "Fix It Now or Fix It Later" (along with the valuable advice from Bob Putnam). From that time on, a consistent friend and advocate for organizational learning has been David Capozzalo from SADAF in Saudi Arabia.

I am grateful to my graduate students at Marylhurst University, who willingly shared their case studies and eagerness to learn. I am in debt to Todd Cook for his assistance with the DVD. The staff and editors at Jossey-Bass, Kathe Sweeney, Jessie Mandle, Mary Garrett, Michele Jones, and Byron Schneider, were extremely helpful throughout the process of writing. Regina Maruca shepherded the book from draft to its final version with her eye for style, flow, and clarity.

I am very fortunate to be married to a writer, so last and most important, I am grateful to Lori Russell, my wife and partner in the writing arts. Taking only the DVD script and suggestions from me, she wrote the fictional accounts of Mark and Brenda. She made them real people through her art, with the hope that you, as the reader, can recognize what we do to get ourselves into defensive routines and what we can do to alter them.

Bill Noonan is an educator and consultant who works with many leading learning organizations. His practice includes facilitation, executive coaching, and conducting workshops, and he collaborated on two Web-based learning programs: *Forging Breakthroughs with Peter Senge* (Ninthhouse) and *Productive Business Dialogues* and *Managing Difficult Conversations* (Harvard Business Review Publishing Company).

Noonan teaches at Marylhurst University in the Business Department, the Art Therapy Department, and the Religious Studies Department; he also teaches the philosophy series at Columbia Gorge Community College. He lives with his family in The Dalles, Oregon.

Defining Defensive Routines

Part One introduces you to the layout of the book, a definition of defensive routines, and the work of Chris Argyris and Donald Schön. A review of their work establishes a common understanding of the basic concepts and the foundational skill set used throughout the book.

Framing the Issue
The Work of Chris Argyris

Innovation, ingenuity, and thinking outside the box are often cited as hallmarks of successful organizations, but in practice, their occurrence is rare. More likely, the "way things work around here" is a litany of missed deadlines, low morale, strained relationships, and inept problem solving. In fact, many organizations manage to operate far below the standards of excellence they strive for. Why is that the case?

No one sits down and says, "Okay, here's our plan for lowering morale in the company." No one asks, "What can we do to run this project into the ground?" We are human beings who desire to succeed, to foster creativity, to be competent, and to value the dignity of work. Yet we find ourselves being ineffective, settling for less, and caught in escalating cycles of unproductive behavior toward each other. We also tend to cover up inefficiency to protect ourselves, and come to see those actions as necessary, realistic, and even caring. How does this happen?

I have written this book to help people and their companies sort out these puzzles of human behavior. My inspiration and the foundation for this book is the work of Chris Argyris. Professor Argyris has dedicated his life's work to the topic of human behavior in organizations. His research has shown that our reactions to conditions of threat and embarrassment create patterns of behavior that he refers to as *organizational defensive routines*. These routines are predictable and ubiquitous in the world of work, and ultimately they do not serve the best interests of an organization. Understanding how each one of us participates in these dynamics is an important step toward creating a productive workplace. Learning how to mitigate or even avoid the resulting discord and loss of productivity is another. My goal is to help you accomplish both. This book, along with its accompanying interactive materials, attempts to make Chris Argyris's work more accessible and practical.

WHAT IS AN ORGANIZATIONAL DEFENSIVE ROUTINE?

Organizational defensive routines arise when we find ourselves under the conditions of threat or embarrassment. In reaction to these conditions, we engage in a characteristic mode of defensive reasoning and behavior. We think, "The problem is not me, but you." If both parties are thinking in the same defensive mode about each other, then the stage is set for some nasty behavior.

Although we would not think of ourselves as being unreasonable or ill intended, we readily concoct private explanations about why others do what they do. We make attributions about each other's motives and intentions and hold other parties accountable for the difficulty when we find ourselves at odds with one another. In the privacy of our own minds, we hold our positions with a high degree of certainty. It is hard to listen when you think the other person is dead wrong. Yet we will be the first to call "Unfair!" if we don't think the other person is listening to us.

None of what we are thinking is spoken directly to the person involved. In fact, when and if we share our emotionally charged assessments, theories, and explanations, we generally do so only with those individuals who we feel will be sympathetic to our views. These private conversations are held behind closed doors, in the hallways and break rooms. Nothing is discussed in public meetings, and rarely, if ever, do the targets of those third-party conversations ever find out what we really think. The result is "open secrets," "undiscussables," or the "elephant in the room." Most everyone can think of some example of this, often accompanied by a juicy story. What is often left out of the story is the teller's complicit participation in it. There is no awareness of how he or she might be involved in creating the open secret, the undiscussable, or the elephant in the room.

These dynamics become a routine part of the workplace culture. Whole departments become encased in assumptions and expectations that feed predictable, vicious cycles of human behavior. As organizational defensive routines take hold of a company's culture, the consequences are increasingly troubling. I have observed companies in which defensive routines proliferate to the point where the organizational culture becomes so toxic to working relationships that the organization's productivity suffers dramatically.

Defensive routines become so ingrained in our social behavior that they become an accepted part of the "way things work around here." What becomes apparent is that the organization, project, or team isn't all that it's cracked up to be. No one is walking the talk, and everyone knows it. When this realization dawns on us, our first reaction is usually sadness, disappointment, or a physical sensation of being let down. People talk of being deflated and dispirited. There is a loss of animation. Animation, by the way, derives from the Latin word *animus* (m.) or *anima* (f.), "soul." That definition holds true here. There is a loss of soul.

But even that isn't the whole story. Along with that loss comes a sense of helplessness. Organizational defensive routines are experienced and reported as being external to anyone's control or influence. We distance ourselves from any sense of personal responsibility. We don't realize that we might be as much a part of the problem as the next person. No one knows how to break the cycle and start afresh. This self-fueling, counterproductive process exists in all organizations and plays out in one-to-one interactions, in groups, and across organizational divisions, time and again, to the detriment of all.

These situations are depressing, to put it mildly. They are also much more common than we'd like to think, in organizations of all sizes, shapes, and geographies. But there is a way to break the cycle. And although the process is difficult, it is doable and very much worth the effort.

HOW I CAME TO WRITE THIS BOOK

I came to know Chris Argyris's work and to write this book through an untraditional route. My academic background is steeped in the liberal arts fields of philosophy, psychology, religious studies, and folklore. Prior to my career as an educator and consultant, I made the rounds in a variety of health care professions, mainly in care of the sick and dying.

I never thought I would be writing a business book. Fortunately, my background, particularly in the study of philosophy, has served me well in this line of work. In the study of philosophy, reflection is a requirement, and critical thinking is an essential tool, just as it is in the field of organizational learning. I have never been attracted to a philosophy that is disconnected from living, nor do I desire to ponder thoughts without understanding their practical implications. I follow the precepts of the philosopher Epicurus, who said, "Empty is the argument of the philosopher which does not relieve any human suffering." Translated into the language of action science, knowledge must be actionable if it is to be at all useful.

I recognized in Chris Argyris's work a program of attraction for those with an appetite for reflection. He prescribes a different way of thinking and acting that holds the promise of greater learning, reduction of error, and a fair exchange between conflicting views. Simply said, he offers us a better, more excellent way of behaving in the workplace. In my world of philosophy, demonstrations of the best of human action are called virtues. The word *virtue* comes from the Latin *virtus*, which is a translation of its Greek counterpart, *arête*, "excellence." The antidote to the vicious cycle of human behavior exhibited in defensive routines is a virtuous one in which we act well or most excellent with each other.

I made the connection between virtues and Chris Argyris's work one night when he spoke to a small group of us gathered at a friend's house. Argyris said, "People think that because I am a social scientist, I am interested in the truth. I am not interested in the truth as much as I am in justice: how to treat people with respect and dignity in the workplace." And at that moment, my heart was won over to his work. From my youthful days to adulthood, I was always involved in issues of justice. My generation acted to correct injustices and instilled in me a firm belief that things could change and that I could be part of that effort.

My confidence in my ability, as one individual, to change the world has tempered over the years, but I still believe in the pursuit of justice. Instead of trying to change the world, I now focus closer to home. Thomas Merton, a Trappist monk who lived and died during the turbulent 1960s, once said, "Social justice is how you treat the person next to you." Every encounter I have has become an opportunity to act justly. That evening, Argyris's statement confirmed a connection between his work and the passion I felt for the cardinal virtue of justice.

Acquiring the mind-set and skill set proposed by Argyris for a more just workplace is a matter of learning new behavior through practice. When watching Argyris interact with workshop participants, I would always hear him say, "So, how would you do it? What would you say?" He was interested in seeing if people could produce the behavior they thought would be effective and well intended. He, like other practitioners of action science, was also offering the person a chance to practice.

We learn to do something well by doing it. Practice involves the repeated necessary actions for perfecting a craft. It is the cultivation of good habits. There are good "habits of practice," a definition for virtues used by Thomas Aquinas, to be found in Argyris's work. Like any virtuous activity, these habits of practice don't come naturally, but come about only by doing them. Practice is something we can do, and if we do it well, we can alter the destructive path of defensive routines.

FROM WORKSHOP TO BOOK

In 1998, I had a chance to engage in a full-time practice by working an entire year as an external consultant to Shell Oil Company's Learning and Transformation Services. As part of my work there, I developed a two-day workshop called "Unlocking Organizational Defensive Routines," designed to focus on the interpersonal nature of organizational defensive routines and the practical skill set needed to unlock them. I conducted the workshops while at Shell Oil and, beyond my tenure there, for other companies both nationally and internationally.

On a visit to Shell Oil, Chris Argyris came across my workshop manual and contacted me with the idea of transforming the workshop into a book format. And that is what I have done. Sample lectures have become chapters. The exercises and video scenario, "Fix It Now or Fix It Later," are incorporated into the book in order to facilitate the same aim of the workshop: to help you understand your role in organizational defensive routines.

My intentions in this book are to render the work of Chris Argyris into the everyday language of personal interactions. I hope to faithfully represent his work at a conceptual level and, more important, make it come alive for those who wish to put into practice the skill set and concepts based on his research. In this endeavor, I hope to fulfill what I believe is his true desire for his work: to make it actionable.

I should note, however, that although the concepts and skill set found in this book are Chris Argyris's intellectual property, I do bring to his work my own experience. As of this writing, I have been a practitioner of his work for more than fourteen years. I have striven to put into practice the thinking and actions prescribed by his research. In this book, I offer up my own mistakes, practical suggestions, and way of thinking about his work so as to help you practice it better.

THE STYLE OF THE BOOK

Organizational defensive routines have been the subject of many scholarly articles and books, but this is not one of them. This book contains no longitudinal studies, empirically based research, or extensive quotations from the field's literature. Although these methodologies of academia are valuable, they run the risk of objectifying organizational defensive routines as a phenomenon to be studied apart from our own involvement. I want to avoid creating any further distance from this human reality that is already designed to remove us from any accountability for its existence.

For this reason, I am not writing in an academic voice, but a personal one. I will rely on examples of my own thinking and acting to demonstrate the qualities of defensive reasoning. I will share case studies and stories from my consulting practice to illustrate this fundamental human dynamic we have in common with each other. I hope that the use of my personal voice will evoke a sense of identification on your part. If it does, then you will stand a greater chance of altering the defensive routines in which you participate with the people in your daily life.

Use of Metaphors

My personal voice gravitates toward the use of metaphor. I like playing with metaphors. They appeal to more than just our intellect. They tickle the imagination, evoke emotions, and establish common meaning quickly. Metaphors help us grasp complex realities and apprehend their entirety in a single image. In the words of Paul Riceour, a French philosopher of linguistics, metaphors "yield a surplus of meaning." Imaginative metaphors can tutor our imaginations and thoughts in new directions.

I hope to expand the metaphorical vocabulary for how we think about organizational defensive routines. Currently our language is bound up in the mechanical imagery of controlling and fixing them. We need metaphors to help us dispel their "aura of externality" so that we can more easily discover our own complicity. The right metaphor can help us find a new direction for freeing ourselves from their destructive impact.

Use of Storytelling

In this book, I also use storytelling as a means of making sense of organizational defensive routines and as a teaching tool. Traditionally, business books have used case studies as a format for teaching business principles. They are a form of story, but objectified and removed from the reader. This approach is valuable to a cognitive comprehension of various business issues and challenges. In fact, a little distance helps the process of moving from the concrete to general principles.

In the case of organizational defensive routines, however, "a little distance" can only further reinforce the perception that they are an external reality existing outside our personal influence or involvement. As previously mentioned, I wish to avoid this message, so I am relying on a fictional narrative instead of an abstracted business case. Fictional narrative has a greater potential to draw you deeper into the complexities of human interactions. Identification with the characters opens up the possibility of introspection—to see how similar or dissimilar you are to them.

The Fictional Narrative

The fictional narrative is called "Fix It Now or Fix It Later." The business context is specific to the oil industry, but the problem is generic to anyone who has had to face the decision to fix a soon-to-be-failing piece of equipment. Have you ever heard a small squeak or, worse, a slight grinding sound when you hit the brake pedal in your car? If you have, you might have thought something like, "Oh no, not now. I don't have time this week to be without my car. Besides, this is a bad month for a repair bill. I wonder if I can wait two weeks." You might wait the two weeks, get the brakes fixed, and move on. But then again, you might find yourself at some point pushing the brake pedal to the floor, not stopping, and smashing into the car in front of you. When you hear that first squeak, do you fix it now or run the risk of failure? The fictional narrative in this book begins with the characters facing just such a "squeak."

The characters in the narrative are dealing with a plant in the midst of a turnaround. During a turnaround, an entire unit is shut down for scheduled repair and maintenance. When the unit is down, it offers the opportunity for inspectors to examine equipment and perform tests on areas normally not accessible during full operation. During the current turnaround, an inspection report revealed additional problems. An exchanger is predicted to fail sometime in the next eighteen months, six months before the next scheduled turnaround.

An exchanger transfers heat out from one system into another. A common example is a car radiator. In the radiator, heat is transferred from the water to the air and out of the system. The water cools down and returns to the engine to repeat the cycle. Similar to a blown radiator, a malfunctioning exchanger can cause the system to overheat, resulting in serious damage to equipment.

The choice is to fix the exchanger now or to continue operating it, with the risk of failure. By taking the risk, Sales can deliver on its commitment to the customer, defer the cost of the repairs, and maintain the schedule as planned for the turnaround. At the same time, taking the risk might result in an unpredicted failure. Failure would impact the current operational budget, incur greater repair costs, cause hardship for the employees, and possibly damage the environment.

The Characters

The main characters are Brenda, the sales manager from the corporate office, and Mark, the operations manager for the plant. Brenda Fields is in her early forties and a career professional with the company. Early in her career, she worked as an operations manager. She has a strong technical background. Her knowledge of operations and distribution systems prepared her well for advancement in the business division. She is responsible for a related line of products that focuses on a specific group of customers. She oversees the capital budget, customer relations, and contract negotiations with customers. She goes to bat with senior business leaders for capital infusions for the plant.

From her vantage point, she sees the bigger picture of the business that takes into account the customer, technical operations, the marketplace, and the competition. She is willing to take risks. She is accountable to the senior leaders and business center.

Mark Listman is in his mid-thirties, working in his first managerial job. An operations manager is an entry-level management position. He has been with the company for nine years, having joined straight out of college. He has held two or three line positions in various technical fields.

His main responsibility is to manage one of the plant's product lines at its optimal capacity, safely and at the least possible cost. He is environmentally sensitive yet prudent. He is one of several peers reporting to the plant manager, Walter Burton, who carries the overall responsibility for the entire plant.

As you enter into their world, you may notice yourself taking sides with one or the other character. If you do, take note of the point in the story where you identify or side with Brenda or Mark. Similar to the defensive routines you come across at work, taking sides will only draw you into the defensive routine further and will ultimately render you ineffective. Instead, as you read along, see if you can track how both Mark and Brenda are contributing to the difficulty at hand. If you can, then you are well on your way to understanding how to intervene in defensive routines.

WHO IS THIS BOOK FOR?

You know that you're in the middle of an organizational defensive routine when you hope and pray you don't run into so-and-so today or, worse, have a meeting with him or her. Your head imagines what your organization is capable of, but your heart sinks with the thought of the "way things really work around here." If there is still an ounce of hope in you that things can change, then you have picked up the right book.

This book is not written for managers alone, nor is it written solely for consultants or coaches. Throughout the book, when you see the word "practitioner," understand that it means anyone who wishes to change things for the better. Practitioners exist in all positions and at all levels of an organization. They are managers, project leaders, internal OD consultants, Human Resources staff, and external consultants. They are also employees who have no managerial experience, but a desire to improve their workplace and their own contributions at work.

Anyone who comes in contact with organizational defensive routines will benefit from the exercises and easy-to-understand concepts found in this book. The book includes a DVD that supports the exercises, skill set, and concepts. You can use the DVD and chapter exercises in work group and team settings, as well as in your own private reflection. Any insight you gain into your participation in defensive routines will prove invaluable to you as a practitioner. To the degree that you can use the book's helpful hints and skill-building exercises to improve your own practice, the book will have succeeded in its main purpose.

In other settings, college professors will find the book's exercises and pedagogical methods helpful in creating more practice-oriented and interactive classroom presentations.

THE LAYOUT OF THE BOOK

Throughout the book, I will be referring to the terms, concepts, and skill set covered in Chris Argyris and Donald Schön's corpus of work. I will briefly introduce these concepts in Chapter Two. I will also address the initial misunderstandings or errors beginners often fall into when they first translate the concepts and tools into practice.

Chapters Three, Four, and Five open with narratives that show the characters, Mark and Brenda, exhibiting common characteristics endemic to the rise and maintenance of defensive routines. In all three chapters, the opening narrative fills you in on the back story to the business meeting available for viewing on the DVD. The opening narrative also serves as a jumping-off point for reflecting on the typical ways we react to the conditions of threat and embarrassment that commonly give rise to defensive routines.

Chapter Three explores the various types of conditions of threat and embarrassment. Chapter Four focuses on our internal reaction to potential threat and embarrassment and the need to maintain control. I discuss Chris Argyris's Model I, with its accompanying aims, beliefs, and values. Chapter Five covers the various bypass and cover-up strategies used to keep defensive routines in place.

In Chapter Six, Mark and Brenda's story culminates in a business meeting. Before reading Chapter Six, insert the DVD into a DVD player or computer and watch the business meeting take place. You can observe the full spectrum of interpersonal, team, and organizational defensive routines. Because of the magic of video, you will always be able to see a replay of the meeting and hear the characters' private thoughts. Their private thinking will reveal the typical kind of thinking that promotes defensive routines.

Chapter Six in effect marks the turning point in the book. The book's focus shifts from understanding how defensive routines come about to learning what to do with them. The technique of mapping, introduced in this chapter, demonstrates a method of tracking the interlocking patterns of defensive routines. This technique gives the practitioner a tool for presenting defensive routines that minimizes the tendency toward blaming and emphasizes the contributions of all participants. (The methodology for mapping is explored in detail in Appendix A.)

Chapter Seven describes the challenges that individuals, teams, and organizations must face in order to de-escalate defensive routines. This chapter, which opens with Mark and Brenda beginning to unravel their own defensive routines, focuses on self-reflection and the ways in which people can begin to engage their differences productively.

In Chapter Eight, we see a demonstration of the behavior capable of mitigating the negative effects of defensive routines. Here, Mark, Brenda, and their team are now able to model a productive conversation. In conjunction with working on the chapter exercises, you will be able to observe scenes from a business meeting where Mark and Brenda are able to move the dialogue forward to a positive outcome.

Without a change in mind-set, though, Mark and Brenda would not have been able to engage in mutual learning. Chapter Nine introduces the four key thought enablers that support the thinking needed to produce the kind of action we saw in Chapter Eight. In the business fable, DVD scenes reveal how and where Mark's and Brenda's transformed private *thinking* shows its influence and makes the productive *behavior* possible.

Chapter Ten is a meditation on the value of learning from mistakes. We've seen how people can diagnose and reverse an organizational defensive routine. But how can defensive routines be minimized, or even avoided, again and again? Chapter Ten offers thoughts on what makes it difficult to learn from mistakes and how to view them differently in order to correct them sooner and more easily.

Finally, Chapter Eleven is written for practitioners who wish to use the book's exercises in a group setting. I offer up my own mistakes as reflections on the pitfalls and common obstacles practitioners encounter when teaching the material or conducting a session where defensive routines exist.

⌒

Defensive routines play out in our interpersonal working relationships. Any alteration or reduction of defensive routines takes place in the same arena of human interaction. Therefore, how we relate to each other is the greatest leverage for change. The medium in which we work together is conversation. If we can improve the quality of our conversations, we can alter the dysfunctional nature of defensive routines and further organizational learning and success.

The Foundational Skill Set

Whether we are on the phone, in meetings, or in cyberspace, we are constantly exchanging ideas, gathering information, and putting plans into action, all through the medium of conversation. Our successes and failures depend on the quality of our thinking and communication.

Yet people have often said to me, "I don't have time to think." They say that although they are aware that their communications are unfocused and sometimes even misleading, they feel unable to analyze the problem and change their approach. Time is too dear; pressures are too great.

For these individuals, communication takes a backseat to the work at hand, even if the work at hand is steered and sometimes derailed by the poor quality of communication. Many times I've seen individual, team, and enterprise-wide change initiatives fail to deliver results because the groups involved lacked the critical reasoning and conversation skills necessary to achieve their vision.

Alternatively, most of the successful professionals I have encountered practice what Chris Argyris of Harvard and Donald Schön of MIT refer to as *double-loop learning*. In double-loop learning, the first loop is the common rapid-fire approach to solving problems, namely, to react by changing the course of action when something doesn't work. The second loop takes into account the thinking, values, and assumptions behind all the actions. If the actions were ineffective, these professionals examine the thinking that fueled those actions and how it can be changed

Double-loop learning relies on a skill set that invites challenge to our own thinking while also challenging the thinking of others. There are three tools presented in this chapter that together form this skill set. They are the Left Hand Column, the Ladder of Inference, and advocacy and inquiry. These tools were developed by Argyris and Schön in the mid-1970s as part of what they refer to as Model II thinking and behavior.

Using these tools can help people secure valid information on which to base decisions. They inject vitality and relevance into any exchange of views. Finally, they help people ensure that the best collective thinking is gleaned from multiple perspectives. Together, they are the antidote to defensive reasoning; they provide a substantive foundation for productive conversations.

I should note that the concepts and tools presented in this chapter reflect the initial work done by both Argyris and Schön. Beyond his initial work with Schön, Argyris continued his own research with a concentration on organizational defensive routines. The remaining chapters incorporate Argyris's subsequent research, which has continued to this day, along with the insights I have gained as I continue to study and apply this work. Throughout the book, I also rely heavily on the work of Action Design, a partnership of three former students of Chris Argyris: Robert Putnam, Phil McArthur, and Diana Smith. These individuals have advanced Argyris's work with additional concepts and a pedagogy for teaching his material. Action Design, in fact, coined the term that I prefer to use when describing Argyris's Model II thinking and behavior: the Mutual Learning Model.

The three tools are summarized in brief in the following box. They are explained in much greater depth in the rest of this chapter and are revisited throughout the book. If you are already familiar with these tools, you may be sorely tempted to skip this chapter, but I strongly recommend resisting the urge. For years, I sat through presentations on the Left Hand Column, the Ladder of Inference, and advocacy and inquiry. Prior to each presentation, I had the thought "I know this stuff." Yet without exception, I always heard something that deepened my understanding of the skill set. Each presenter provided a unique language of expression. I began writing down a phrase or image that seemed to capture a meaning better than I had in my own lectures. Each time, I said to myself, "I could use that."

My hope is that even if you are familiar with the tools, and even with the broader scope and depth of Argyris's work or that of Action Design, you will find something useful in this chapter. I will review the common errors and misrepresentations of the material often made during presentations and in beginning practice.

A Snapshot of the Three Tools

Tool: Left Hand Column

Purpose: The Left Hand Column (LHC) is a reflective tool that helps us monitor the thoughts and feelings we have that we deem unsuitable to share publicly. Used effectively, the LHC helps us process these private thoughts and feelings into information that can be useful in a productive conversation. The results are

- More information on the table for discussion
- Honest discussion of issues (fewer hidden agendas)
- Minimized emotional volatility
- Suspension of judgment
- Healthy mistrust of one's own thinking
- Identification of unchecked assumptions

Tool: Ladder of Inference

Purpose: The Ladder of Inference helps people identify what information or facts are used as the basis for their reasoning process. It also helps people understand how they interpret that information and how they apply their interpretation to the issue or problem at hand. Used effectively, the Ladder of Inference enables people to see how each other's thinking diverges on important issues and still to remain focused on discovering the relevant information contained therein. They can also test that information for accuracy and make an informed decision or conclusion. The results are

- An improved reasoning process
- Greater utilization of diverse thinking
- Minimized point-counterpoint conversations
- Greater confidence in the information used to make decisions and draw conclusions

THE LEFT HAND COLUMN

The Left Hand Column (LHC) is a shorthand reference to a technique Argyris and Schön created for reflecting on our thinking "after the fact." Essentially, you practice the technique by writing down a recollection of a conversation that proved to be difficult, didn't yield your desired results, or went in an unanticipated direction. On the right side of the page, you write down a sample of what was actually said (RHC); on the left side, you write down what you thought and felt, but did not say (LHC). The paper then becomes an artifact for reflection. The idea is to consider it later on (with a cool head and as much objectivity as you can muster) and look for telltale signs of thinking and actions that led to undesirable results.

What do our private thoughts reveal? Often the LHC illuminates unresolved tensions, suppressed feeling, and loss of information potentially vital to decision making. But these discoveries don't necessarily mean that we should share all our private thoughts! If we share them "as is," the results may be undesirable. We could make things worse by unduly upsetting people or placing ourselves in a vulnerable position. This is a basic dilemma of human communication—we often feel damned if we do and damned if we don't.

The goal, then, is to increase our awareness of this dilemma and the actions we take to filter our private thoughts. A careful reflection on our private thoughts and feelings, using the LHC, can help us process those thoughts and feelings into information useful in a productive conversation.

When first introduced to the Left Hand Column, many people express an eagerness to move LHC material quickly into the RHC. People want to know how to express what they are thinking and feeling in a productive way and in a public forum. Their immediate goal is "translation." This enthusiasm is admirable, but it can also be dangerous. Rushing to "reword" the LHC bypasses an essential step in the process: the difficult work of first truly understanding one's thinking as it is conveyed in the LHC.

This step is critical, because an examination of what is written in the LHC often reveals three prevailing, embedded assumptions:

1. The other person is the problem.

2. One's conclusion is factual.

3. One's view is complete rather than partial.

Until people see how these three assumptions are operating in their LHC, it is difficult to start the work of transforming LHC material productively. There is a tendency to see what is in the LHC as what is really going on. Thus beginners make the mistake of stating, "Let me tell you what is on my LHC" and then blurting out whatever is in their minds. I have seen this error reinforced by trainers who mistakenly think the LHC is an action tool. In a workshop, I once heard a trainer say, "If you are in a meeting and you have some LHC thoughts going on, all you have to do is say, 'I have a left hand column thought on that, and it is . . .'" When you hear something like that, you can usually take it as a signal to get ready for an emotionally charged doozie of a thought.

This error becomes frightening when permission to blurt out one's LHC becomes institutionalized. A manager once told me of her company's "Left Hand Column" meetings. The company practice was to have a regular business meeting with pads of paper for each participant. Each participant was to keep a record of his or her LHC thoughts during the course of the meeting. At the end of the meeting, everyone was asked to go around and share their LHC thoughts. After continual blowups and meetings running over time limits, people started to "pretty up" their LHCs and create Far Left Hand Column thoughts that they would share privately with others after the meeting.

In organizations that teach the LHC, "What's in your LHC?" has become a shortcut for saying, "What are your private thoughts?" Although it is language that can be used for a shared common understanding within an organization, its popular usage risks the reification of the original tool and the reinforcement of a common misunderstanding. A participant came up to me after a module on the LHC and said to me, "One of our managers yelled at me during a meeting, 'I want to know what is in the left hand corner of your brain!'"

The manager, wanting to know the man's private thoughts, instead communicated an innocently naïve understanding of the LHC as something that actually exists somewhere in our brains. Although the manager's notion of the LHC is a bit comical, it's not at all useful, and unfortunately, that interpretation of the LHC is in play in many organizations. Too often, I hear people talk about the LHC as if it were something tangible.

All of which leads me to emphasize, as much as I can, the importance of using the LHC as a reflective tool. The following box, "AWARE," offers one way to think about the tool and what it can help you accomplish.

Many important things go unsaid during meetings. They are discussed in the hallways and in "behind the scenes" private caucuses. Decreased effectiveness and lost time are two results of a group's inability to discuss what its members see as truly the problem. People want to be able to say out loud what they truly think and feel. This cannot happen until they become AWARE of their private thinking.

First, you need to develop an awareness of when your private thinking becomes toxic and worthy of censorship. In those moments, if you are unable to productively share what is in the LHC, it is best not to share it. The most you can expect is a prudent restraint once you know you have been triggered. Later, an "after-the-fact" exploration of your trigger points will eventually lead to a quicker recognition the next time your buttons get pushed and, you hope, a faster recovery.

AWARE

Awareness of your private thinking is the main purpose of the LHC tool; the tool does not give you permission to blurt out everything you think and feel.

Weigh the risks and benefits of sharing your LHC.

Assumptions that you hold with great certainty about others' being the problem and having bad motives decrease the chances of having a productive conversation.

Reframe your thinking; assume you are not aware of or do not understand others' motives, reasons, and data.

Explore what it is about you that triggered the thoughts and feelings in your LHC.

The ability to share your private thoughts increases as you become more accomplished in the use of the Ladder of Inference and the craft of producing quality advocacy and inquiry. As your skill increases, the more information can get out on the table for discussion in an honest and direct manner.

A quicker route, of course, would be to think differently altogether. Doing so, however, requires mastery of all these tools, which leads to a new level of fluency of thinking, action, and mutual learning. The key thought enablers described in Chapter Nine represent a few of the mental shifts of frame needed for mutual learning to take place. Ultimately, an honest appraisal of the limits of our own thinking should lead us to suspend our harsh judgments of others more often and develop a healthy mistrust of our own thinking. By reframing others in a different light, we can act differently toward them and improve our chances of getting better results.

THE LADDER OF INFERENCE

No matter how many times I hear it, I'm always amused when people refer to the Ladder of Inference as the "Ladder of Influence." This may be a Freudian slip betraying the person's mind-set, but I think that it is just as likely that they are unfamiliar with the word *inference*. The word is not in our common lexicon of daily usage, but it is what we do every day. We are constantly observing and taking in information. From the particulars we observe, we draw general conclusions. We infer meaning from the information we gather.

The Ladder of Inference is an important tool because when we are in the throes of a defensive routine, we don't stop and think about what we are thinking. Essentially, the Ladder of Inference is a metaphorical tool designed to help people understand and describe their use of inductive reasoning. Given what we see, what conclusions do we draw? Take the following example: if I see on my neighbor's porch a pile of rolled-up newspapers accumulating over a period of days, I can infer that he is not home. This inference is very probable and most likely the case, but it is not absolutely certain. Other inferences from the same data are possible. The neighbor could be ill or, worse, lying dead in the house. My inference can be validated only upon inspection.

Inferences deal in probabilities, but in general, we don't spend much time or energy confirming them. Instead, we tend to confuse our inferences with the facts. This is due to the amazing speed of our thinking process (a great thing), but there is a considerable downside. We think so very quickly that we're not conscious of all that goes on in our heads. We can walk into a room, size up what we see happening there, and respond almost instantaneously. Our quick thinking helps us make sense of our everyday experiences. Yet the same qualities that make our thinking so efficient also have limits.

We tend to consider our conclusions factual and obvious. It's as if a little voice inside our head were saying, "Of *course* this is what's happening. Isn't it obvious?" We may even wonder why others can't see how right we are. We expect them to see the obviousness of our thinking, and get frustrated if they don't share our views. Because our thinking seems to just pop into our heads, we never take the opportunity to slow down enough to see how we got from "there to here." Instead, we talk to each other from on top of our respective ladders. From on top, we think we are communicating well; in reality, however, we are only trading abstract conclusions back and forth.

The benefit of the Ladder of Inference is that it enables us to reflect on our thinking, separate fact from conclusion, and appreciate the limits of our thinking. The following box, "JUMP," summarizes the essence of the tool.

The Pool of Data and the Rungs on the Ladder

The most common depiction of the Ladder of Inference is one of a ladder standing in a pool of "data." For our purposes, *data* is all the available information, facts, and sensory stimuli that surround us in our everyday world. Our world constantly generates data. All data shares certain key characteristics:

- Data exists in limitless quantities—more than our minds can hold. That's why it is impossible to focus on all available data and why we necessarily select some data from the pool. An image of an ocean may be more fitting than a pool.

- Data is observable. You can see it. I can see it. Everyone can agree that the data exists independent of our interpretations. This means data is "hard," as if a video camera could capture its sights and sounds. Data includes spoken words, tone of voice, and gestures, as well as accounting reports, written memos, saved e-mail messages, statistical reports, tests, and marketing results.

- Data is often unintelligible unless we interpret it. For example, the stock market can drop 300 points in a day. That is simply a fact. The fact becomes significant only after we interpret and respond to it. Some may see it as a necessary correction; others might see a 300-point drop as a signal of serious trouble in the market and decide to stop investing in stocks.

We process data just as constantly as the world generates it. However, we can't take in *all* the information available to us. If we tried, our brains would short-circuit.

Each rung of the ladder represents a step we take to interpret data and arrive at a conclusion. The higher we climb on the ladder, the more general or abstract our thinking becomes, and the greater the chance that we and others in a conversation could be using different data or using the same data but interpreting it differently.

On the bottom rung, we *select data.* As I mentioned, it's difficult, if not impossible, to pay attention to all the information, facts, and sensory stimuli that bombard us in any given moment. Imagine what our lives would be like if we had to examine and interpret every piece of data we encountered. We'd become overwhelmed and paralyzed. Instead, as information comes in, we engage in a kind of selection-and-interpretation triage. We choose to focus on some bits of data and not others. Sometimes we consciously choose what we select or ignore; at other times, the choice feels spontaneous and intuitive.

Moving up the ladder, we begin to *interpret data.* That is, we assign meaning to the data we've selected. We interpret what we see, hear, read, and so forth. For example, we may hear certain words someone else says. Instantly we paraphrase in our own minds what we thought we heard. Often we inject our own meaning into those words, different than what the other person meant. Our interpretations are powerfully shaped by what's going on in our surroundings at the time, as well as by our expectations and past cultural and personal experiences.

At the top rung of the ladder, we *draw conclusions.* Our conclusions are the final outcome of our reasoning process. From the top of the ladder, our conclusions appear clear, obvious, and valuable to us, but not necessarily to others. When we state our brilliant ideas, we might not mention the reasoning that led us to those ideas. We might not cite the facts that we've selected. We feel no need to do so because the validity of our conclusion is so obvious to us.

Consider the following scenario: I'm delivering a performance review to an employee. As I'm discussing the person's performance, I notice that she's looking out the window *(select data).* I think to myself, "Hmmm . . . she doesn't seem to be paying attention" *(interpret data).* I decide that she's not interested in what I have to say, and begin questioning her commitment to her job *(draw conclusion).*

That's my view from the top of my ladder. Is it accurate? Could be. But it could also be very far off the mark. The employee may see something strange going on outside. I might have mayonnaise stuck to my cheek, and she's too polite or nervous to say so, but also doesn't want to stare. I may be intimidating her with my criticisms; I may be embarrassing her with my praise. If I don't stop and reflect on alternate possible interpretations, I'm doing both of us a disservice.

Mental Models

The way in which we climb our ladder is strongly influenced by our *mental models*—our values, assumptions, and beliefs about how the world works. To complete the visual image of a ladder, one can think of these mental models as the ladder's sides. Like the sides to a ladder, mental models hold the steps of our reasoning process together in a structured and coherent way. For example, if you hold the mental model "think positive," you might tend to notice only the happy or beneficial events taking place around you. Thus you might well conclude that the world is generally a good place. By contrast, someone who holds the mental model "expect the worst" would notice very different things and interpret them in a way that fits the mental model. In each case, the selection of data, the interpretation of that data, and the final result (the conclusion) make perfect sense to the person holding the mental model.

We form mental models based on our accumulated experiences. For example, if you witnessed a car accident as a child, you might form the mental model that automobiles and streets are dangerous. Your model might serve you well by prompting you to be particularly careful when crossing the street. We also inherit mental models from our parents, teachers, and culture. In some cultures, for example, the mental model "respect your elders" powerfully influences how people relate to authority figures. Whether formed from personal experience or inherited, these models become blueprints for future actions.

We usually form or inherit mental models without conscious awareness. They seem to be simply a part of the workings of the world. We are thus not always aware of which ones are currently influencing our thinking or how they influence our actions, and we rarely think to examine them. And although when we form a mental model it is generally useful to us at the time, many of them eventually outlive their usefulness. For instance, if your mental model about cars and streets prevented you from learning to drive, it would place serious constraints on your social and professional life. Or if new regulations about driving were to make cars and streets much safer than before, your mental model might no longer be necessary. Unexamined mental models can also pose problems for us in the workplace. When we find ourselves embroiled in a difficult situation or conversation, mental models that aren't necessarily conducive to productive conversation may affect our thinking and thus our actions.

We can benefit greatly by periodically examining and testing our mental models—and revising them if it turns out that they *have* outlived their usefulness.

The foundational skill set is the ideal method for examining our mental models. It comprises the tools of reflection that bring unspoken assumptions, tacit values, and evaluative criteria to the table for public discussion.

A Domestic Example of the Ladder of Inference

Consider another example, this one taken from my own life. In my household, my wife and I take turns doing the food preparation or the cleanup each year at Thanksgiving. A couple of years ago, it was my turn to do the dishes. I was sitting on the couch after the Thanksgiving meal, overdosed on turkey. I looked over at a stack of dishes that resembled the skyline of Manhattan. The only way I was going to get through this job was to put on a hard and determined mind-set that banged out a steady drumbeat of CLEAN, CLEAN, CLEAN in my head.

I got to work and was making progress. I looked over and saw a pot with a turkey neck, heart, and giblets swimming in a brown liquid. I thought to myself, "No one eats that stuff. They are useless meat products." In a nanosecond, I took action and flushed the whole thing down the garbage disposal. A few moments later, my wife came up the stairs and asked me, "Did you throw out everything that was in this pot?" With pride in my voice, I said, "Yes, and look how well I am getting through the dishes." She screamed, "How can you be so stupid?! You threw out the turkey broth. Now we can't have turkey soup. Don't you ever throw anything out again unless you get my permission." At that moment, I didn't exercise my best communication skills, because I responded with, "If you don't want something thrown out, you'd better tell me in the first place." Anyone can fairly accurately predict where that conversation went.

From my wife's perspective, I was pretty stupid, but I didn't intend to wreck the turkey soup. I am a good cook, and I know the value of broth for soups. In that moment, I didn't see the broth. My frame of CLEAN selected the data of a turkey neck, heart, and giblets. I deselected the brown liquid. I interpreted the data as something that no one eats. I drew a conclusion that they were useless meat products and were to be thrown out.

My wife saw the situation a little differently. She had another Ladder of Inference going. Together, we had what is called "dueling ladders." She selected the brown liquid with the interpretation that the broth is important to making soup and therefore concluded that it should be preserved. Our communication took place on top of our respective ladders: "Useless meat products; throw them out" versus "Valuable broth; keep it." As in the case of many dueling ladders, we selected different data, made interpretations, and came to two very different conclusions.

A Cautionary Word

To those familiar with the Ladder of Inference, the phrase "being on top of your ladder" has become code for insinuating that the speaker is being abstract, general, and vague. But beware of the kind of jargon that oversimplifies or distorts the real meaning of the tool. I had one participant at a workshop tell me that he was taking the workshop to understand what the Ladder of Inference was all about. Someone at a meeting had screamed at him for being on top of his ladder. He felt punished for what he had said and had no idea what the phrase meant. Nor did he want to approach the person later on and find out!

After introductory workshops, many enthusiastic beginners become the Ladder of Inference police. As such, they can do a lot of damage. They resonate with the concept in broad strokes, but in practice, they jump to the inaccurate conclusion that there is something wrong with being on top of the ladder. It is natural and normal for us to live on top of our ladder. Our quick and efficient thinking enables us to function in the world. It is when we get into difficult situations where multiple views surface that it is appropriate to slow our thinking and reflect on how we got to the top of our ladder.

I have found it important to continually emphasize the fact that the Ladder of Inference is a metaphor. As with all metaphors, taking the image literally is a misplaced understanding. It is not meant to describe the biochemical neural pathways of the human brain. Each rung on the ladder represents a step we take to transform observable data into conclusions. Mark Twain made the point when he said, "Give me the facts first and then you can distort them all you want." We get the facts first, then immediately begin the interpretive process. The higher we are on the ladder, the more general or abstract our thinking becomes. The more abstract our thinking, the greater the chance that we and the person or people we're talking to could be selecting different data or using the same data but interpreting it differently—thus arriving at different conclusions.

That's why, although the concept of the Ladder of Inference is immensely appealing upon first introduction, the question soon arises as to how we can possibly keep track of the multiple ladders of inference stacking up in our minds, not to mention the thousand more in others' heads. The answer is simple: it can't be done. Nor should it!

I am fond of quoting my friend and colleague Diana Smith, who says, "You can't engage every thought that comes down the line." The Ladder of Inference is not a tool for all occasions. There are appropriate times when putting it into use can be most productive.

Where can it be employed most productively? One appropriate use is to break stalemates. Point-counterpoint conversations are common in business meetings. We've all witnessed (or participated in) a volley of points traded back and forth with the familiar "Yes, but" retort. The conversation ends with a polite agreement to disagree, but no resolution. The Ladder of Inference, when used effectively, can help people see how each other's thinking diverges on important issues. Using the ladder, people don't avoid conflict, but rather engage their differences by discovering the different information used to arrive at conflicting conclusions.

For example, consider what happened at this meeting between a group of bank managers. Midway through the meeting, which was about their marketing plan, one manager said, "There are people who are willing to pay more for better service." I was facilitating the meeting; immediately I thought to myself, "Okay, top of the ladder; what information is she using to support that statement?"

So I asked her a few questions. In her response, the data she selected became apparent. She cited how the bank was paying less interest on deposits, yet charging more for its loans (thus increasing its margin), the bank's market share had grown in the last year, and it was spending less on operating costs. Her interpretation was that more people were choosing to bank with them even as they increased their margin and lowered their costs. On the basis of her selection of data and her interpretation, she concluded that the reason people were continuing to bank with them was the service. Everyone around the table agreed on the data she had selected. The pursuing discussion focused on how others interpreted the same data and came to different conclusions.

Conclusions are often presented as factual when they are actually inferential. The Ladder of Inference helps individuals discover the hard, observable facts that can be verified independently of anyone's interpretation. Conversations remain focused on discovering the relevant information contained in the thinking. Information is tested for accuracy and serves to make an informed decision or conclusion.

The Ladder of Inference helps people use the diversity of thinking in a group by identifying what information or facts they are selecting to be important and how they add meaning. The results are an improved reasoning process and a reduction in the time from idea to decision.

ADVOCACY AND INQUIRY

How often have you had an idea that is clear, brilliant, and exactly the right direction to take? At least that is how it sounds as it bounces around inside your head. Yet when you speak, particularly during a conversation when you feel on the spot, you ramble on and on trying to connect the spoken word with the thought that was crystal clear in your head only moments ago. A playback of what you actually said would reveal a muddled string of disconnected, vague, and general statements. You punctuate your final comments with "This will work; I know it will. Trust me—it's the right thing to do." In response, others pass the verdict of irrelevance on your idea by saying, "That's an interesting idea; let's send it to a subcommittee for discussion."

Other times, the best information available remains inside your head, residing in your LHC, unable to be made public because of how it would sound if it came out of your mouth uncensored. Whether you are dealing with a muddled thought or censored information, the ability to produce a high quality advocacy is an extremely valuable skill to develop.

Advocacy is expressing a view or making a statement about your position. *Inquiry* is exploring the views of others through questions. Advocacy and inquiry are the basic units of a conversation. How you state your view and inquire into others' perspectives determines the quality of the conversation. When your advocacy reveals the steps in your thinking and gives specific examples, it promotes learning. High quality inquiry seeks alternative views, probes the views of others, and encourages challenge to your own view.

Thus, for our purposes, advocacy and inquiry are essentially two distinct parts of a single tool. The following box, "BALANCE," illustrates a way to understand the essence of advocacy and inquiry at a glance.

BALANCE

Balancing your advocacy with inquiry will foster mutual learning.

Ask for alternative views.

Look for examples that illustrate your view.

Ask for others' reasoning and data.

Not all advocacy and inquiry are equal. High quality advocacy and inquiry bring others' reasoning and data to the surface.

Challenge your own view with inquiry: "Do you see it the same or differently?"

Explain the steps of your reasoning by using the Ladder of Inference.

Advocacy

There is a difference between saying, "There is no way this project is going to succeed" and "I heard Fred say that he couldn't give this project the attention it deserved. Without his support, I have doubts about the project's success. Do others place the same or a different degree of importance on Fred's role?" A productive advocacy helps others see what data you have selected, the meaning you've attached to that data, and the conclusion you've drawn. Your Ladder of Inference is made visible.

A high quality advocacy is a clear and compelling presentation of your point of view. Clarity in thought and speech delivers a precision of meaning and a focus on what really matters to you. A high quality advocacy guards against misunderstanding that comes from talking in generalities and abstractions. The goal for presenting your view clearly is not to win an argument but to disclose your thinking in a way that is helpful to others' learning. A high quality advocacy can establish the inherent reasonableness of your thinking, increase the efficiency in which information is exchanged, and promote shared understanding. Others are able to see how you arrived at your position in a way that is simultaneously compelling yet subject to challenge.

But how can you craft high quality advocacy? One of the easiest and best ways to strengthen the quality of your advocacy is to offer an example. When it comes to presenting your view, there is usually ample room for an example. By illustrating your view in this way, you metaphorically drop down your Ladder of Inference. Productive conversations take place "low on the ladder" by sharing concrete information rather than vague and general concepts.

Concrete examples are also easier to confirm or refute because they are observable and more apt to be remembered by others. Claiming that the morale at the company is suffering is a conclusion that could be debated, but citing the HR report on last quarter's employee turnover is directly accessible and observable.

Not every example improves the quality of your advocacy. A lengthy illustration may lose your listener in the details. Finding a good example is like Goldilocks tasting the porridge: "Not too hot, not too cold; just right." So when you're selecting a "just right" example to illustrate your point of view, ask yourself,

Does my example describe a pattern or trend? An example that represents a single, isolated event can be easily dismissed as marginally relevant, of low impact, or a personal preference.

Is my example easily accessible and observable by others? If not, it may be difficult for others to support the connection between your example and conclusion. Without the ability to verify the example, others can only rely on your word. This may work fine for those who trust you completely, but your credibility may not be universally accepted. You have a better chance to build your credibility with others when they are able to verify what you are seeing.

A good example is brief, precise, and vivid in its description. It is essentially a short story. You don't want to bog down the listener with minute details, yet you can't afford to be vague, especially when describing human behavior. Saying "An example of when you were not a team player was when you blew off John's idea" is not an example, but a conclusion.

It is best to use conversational data when describing human interactions. In the previous exchange, an example that cites the conversational data would be "An example of when you were not a team player in my mind was when you said, 'That's a stupid idea, John, and it will never fly with corporate.'" Conversational data is your best recall of the dialogue.

Get into the habit of repeating the conversation between yourself and the other by saying, "He said, then I said." In lieu of a tape recorder, your memory is the best available recall of the conversation, but it is by nature selective. It is always important to add the inquiry, "Do you recall it the same or differently?" after re-creating the conversation for the other person.

The best examples are neutral, descriptive statements. We have a tendency to "juice up" the story when describing human interactions in order to favor our point of view. We quickly add our own inferences to what we observe without knowing we are doing it. There is a difference between saying, "She wouldn't take no for answer," and "She said, 'At this point in time, we are going forward with the project unless unforeseeable circumstances cause us to change course.'" It is understandable how one might reach the conclusion that she wouldn't take no for an answer, but the meaning behind her actual words includes the possibility that she might change her mind in the future.

Crafting a high quality advocacy is not a guarantee that your view will prevail, but it stands its best chance by being clear and explicit. More important, getting your reasoning process out on the table for discussion increases the chances that others will learn from your point of view. If they do the same, then there is more information available. Additional information leads to better decision making. Better decisions increase the likelihood of a more effective implementation.

Inquiry

The quality of inquiry is equally important. There is a difference between "You agree, don't you?" and "Do you see it differently?" The first inquiry seeks a confirmation; the second actively encourages challenge. A quality inquiry helps others "down their ladders" in a way that doesn't evoke defensiveness, grill them for information, or make them feel pressured to prove a point.

An effective inquiry can be simply to ask, "Could you give an example?" Often your listener will give a response that specifically identifies the data he or she has selected. Well-crafted inquiries also invite alternative views and new information. Asking a group, "What may we be missing?" or "What obstacles can we anticipate if we take this course of action?" actively invites challenge and keeps thinking agile.

Here are a few additional examples of productive inquiries:

Do you see it the same or differently?

What did I say that triggered your thought?

How do you understand what I am proposing?

What is your reaction?

In a number of programs, I have seen the exercise "Why, why" used to instruct participants on how to ask high quality inquiries. This exercise is drawn from the systems thinking chapter in Peter Senge's *The Fifth Discipline Fieldbook*. Here's how it works in brief: one person states a view, and the other simply asks "Why?" The first person offers another statement, to which the second person again responds with "Why?" This goes for several rounds until the first person discovers the deeper layers of causality operating within a system.

Although this technique works for the systems thinking discipline, the practice of asking "Why?" has limitations when it comes to crafting high quality inquiries. Quality inquiries generally don't use Why questions because such queries tend to make listeners feel pressured to prove their point or justify their position. Also, people tend to respond to Why questions with fairly abstract explanations, such as "because our team's capacity is insufficient." A person's causal theory or explanation of "why" is usually an evaluation of what is good, bad, right, or wrong with the situation or issue. It may be useful information, but it remains fairly abstract.

After one "Why, why?" exercise, I asked a participant, "What is your understanding of the exercise and being asked 'Why?'" His response was, "You need to justify that what you said supports the original Why or supports what you had previously said." His response fed my concern about how this technique may be practiced in the workplace. Asking someone a series of Why questions can easily create a defensive reaction in the recipient, who thinks he or she needs to prove or justify his or her point to the person asking the question.

I would not put a ban on asking Why questions. In the right context, tone of voice, and interpersonal relationship, a Why question can help a conversation get to the same productive place as a high quality inquiry. Yet a high quality inquiry can get the conversation there a lot quicker. Asking questions starting with "What," "Where," and "How" elicit more descriptive responses, and result in more concrete information. And again, with more information come better decisions and effective results.

Balancing Advocacy and Inquiry

An exchange of high quality advocacy and inquiry generates mutual learning so that ideas are not bought and sold, but shaped and molded by the collective thinking of the group. Assuming you are obviously right and embarking on the task of convincing the other person that he or she is wrong only works if the other person agrees with you. Often the other person holds the same mind-set, and the results are both predictable and disappointing. When you instead assume that your viewpoint may be missing something that others see, and realize that your view may hold something that others have missed, the quality of a conversation will be dramatically different than the win-lose variety. This kind of conversation engages participants in disclosing their viewpoints so that others can learn and eliciting information from other people's perspectives, both of which promote mutual learning.

How many times have managers and their teams left a meeting thinking that they all had a common understanding of what needed to be done, only to discover later that everyone went off in different directions? Too often managers and team leaders make the assumption that their teams have clearly understood what they have asked. They fall short on the advocacy end of things by staying at the "headline" level of an issue and failing to use examples. And they follow up with a question such as, "Okay, does everyone know what to do?" instead of a higher quality inquiry that asks, "What is your understanding of what's to be done?" and yields a more accurate check for shared meaning and understanding.

Clearly, a balance of high quality advocacy and inquiry results in the highest caliber of communication. But what does a balance look like?

The term *balancing advocacy and inquiry* has both a quantitative and qualitative meaning. On a quantitative level, it is desirable to ask questions as well as make statements. If a conversation is all statements (advocacy) there is probably little learning going on. It is more likely that everyone is pushing his or her views. At the same time, however, there needn't be a rigid adherence to ensuring an equal amount of statements and questions. (Aside from anything else, this would extend meeting times beyond their reasonable limits.) What should be evident is a skillful use of questions that surface information from various perspectives or invites challenge to one's own perspective.

My favorite "balancing" questions are "What is your reaction to what I have said?" "Do others see it the same or differently?" and "What might I be missing?" I don't ask them after every statement I make, but they are useful on certain appropriate occasions, such as when there is

- A potential disconnect in how people understand what others said or meant

- A suggestion or proposal for action that could potentially create difficulties

- A difference in how people are describing a problem

On these occasions, balancing advocacy with inquiry promotes learning. This technique helps the dialogue move forward by continually surfacing more information from various perspectives. Balancing advocacy with inquiry also acknowledges the partiality and limitations of your own thinking. It is the difference between ending your advocacy with "You agree, don't you?" and "Do you see it the same or differently?"

Argyris said, "You must simultaneously be aggressive and vulnerable with your viewpoint." He calls for a dynamic tension between our views and their limitations, the necessity of getting our viewpoint on the table for discussion in a way that allows for productive challenge. The following chart, "STATE and ASK," illustrates an effective approach to balancing advocacy and inquiry in practice.

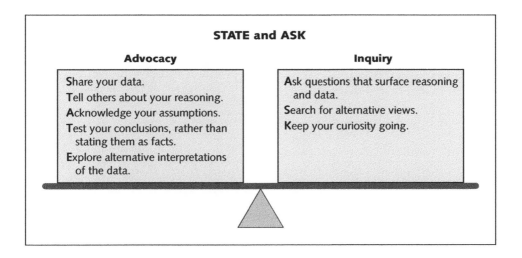

STATE and ASK

Advocacy	Inquiry
Share your data. Tell others about your reasoning. Acknowledge your assumptions. Test your conclusions, rather than stating them as facts. Explore alternative interpretations of the data.	Ask questions that surface reasoning and data. Search for alternative views. Keep your curiosity going.

The terms *high quality advocacy* and *high quality inquiry* may sound like fancy ways of saying "stating your view" and "asking others for theirs." They actually mean something more. They challenge us to raise the bar on the effectiveness of our communication and interaction with others. What you will soon discover, if you haven't already, is that what appears to be common sense is actually very hard to achieve.

❦

In Chapter Three, we enter the world of Mark and Brenda, the main characters in the fictional narrative "Fix It Now or Fix It Later." As I've said, this narrative provides a backdrop against which to explore the sources of defensive behaviors and the ways in which people can overcome them.

With an understanding of the three tools described in this chapter, you will be able to see how the characters' thinking influences their actions, how quickly they jump to conclusions, and, in the limiting environment of e-mails and voice mails, how poor-quality advocacy abounds and no inquiry exists.

Mark, Brenda, You, and Me

Bringing Defensive Routines About and Keeping Them in Place

Part Two describes how defensive routines come about and are kept in place by our defensive reasoning, our actions, and a set of socially sanctioned values. Chapters Three, Four, and Five each begin with a scene from the case study "Fix It Now or Fix It Later," in which the fictional characters Mark, Brenda, and their colleagues exhibit typical defensive reactions and behaviors. These scenes are followed by a summary-level interpretation of the characters' conversations and a discussion of the issues in general. At the end of each chapter, there are exercises to help you "turn the lens on yourself" and consider your own experiences.

Conditions of Threat and Embarrassment

FIX IT NOW OR FIX IT LATER, SCENE ONE: THE BAD NEWS

Josh, the plant's inspection and pressure equipment manager, appeared at the door, a mug of coffee in one hand and a yellow legal pad in the other.

"Hey, Mark, do you have a minute?"

"Sure Josh." Mark pushed back from his desk. The chair creaked as he leaned back. "What's up?"

"Just wanted to give you a progress report on the inspection. We've found a few problems."

Mark settled in for the news. Problems were expected. That's why they shut the plant down every twenty-four months to give the safety inspectors a chance to check equipment they couldn't get to when the unit was at full operation. "Anything serious?"

"Most of it is minor, but there is one big issue. We've got higher than expected wear on one of the exchangers."

Mark tried to read Josh's face, but his expression gave nothing away. "How bad?"

"Needs to be replaced."

"Now?"

"It has about another eighteen months max."

Mark nodded. No way would they be able to push the repairs to the next turnaround two years from now. A worn exchanger was like a ticking time bomb. An unplanned shutdown due to equipment failure that should have been anticipated wouldn't sit well with Walt, the plant manager, and the repairs would blow his budget to pieces. Most important, there was the safety of his crew to consider.

"How long before we can be up and running again?"

"We've got the crew, and the parts can be ordered. It should only extend the turnaround an extra week," said Josh.

"Not great, but it could be worse. I'll make the recommendation to Walt and call Brenda with a heads-up so she can smooth it over with our customers."

Josh nodded. "I'm going to get back to work."

Mark picked up the phone and dialed Brenda's private line. He hadn't spoken to his former colleague in several months. Brenda had started in a technical position at the refinery a few years ahead of him and worked her way up as far as she could in the plant before transferring to Sales about a year ago. Since then, he had rarely talked to her in person. It seemed she was always in a meeting with a customer or on a plane headed for one. They communicated by voice messages and e-mails.

After the perfunctory two rings, on came the tape.

"Hello, you've reached the office of Brenda Fields. I'm not in right now. . . ."

As he waited for the beep, Mark stared at the photo of the plant on the wall across from his desk. Shot from an aerial view, the massive refinery looked solid and streamlined, without a hint of the complexities that lay within. It had been a gift from the crew when he'd been promoted to operations manager.

"Hey, Brenda, it's Mark Listman over at the plant. Our inspectors have found some faulty equipment that needs replacing before we can complete this turnaround. Looks like it's going to delay our going back on line by about a week. Give me a call."

Balancing an overstuffed briefcase, laptop, and sugar-free triple-shot skinny no-whip latte, Brenda hit the automatic door release with her elbow and strode through the oversized oak doors and into the corporate offices. Her own desk was piled with papers and files that had accumulated while she was out of town, and few of which she expected to deal with before leaving again for the airport in two hours. She deposited her bags on the floor and fired up her computer. As it loaded, she hit the speaker on her phone to retrieve her voice messages. Twenty new ones since she checked them last night at the airport after arriving from Houston.

She scanned her e-mail as she listened to the first five requests—all minor issues she could handle when she returned to town tomorrow night. The sixth was from Mark Listman, an old colleague and current operations manager at one of the refineries.

Brenda typed a quick response to an e-mail, then took a sip of her coffee as she listened to Mark's message. The words "faulty equipment" pulled her focus from the computer screen to the phone.

". . . delay our going back on line by about a week."

"What?" Brenda slammed her cup down on the desk, and a stream of hot brown liquid shot out onto her jacket sleeve.

"No." She stood up, letting the coffee drain down her hand onto her desk. Mark's voice continued. Something about making the customers understand.

"No, no, no." Brenda looked around for something to wipe up the mess soaking into the papers on her desk. Finally she grabbed a fistful of tissues from the box and threw them over the puddle.

What was Mark thinking? She'd been working on these accounts for months, promising them the product as soon as the refinery came back on line. She dabbed at her jacket sleeve with a tissue, but the coffee had already left a spot.

She should have known it. There hadn't been a turnaround yet when Operations hadn't tried to extend the deadline for some sort of added repairs. She'd worked at that same refinery, so she knew what they were trying to do. Making repairs during a turnaround saved Operations a lot of cash out of their budget.

Brenda shook her head. Mark was a stickler for safety. He backed his crew and held his ground. She admired him for that. But now that she worked in the corporate office, she was tired of their attitude, of them acting like they were the company, like nothing else mattered as much as their refinery.

Brenda knew it was her technical experience at the refinery that gave her the edge. She could talk details with the big guns and massage the relationships between Operations and the customers. She also knew there were lots of ways to make things move faster, that not every repair needed to be done during a turnaround. If Mark could wait even a few months to make the repair, she could deliver on time. He had said only that there was a problem. Who knew what they would find when they really got in there? Three-quarters of the way into any turnaround, there were always more problems, more delays, more money needed for capital expenditures not in the budget. How long would it really take before they were up and running again? Too long for her accounts to stick around. She had to make sure Mark understood that the customer came first this time.

She sent off a quick e-mail promising she'd call to discuss options with him when she returned from her trip, then mopped up the rest of the spilled coffee and dumped the soggy wad of tissues into the trash can.

SUMMARY: SETTING THE STAGE FOR DEFENSIVE ROUTINES

There is a lot at stake for Mark and for Brenda, on both personal and business levels. The choice they face is to risk running the bad exchanger to failure or to fix it now. On one hand, by delaying the repairs, the plant can deliver on its commitment to the customer, defer the cost of replacing the exchanger, and maintain the schedule. On the other hand, the delay might result in an unanticipated failure. This possibility would impact the current operational budget by incurring greater repair costs, creating environmental problems, and causing hardship for the plant employees.

Brenda had made a promise to her customers. Not delivering a product as scheduled is a direct threat to the business. From a personal standpoint, she sees her professional reputation on the line. She will have to take the heat from the customer, not to mention the glare of her peers at Corporate if she loses the account. This plant's unscheduled delay jeopardizes the company's future relationship with its biggest customers. The loss of any major customer would have a dramatic impact on the corporation's bottom line. She can't allow this to happen. Operations can fix the exchanger later.

Although acutely aware of his responsibility to deliver product to the customer, Mark's immediate concern is his crew and their ability to operate his segment of the plant. The inspection manager and his crew have sold him on the need to fix the equipment. On-line failure is messy and uncontrolled, and brings with it the accusation of insensitivity to workers' safety. If Mark goes against his team's recommendation, it would further confirm their belief that the corporate head office never listens to line workers. Nothing he could say would change their perception that he was a mouthpiece for corporate interests and short on concern for his team's safety. Worse yet, he would have a hard time living with himself knowing that this is the right time to replace the exchanger. The plant is down for the turn-around. Now is the time to fix it.

Brenda and Mark are also players within a larger organizational setting where well-entrenched assumptions influence how each of them view the other. Operations is on the front line of production. They are the ones who have to wake up in the middle of the night to fix leaking equipment. They have to explain cost overruns, assess safety and environmental risks, and deal with union leadership. Sales sees Operations as removed from the customer. The phone doesn't ring on their desk with an irate client. From the point of view of Sales, Operations is risk adverse and not willing to take the chances needed to remain competitive in the marketplace.

These conditions have set the stage for the rise of defensive routines. Depending on which way the decision goes, Mark or Brenda will be in a position where his or her competency might be held in doubt. That possibility holds potential embarrassment for each of them. There is a threat to what Mark and Brenda respectively hold as important and critical to the business. Each person sees himself or herself as acting sensibly and upholding the values of loyalty, integrity, and prudence, but may not necessarily think the other possesses the same values.

MARK AND BRENDA ASIDE: CONDITIONS OF EMBARRASSMENT AND THREAT

Although the circumstances Mark and Brenda face may be unique to their business problem, there are salient features of potential embarrassment and threat that all of us share and have experienced in a multitude of situations.

What does it mean to be embarrassed? When do we fear being embarrassed? It's important to understand that embarrassment cannot live in a vacuum; embarrassment has no potency without public exposure. Thus the experience of embarrassment does not depend on whether or not I care about what others think of me. Instead, the awkwardness of embarrassment comes when others see or hear what I would have preferred they did not.

In other words, when an inadequacy, mistake, or contradiction has been exposed, I look bad. And whether "looking bad" is an accusation made by others or a label I assign to myself, the result is the same. I feel embarrassed. Think of a time when you were embarrassed. Recall the physical sensation. Feel the eyes of everyone in the room on you. The heat of attention generates a warm flush in your face. The burning sensation is your vocal chords frying. You can't find anything sensible to say. All your blood is rushing to your head.

You're going to go into either "flight mode" or "fight mode." That is, your brain might send the message "Let's get out of here," or send an alternate message, something along the lines of "What are you looking at, buster?" Your response may be an outcry of injustice or a silent, embarrassing moment of acknowledgment. In either case, it is plainly an uncomfortable emotional state.

Threats can cause similar reactions. Whether actual or perceived, a threat signals danger and intends to inflict damage. Fortunately, in our day-to-day business interactions, the damage is rarely physical. Instead, our sense of competency is under attack. This is not to be minimized; it can be devastating. Competence is the requisite or adequate ability to get done what needs to be done and to do it effectively. We like seeing what we do turn out well. When others acknowledge our performance, achievements, or ideas, we feel good about ourselves. Even without public acknowledgment, we can still feel the personal satisfaction of a job well done. We operate best when feeling competent.

What happens when our competency is threatened? A typical situation occurs when another person makes a negative evaluation of our actions. The evaluation could be true or false. If we know it to be true, embarrassment may take front and center in our minds. If we believe it to be false, the alarm bells ring, and we scream, "Unfair!" We don't like being represented differently in the eyes of others from how we see ourselves. So we might find ourselves garnering all the reasons we can to defend our competency against others' accusations. There wasn't enough time. There were unrealistic expectations. What happened isn't an accurate measurement of what I am able to do. In reaction to a threat, we take a defended position.

Some of us don't need the aid of others' criticism to devastate our sense of competency. We have our own inner critic. We might see ourselves acting sensibly in the moment, but later on, when we look back, we think about how insensible our behavior was. In retrospect, there is that sinking feeling when we realize that there is a gap between what we believe to be true about ourselves and what our actions seem to reveal. The critical voice of others, in that case, only confirms what we know to be the worst about ourselves.

Conditions of threat and embarrassment arise in a variety of situations. They can be unexpected or anticipated. People close to us can trigger them, and so can total strangers. We can find ourselves in the midst of daily events, whether minor or major, where either potential embarrassment or threat exists. Although the context may differ, there are common identifiable themes of threat and embarrassment.

In the following cases, five people share their experiences when under the conditions of threat or embarrassment. In these short recollections, they reveal what was at stake for them in an uncomfortable situation. Each case takes up one or more themes typically found in conditions of threat and embarrassment. As you read, pay attention to any point of resonance you might have with them. Those points could be clues to how your own defenses get triggered in similar situations.

Case 1: The Temperature Is Rising

One member of a work team is talking to his manager, delivering the bad news that the manager's pet project is failing. The team member has done everything he can do, but others are not pulling their weight. The project needs leadership, and the manager must step in and hold everyone accountable. The team member drops by the manager's office unannounced. Note the use of the LHC to divulge the thoughts behind the team member's words.

What was thought and felt, but not said by the team member (TM)	What was actually said
	TM: You got a minute?
	Manager: What do you want?
He looks tense. I can't lose control of this conversation.	**TM:** I thought you should know that the project has hit the wall. I've done what I can, but I really need help with the assessment phase.
	Manager: Maureen is doing that.
Why is it that I'm the one who looks ineffective when I am the only one moving forward with this project?	**TM:** Well, she is dragging her feet. So, I'm telling you it isn't getting done. Someone needs to be a leader on this project and hold people accountable. That's either me or someone else.

Wait a minute, why is his face red? He is frowning at me. He is leaning across the desk in a threatening way. It feels like he is suggesting that I'm the one not accomplishing the work.

He didn't say that nicely.

His face is really red now. He won't look at me, and I can't look at him. I'm so mad. What a weirdo. I've got to keep my emotions in check. It feels like I'm the scapegoat. It isn't fair.

What a dork. He has no idea what I'm talking about.

I'm not lying. I really mean it.

Manager: That's my job. I hold people accountable. If someone isn't doing their work, you can bet I'm going to do something about it.

TM: But you act like you don't want to hear it. How are you going to know the project is at a standstill if no one tells you?

Manager: Who says it's at a standstill?

TM: I do. I'm the only one working on it. But I can't do it anymore. That's what I just told you.

Manager: I talk to Maureen every day. She has said nothing about it being at a standstill.

TM: It feels like we are talking in circles. You say you want to know if there are problems. I tell you there are problems, and you get mad at me. Aren't you worried?

Manager: No, I am not worried. It needs to get done by the end of the year.

TM: That is not going to happen.

Manager: So *you* say.

TM: That's it. Take me off this project.

Manager: Oh no, you're not getting away with that. You started this, and you are going to finish it. I'll take you off when I feel like it.

He's laughing. What is he? Some sort of sadist? He is such a creep! This is torture!

TM: You are torturing me. You don't let me do what needs to be done, and you don't let me off the hook either.

Manager: I told you that I am the heavy. You just do your job. I expect people to tell me when someone isn't doing their job.

This guy is so out of touch.

TM: But I do that and you get all mad at me. You shoot the messenger.

The conversation between the manager and the team member spiraled out of control. The emotional heat from the exchange hit the boiling point.

The conversation started innocently enough. The team member was dutifully going to deliver the bad news about the project. He saw himself on the precipice of a fiasco. By acknowledging that he had done all that he could do and needed help, he ran the risk of looking ineffective. This emotional reality remained unstated. Instead, he laid out a challenge to his manager: "Someone needs to be a leader and hold people accountable." Judging from the manager's response, "That's my job," the manager could very well have heard the team member's statement as telling him that he was being negligent in the performance of his responsibility. The manager's reddened face was a cue that emotions had been triggered.

They exchanged high-level assessments of whether or not the project was at a standstill. The team member accurately described the process as "talking in circles." With each rotation, the emotional temperature rose. The team member's private thoughts (LHC) escalated with multiple negative judgments about the manager. Although the manager's LHC is not available, it is reasonable to guess that he held an equal level of negative attributions about the team member. By the end of the conversation, it was harder for both of them to contain their negative thoughts. They leaked out in a series of accusations, blaming, and demands. In the end, the team member stormed out of the manager's office.

This scene gets played out in numerous different contexts. The slightest suggestion of "You are not doing your job" or "I may look bad" sends out the emotional alert signal to be on guard. All parties struggle to keep the emotions in check, but with no improvement in the quality of the conversation, the feelings are unleashed. Things get awkward.

After the emotions have cooled, the embarrassment lingers. One's mind runs a continual replay of the scene as if the memory were caught in a perpetual loop. There is a disbelief that things got so out of hand. There is a sincere desire to hit the rewind button and have a chance to do it over again. The feeling of embarrassment evolves into a generalized awkwardness and dread at the thought of the next encounter. In the end, there is a firm commitment never to let one's emotions get out of hand again. Getting emotional and letting things spin out of control are too embarrassing.

Case 2: Getting Grilled

There is no doubt that things can go wrong in business. When they do, future success depends on correcting the mistakes in order to ensure that they don't occur again. For anyone involved in the investigation into what happened, the experience of being "called on the carpet" and grilled for information can be mortifying.

In this case, a finance director has some explaining to do when he is called into the VP of finance's office and has to account for a financial report that showed cost overruns.

What was thought and felt, but not said by the finance director	What was actually said
	VP: We are here to talk about these financials. They are abysmal.
Yes, they are awful, but what did you expect me to do in two weeks?	**Director:** Yes, they are what we expected after our conversation last month.
	VP: It looks like your whole team is running free and not watching what they are spending. Why has line item 12 gone up so high?
You make them sound like they are trying to spend money like water. We are just trying to figure this whole thing out.	**Director:** I can't say for sure. We did discover a significant error in coding, so these reports may not be accurate.

VP: That doesn't help the bottom line. Why did your team buy more color printing cartridges after we said no more color printing?

How the hell should I know? We are not the only ones making mistakes around here. Your staff is making them too. You expect me to report on inaccurate information.

Director: I don't know. I will have to look into this further before I can give you an accurate answer.

VP: Why did you buy so much *x?* Does your team really need that much?

Oh good, another question I can't answer. Just how ignorant am I going to look before the meeting is over? If he asks me one more question I can't answer, I'm going to barf.

Director: I don't know. I will have to check back with you.

VP: How come we paid so much for mileage reimbursement?

The director was peppered by questions from the boss. The boss wanted answers. The director was unprepared and couldn't provide them. Not knowing the "why" to "Why are things going so wrong?" only made the situation worse. In the end, if the director was going to give it the old heave-ho, he probably hoped he'd toss his cookies in the boss's direction for making him report on inaccurate information and not sharing the blame.

Make no mistake about it, admitting to mistakes is embarrassing. We look like we don't know what we are doing. It is worse when we actually don't know what we are doing, when we are asleep at the wheel or just plain over our heads. The embarrassment brought on by an admission of error exposes our inadequacy. It is a blow to our sense of competency.

Case 3: Questioning My Ability

On occasion, there is the "no doubt about it" attack on someone's competency. The person levying the charge is direct and brutal.

In this case, a human resources manager has to hire a team quickly to work in the mail room and document production center of the company. For many years, this service had been outsourced, but the finance director asked that this support service be provided internally. Due to the contract with the outside vendor, none of the previous contractual employees can be hired. The recruiter has three weeks to assemble a team before the old service contract expires. The finance director stops by the Human Resources office to see why there has been a delay in hiring a new team.

What was thought and felt, but not said by the human resources manager (HRM)	What was actually said
	Director: What's going on with the hiring process? Can't you do a better job of finding us good candidates, or do I have to do it myself? There must be lots of people out there wanting jobs. How hard can it be?
He is already drawing conclusions, and we still have three weeks to go until the contract employees are gone. At this point, he hasn't even heard my plan.	**HRM:** We are still three weeks away, and I am scheduling interviews. I have already reviewed a number of qualified resumes. It will happen, don't worry.
	Director: Sure—you are going to find a bunch of losers just like the last receptionist you hired.
I am getting angry and taking this personally. He is questioning my ability to do my job and is doing so completely out of context. In an effort to get the conversation back on track, I'll repeat what I said to defend my position. I am feeling threatened.	**HRM:** You can hold me completely accountable for all hiring actions. I take my job seriously, and I am an experienced professional. When you make reference to the quality of candidates I am hiring, then you are talking about my ability to do my job, and this is personal. Again, it will happen.

Okay, he is really off base now. I simply refuse to continue this conversation until he calms down. It has already gotten way too emotional.

Director: This office is a mess.

HRM: I refuse to continue this conversation until you are ready to rationally listen to my plan.

For the human resources manager, there was good reason to get defensive. The finance director's approach was provocative and threatening. He spewed a torrent of insults at her. She could learn nothing from his statements about how she might possibly not be finding good candidates for hire. To her credit, she didn't respond in kind and placed a limit on the conversation.

What is illustrative about her case is the clarity and honesty found in her private thinking. She was aware of her anger and cognizant that her competency was under attack. Her reaction was expected, normal, and needed when under direct attack. We'll hope that later she was able not only to have a conversation where she could present her plan, but also ask him questions that might surface more productively his concerns about Human Resources' hiring practices.

When others openly question our ability to get the job done, it is normal to feel defensive. The threat is real, and the reaction understandable. The goal is not to eliminate the defensive reaction but to take the first step and become aware of it.

Case 4: Reputation Is on the Line

This fourth case takes place within the context of decision making where high-stakes business risks could result in something going wrong. The conflict involves a regional sales manager and her boss, the director of sales. The director of sales has taken an already low-priced product and cut the price to a zero margin point. His thinking is that if he bundles the product with a high-margin offering, the resulting package will boost sales. This program requires the regional sales manager to install product bundles at customers' sites. She was asked to hire additional staff. She delayed the hiring because she doubts the effectiveness of the sales plan. Here, the director of sales meets with the regional sales manager.

What was thought and felt, but not said by the regional sales manager (RSM)	What was actually said
	Director: I heard from Human Resources that you haven't hired anyone yet. What's stopping you?
I don't think the sales projection is realistic. This seems to be a forecast based on faith rather than analysis.	**RSM:** I want to see the sales orders start to increase before I bring anyone new on board.
	Director: You understand that you will be responsible for not meeting revenue plans if you don't have the staff to install the bundled products.
Can I throw him out a window and make it look like an accident?	**RSM:** I think we should look at the rate of order backlog growth and hire based on that. Why risk hiring additional people if we may have to let them go later?
	Director: I told you we will get the orders. Just do your job and make sure we can take the revenue.
Arrogant [expletive]. What is he risking in this project? I've got all the exposure and risk. This is stupid.	**RSM:** What if the orders are slow coming in? Then we have to kill our margin and decrease overall sales. We lose big-time.
	Director: That won't happen. If it does, we will worry about that then.
I can't hire more people without a firmer commitment. If I can't find a high window, I might be able to find an elevator shaft.	**RSM:** I'm planning on hiring one person now and holding off until the backlog supports the additional two people. This will provide longer-term support.
	Director: You know the plan and yet you refuse to follow it. When will you become a team player?

As in many LHC-RHC case studies, what is not said is more telling than what is said. Although the sales manager was not serious, her internally stated intent to commit murder is an indication of the intensity of her feelings toward the director of sales. In her mind, he has engineered a setup for failure. Any failure will reflect badly on her, and she doesn't want to take the risk. Her reputation as a competent sales manager is at stake.

Instead of raising the issue of realistic as opposed to out-of-line sales projections, the manager tells the director that she has made a unilateral decision to wait and see if the sale orders increase before hiring additional staff. Judging from the sales director's response that he is absolutely confident that the orders will come, he experiences her decision as open defiance. He comes down with the hammer by pointing out the consequences of her failure to meet revenue plans. He orders her directly to "do her job." The emotional amperage in the conversation increases. She sees him as a major obstacle whose plan shifts the risk away from him and onto her. She persists in her view until finally he passes the verdict that she is not a team player. The irony is that in her attempts to safeguard her reputation, she now finds her reputation tarnished with the label of "not a team player."

Unless the director of sales has been trained in the Attila the Hun School of Management, senior executives don't implement plans designed to destroy their middle managers' reputation in order to enhance their own. Most likely, the director of sales sees himself as trying to create alignment with the marking plan. This thought is beyond the sales manager's negative frame of the director. She spends her time trying to convince him of her strategy. What she does not raise is how his strategy creates risks for her and potential exposure to failure. Raising the subject of personal reputation can be embarrassing because she might appear as concerned only about her own personal interests, yet self-interested concerns come into play all the time in business decisions.

Business decisions made today have an impact on future endeavors; the risks may or may not pay off. When people consider who bears what risks and the consequences of potential failure, there are implications for the careers of everyone involved. Reputations are on the line. A severe threat to reputation can jeopardize a person's financial security and career advancement, and such threats are not taken lightly. Rarely is this item of self-interest put on the table for discussion, yet it influences conversations all the time.

Case 5: Wrongly Accused

This case illustrates the threat that comes from the perception of being wrongly accused. In this company, a new program for compensation changed the rules for bonuses. Previously, sales staff received bonuses based on the sales price. The new incentive program pays on the basis of the amount of margin sold and paid at the date of the sale. The general manager (GM) delivers the news to the sales manager (SM) that he and his team will not be getting a bonus under the new system.

What was thought and felt, but not said by the sales manager (SM)	What was actually said
I have talked to you numerous times about getting paid a bonus on this job, and you have been evasive. You are trying to take our bonus away.	**SM:** Our last sale was booked in December. Until our new incentive program, I understood we would be paid a bonus on this booking, but I don't see it on the bonus list.
	GM: Because of the track record of losses on jobs in your office, no bonus will be paid until the December sale closes. Also, after all the discussion we had on booking jobs, I can't believe you went ahead and booked the new job with ExVita without talking to me first. I thought I was clear about passing these jobs by me first.
I should not be penalized in Sales because jobs are not managed properly in the field. This is wrong and unfair. I gave you the estimate on the new job, and you approved it. You've changed the rules. The money we made on the sale makes you look good, but I lose thousands of dollars in bonuses.	**SM:** This is unfair. This is not how the new incentive program works. I am going to the regional general manager and see what he has to say about this.

From the sales manager's point of view, not only did he get cheated out of his bonus, but the blame for the team's track record and booking the last job is laid at his feet by the general manager. He sees himself as being penalized for others' poor performance in the field. He stands accused under false charges. To him, these indictments are unjust and without merit.

Being wrongly accused is a combination of threat and embarrassment. It is embarrassing to be singled out for a mistake. If the fault falls on me and I don't think it belongs there, then the protest of "Unfair!" becomes the first rallying call to remove the misplaced accusation. For someone to say that I did something other than what I saw myself doing is an ugly mismatch between his or her perception and my reality.

The other's perception is a direct threat to my version of reality. Because it is my reality, I should know what I do and don't do; therefore the accuser is wrong. I level the charge of ill intent against my accuser. As in the case study, the general manager becomes a devious manipulator of the rules hell-bent on fixing the blame on the sales manager in order to make himself look good. When one thinks he or she is falsely accused, the accuser becomes the perpetrator of injustice.

People can be wrongly accused, and if that's the case, we can hope that the accuser modifies his or her view when the mistake is revealed. But in the sort of scenario described here, the source of the problem is a misunderstanding and not a malicious witch hunt or search for a scapegoat. What often feels like being wrongly accused is actually a misunderstanding or a poor attempt by someone delivering critical feedback. Thinking about the situation this way isn't possible, however, when the accused launches a campaign of protest and vindication using every available means of defensive reasoning in the mind's arsenal.

CONSTANT THEMES

In the five case studies, one constant was the presence of a threat or potential embarrassment. In some cases, it was obvious from reading the dialogue on the right hand side. In other cases, the existence of threat or embarrassment is evident only because the case writer revealed his or her private thinking in the LHC. For most of us, the reality of threat and embarrassment plays out in the privacy of our own minds.

Although we might not find ourselves in exactly the same situations as the people portrayed in the previous cases, we will continually find ourselves in situations where the conditions of threat and embarrassment seize our minds. If we are accused of being insincere, our integrity is called into question. If someone treats us in a way we deem to be unjust or unfair, it is cause for protest. An entire collection of faux pas, blunders, and wholesale catastrophes await us ready to give rise to threat and embarrassment. When they occur, we are ready with an alarmed response.

Differences in Views

We are ready to take the defensive even when there is a simple disagreement in views. For example, knowing that my view is different from yours, I anticipate a negative response. I might think to myself, "She is not going to like this." I hesitate to share my ideas for fear that doing so might upset you. Getting upset can be distressing. There is a chance you might get angry. It could start an argument that would end in a deadlock. I don't want to go there. It could get messy. Emotions would flare up. It would be embarrassing for both of us if things got out of hand. Better to avoid.

Whether the issue has grave significance or is a minor debate, the difference in views poses a threat, especially if the matter is framed as a win-lose situation. Either you have to change your mind (preferable), or I have to change mine. The severity of the threat is in proportion to how obvious I consider my own thinking. The more obvious and clear my thinking is to me, the more I consider your thinking as interference if it doesn't jibe with mine.

When you raise a point of view different from mine, I can easily find myself reacting, "What doesn't he get? It is so obvious." After all, I am right and you are wrong. Although I might acknowledge publicly that I could be wrong, I privately doubt it. If the difference between us is slight, I may be polite and respectfully disagree, but walk away trash-talking you in my mind. You can be assured that I will be looking out for you next time.

The stakes get higher when I hold a negative evaluation of something you said or did. I could very well be doing or saying something that contributes to the problem at hand, but that is not my focus. I am only interested in selling you my version of what happened. If you don't buy it, you will get defensive. My pointing out what you have done wrong can be embarrassing for you, and surely you will get defensive . . . and that is not good; at least that's how people tend to think about it. Getting defensive is something bad.

Differences in thinking can be huge when passions run deep or when a belief has a hold on us instead of the other way around. Everything goes black and white, with very little room for gray, much less color. The threat that comes with big differences is often accompanied by a history. We all know what others are going to do without their knowing that we know. Ask how one can be so certain of another's intentions and future behavior, and you will hear "He has always been like that" or "She does it all the time." Inoculated with certainty, we respond to the other person in a manner consistent with the negative frame we have of him or her. Differences become not only sealed but also expected and predictable.

Differences, be they small, huge, or predictable, do not always result in conditions of threat or embarrassment. Some will be triggers for certain people and not for others. Regardless, when differences do activate threat or embarrassment, we react in similar ways to protect ourselves.

Protective Strategies

Our reactions to threat and embarrassment are protective strategies. Daniel Goleman, the author of *Emotional Intelligence,* claims that these reactions are hardwired into our brains. His work honors the role emotion plays in the workings of the human brain. He sees emotion as a mode of knowing that stems from our earliest evolutionary stages, when our emotions and intuitions guided our ability to react in situations where our lives were in danger. During a potentially lethal situation, any pause for reflection could result in dire consequences. Defenses are normal, natural, and even useful. They are the emotional heritage of the primitive "fight-or-flight" response meant to protect us in times of danger. Although there are no longer any saber-toothed tigers nipping at our heels, there are social situations today where the threat (real or imagined) can activate our defenses.

The first part of *Emotional Intelligence* describes how these seemingly independent functions, reason and emotion, are part of the vast interconnected circuitry of the brain. Goleman gives insight into what takes place in the emotional brain when one feels under attack or when a situation poses potential embarrassment.

Under these conditions, the brain reacts instantaneously. Goleman identifies the amygdala as the first part of the brain to respond to a crisis. Its response is not one of thought, but emotion. When the amygdala sounds the alarm, it triggers the fight-or-flight response. He likens this part of our brain to an emergency switchboard operator standing by to send out calls to the necessary protective services whenever the home security system signals trouble.

The word *emotion* is derived from the Latin verb *motere*, "to move," and the prefix *e-*, "away." Emotion moves us into action. Although our emotional brain has been useful in our evolution, Goleman claims there are several out-of-date neural alarms. The emotional brain scans a present experience for a match with a previous one. The match is associative—not always exact—and calls for immediate action undertaken with complete certainty and conviction. We refer to this as getting our buttons pushed, or what Goleman calls becoming emotionally hijacked. Our emotional brain takes over our rational thought. Accuracy is sacrificed for speed of action. Our emotional response is quick but sloppy, not well thought out. If after a strong emotional reaction to a person or situation you find yourself saying, "I wasn't thinking when I said that," you have had the experience of being emotionally hijacked.

Because our emotional mind is associative, Goleman describes it as childlike. On one hand, this gives us the ability to appreciate metaphors, stories, images, and other art forms that speak the vernacular of the heart. On the other hand, the emotional mind operates with a high degree of certainty and in black-and-white categories. "You *always* do that. It drives me crazy." These thoughts tend to be highly personalized, and we perceive events with a personal bias. "This is being done to me."

This childlike emotional mode is also self-confirming. Try to reason with someone who is emotionally hijacked. It is very hard to do. How he or she sees the situation is *the way it is* to that person. The emotional mind selects the data that confirms the individual's view of what is happening, and ignores the rest. His or her feelings become self-justifying with proofs of their own.

CONDITIONS OF THREAT AND EMBARRASSMENT: A CRUCIBLE FOR LEARNING OR JUST CAUSE FOR DEFENSE

In the course of our lives, we will continue to find ourselves under conditions of threat and embarrassment. And, as a result, we will engage in defensive reasoning. It's not possible to eliminate defensiveness from our lives unless we choose the life of a hermit. Our defensive emotional responses are part of the hard-wiring in our brains and in many cases serve us well by alerting us to danger. And, in fact, there can be a very just cause for going on the defensive.

Conditions of threat and embarrassment can also be crucibles for learning. We may be contributing to the difficulty at hand, may possibly have been wrong or mistaken. If this is the case, then it is to our advantage to learn from the situation. To do so, we need to become more deliberate in our response, instead of reactive. The first step is to increase our awareness of how we get emotionally triggered in certain situations. In that spirit, complete the following brief exercises. They are intended to help you identify how you get emotionally triggered. With increased awareness comes better recognition. With recognition comes the choice to do the same or something different.

Exercises

To Defend, Serve, and Protect (Your Face)

Think about an interaction with someone at work. Use your imagination. Let it go wild, but keep it within the context of the business world. Imagine if you will your worst nightmare, a "Mayday! Mayday!" encounter, a conversation that "went south," a time you wish could avoid at all costs. Whether your scenario is completely imaginary or you are the unfortunate soul who conjures up a real event, ask yourself the following questions:

What is the worst thing that could happen to me in an interaction with another person (or people) in a business situation?

In this real or imagined scenario, what is the other person saying to me?

What is my internal reaction?

What threat do I perceive? What is it about this threat that has such a strong effect on me?

My Buttons

Ask yourself, What pushes my buttons? Give an example.
Then ask yourself,

What does someone typically say that pushes the button?

What do I tend to say or do in response?

What results are generated?

What can I do to "interrupt" my automatic reaction?

In the next chapter, we re-enter the case "Fix It Now or Fix It Later," joining Mark and Brenda as they share their reactions to the situation with their respective colleagues. What they say to their colleagues, they would not dare say to each other. Yet how Brenda and Mark think of each other will influence their future interactions. The nature of their current thinking guarantees a standoff. They are squaring off with each other in a way we often do when under the conditions of threat and embarrassment.

Being in Control

FIX IT NOW OR FIX IT LATER,
SCENE TWO: THE WORD GETS OUT

Brenda signaled Alison from across the restaurant. When she'd invited the account manager to lunch, Brenda had intentionally picked a spot out of walking distance from the office to break the news about Mark and the proposed plant repairs. She didn't need anyone overhearing their conversation.

"Sorry I'm late," Alison sighed as she deposited a briefcase nearly as overstuffed as Brenda's onto the booth seat and slid in next to it. "Those guys at EdCon are really going to keep me on my toes. I'm getting calls six times a day."

Brenda liked Alison. She'd worked her way up through the ranks about five years behind Brenda and had suffered the same corporate challenges—having to prove herself on the technical end and then transfer to Sales, only to start back on the bottom rung with the smaller accounts. When Brenda had finally inked the deal with EdCon, she made sure Alison got the account.

"I don't know how you managed it," Alison continued, "but those guys love you. All I hear is Brenda this and Brenda that. After all the delays and problems they've had with other providers, they're in heaven that we can come through for them."

Brenda knew Alison meant well, but every gushing remark made it more difficult to tell her about Mark's suggested delay at the refinery.

Alison took a sip of water. "How long did it take for you to land the account? Two years?"

"I don't count it in years; I count it in lost sleep, destruction of social life, and chunks of my sanity."

Alison grinned. "Hey, it landed you a nice enough bonus to get that little convertible. I'm hoping now that it's my turn with EdCon, they'll bring me the same success."

A waitress appeared at Brenda's elbow with two menus. Brenda took hers and laid it on the table beside her. "Can you give us a few minutes before we order?"

The waitress nodded crisply and headed toward the kitchen.

Alison's eyebrow raised. "What's up?"

"It's about EdCon. I received a call from Mark over at the refinery. During the routine maintenance, his crew found a faulty piece of equipment."

Alison exhaled hard. "Tell me they're still going to be back on line as scheduled."

"He wants to extend the schedule by a week and fix it now."

"A week!" The shrillness of Alison's voice cut through the dining room buzz. Brenda cocked her head in the direction of the two men in the next booth who had turned to stare.

Alison forced her voice to a whisper. "This is the worst possible time. They are counting on us. If we don't deliver on schedule, we'll be no better than EdCon's former providers. We blow the schedule, they'll start shopping around again. The repairs can't be that critical."

Brenda shrugged. "Who knows? He just left a phone message that he had a bad exchanger. Operations always wants to fix problems during a scheduled turnaround. I know worker safety is an important issue, but they never admit to the real reason. They don't want to blow their budget on an unscheduled repair."

Alison slumped back into the booth. "So what do we do?"

"You and I both know Corporate isn't going to let a big client walk. The only delay that is going to happen is with these repairs. Brenda saw Alison's eyes brighten. "Mark's a great manager, but when it comes to the refinery, it's all or nothing. If there's a leaky faucet in the men's room, he's calling to shut down the whole plant."

Alison laughed. "How are you going to handle Mark?"

Brenda looked over her shoulder. The two men in the booth had resumed their lunch. She leaned forward. "I have to be careful here. There's no point in alienating Mark. We have to work with him for the long term. I've e-mailed him that I'm willing to help him come up with a solution."

"Your solution?"

Brenda smiled. "Mark needs to realize that there's more to business than just providing the product when it's most convenient for him."

"When do you talk again?"

Brenda glanced at her watch. Mark's lunch hour, like most of his activities, ran according to schedule. He'd be back at his desk in twenty-five minutes. She signaled the waitress. "Right after I finish the chicken salad I'm going to order."

Mark checked his inbox, but there were no new messages from Brenda. He knew from the insistent tone of her "We need to talk" voice message a few days prior that she wasn't on board with the delay in schedule.

Not that he was surprised. After leaving the refinery for Sales, Brenda had forgotten whose side she was on. Even the jokes they had once shared about clients to let off steam didn't raise a smile.

Mark had considered every option he could think of in the past twenty-four hours to avoid a delay, but the gamble was just too great to bring things back on line knowing there was a problem. Mark had already notified Walt, the plant manager, of his plans. He'd also reminded him of the Workers Comp claims that had strangled the budget last year and how Corporate had been putting on the pressure to bring costs down. Walt knew that if an exchanger failed, people could get hurt. Even if there were injuries, paying the overtime to make the repairs would annihilate any savings they'd accrued so far.

Hearing a knock on his door, Mark looked up. It was John, the operations manager at the south end of the plant. He had his lunch box in hand, on time for their usual noon break together.

"You ready?" he said leaning against the door jamb.

"Let me just close up these e-mails." Mark clicked the mouse, and the messages on the screen disappeared.

"I heard a rumor of a bad exchanger," John said, his body blocking the exit.

"Yeah, the repair will delay the start-up about a week."

"How is Sales handling it? I bet Brenda gave you an earful."

Mark grinned. "Not yet. We're trading e-mail and phone messages back and forth, but we haven't actually had a conversation."

John shook his head. "All this technology, and still no one talks to each other."

Mark shared his colleague's disdain for the so-called time-saving devices that only created more work. Give him a face-to-face conversation any time. That's when the problems were hammered out and the real work began.

"Brenda knows better than most the danger of working with a bad exchanger," said Mark. "No one in their right mind would take that risk." He leaned back in his chair.

John smirked, "Yeah, but never underestimate Corporate. You'd better be careful how you handle this."

"I've already talked to Walt." Mark pushed back his chair and stood up. "Brenda and her sales staff will just have to deal with it."

John stepped aside to let him pass. "Have you ever seen Brenda *just deal* with anything?"

"This time, she doesn't have a choice."

SUMMARY: SQUARING OFF

The battle lines are being drawn between Mark and Brenda. They are now deep into defensive routine. There is a lot at stake. Neither one would admit publicly or even be consciously aware that he or she is reacting out of conditions of threat or potential embarrassment, but both are doing just that. One clear clue is that even as they take up opposing positions, they share a common mind-set: each believes that his or her own view is right and that the outcome will be one winner and one loser. Each also sees himself or herself as being rational and reasonable.

This kind of thinking is a hallmark characteristic of defensive reasoning; it is designed to protect individuals from threat or embarrassment. Argyris refers to it as Model I thinking. Action Design uses the term Unilateral Control Model, which I will also employ in this book. This mind-set is primarily responsible for setting a defensive routine in motion. It is activated as a means of keeping us in control of a situation where we sense ourselves as being under threat or facing embarrassment.

MARK AND BRENDA ASIDE: WHAT CAUSES THE UNILATERAL CONTROL MODEL TO KICK IN?

When we are in control, there is a consistency between our perception of reality and all incoming information. There is no interference or static. We feel that things are going as we hoped and intended. Things are going our way. We know what we're doing. We feel competent.

When subjected to the conditions of threat or potential embarrassment, however, we can quickly feel that control gets away from us. Think about what happens when we suspect that our words have been misinterpreted. Although we realize that we don't have any control over how another person interprets our words, we immediately go on the offensive, insisting that what the other person heard is not what we meant. If the other person counters with "It's what you said," then the exchange can escalate into a "No, I didn't," "Yes, you did" scenario.

Any time the unexpected triumphs over the expected, there is a good chance that someone will start losing his or her grip on control. When a conversation goes to a place I hadn't intended or desired, it feels like the rug is pulled out from under me. For example, I go into a meeting eager to garner support for my plan, and before I know it, opposition to my most brilliant idea takes the center stage of the team discussion. I scrabble to disarm the opposition, but to no avail. My mind sends out the "Mayday! Mayday!" emergency call as my idea is shot down.

Then there are those times when I am carrying on my end of the conversation in a civil manner, and I notice that the other person has daggers in his or her eyes. Something I said clearly must have triggered a reaction, but I am clueless as to what it was. Or I can be listening to another person and seize upon a word or phrase that indicates to me that he or she has no understanding of my position. The person's potentially innocent comment is inadvertently the stimulus to my response of "What in the [expletive] are you talking about?"

My least favorite time for losing control is when I am trying to point out something problematic with what another person said or did, and suddenly I am being told that I am the problem. I see the other person as being defensive and trying to turn the tables. We end up both clutching our respective sides of the issue and trying to wrestle a confession from the other as to who takes the larger portion of the blame.

When these encounters occur, I feel disoriented, disturbed, and distracted. There is momentary bafflement over what is going on. I am not thinking about mutual benefits or outcomes. I can't allow myself that luxury. I am being threatened; I am not in control of the situation, and that is an unpleasant experience.

Being out of control is not a pleasant experience for anyone. We all have different tolerance points and triggering situations and emotions, but we share a common reaction: we try to get a firm grip on the reins of control. When the conditions of threat or embarrassment arise, our need for control shifts into a higher gear. We engage the Unilateral Control Model, in which the predominant concern is self-interest and self-preservation.

We all exhibit the thinking and actions of the Unilateral Control Model. According to Argyris, it is a socially learned prescription of thoughts and behavior that is highly shared among us. It is so ingrained that it appears as a default state of mind. The Unilateral Control Model is not necessarily a bad thing; in fact, it is sometimes necessary. What's important to understand is that the Unilateral Control Model is not our only option, and it is not generally the best tack to take when trying to resolve or minimize defensive routines.

THE MAIN FEATURES OF THE UNILATERAL CONTROL MODEL

There is nothing wrong with being in control. It's possible to be in control and at the same time to work happily with entire teams of people, in which most if not all members also feel in control.

Unilateral control is different. The term *unilateral* is what gives this model its distinctive defensive quality. Being unilateral means there is a one-sidedness to the thinking, and what one person is thinking is *imposed* on others.

Winning, Not Losing

The aim of the Unilateral Control Model is to *win, not lose.* In a defensive routine, no one is thinking that win-win is an option. In conversations, this aim manifests itself as a desire to assert our views and to convince the other person that we're right and the other is wrong. Many of us place a premium on being right. We associate being right with winning and being wrong with losing. We hold our position and argue to win. Moreover, we assume that if we win an argument, our ideas will prevail. If we lose, our ideas will disappear into the black hole of corporate amnesia.

Certainly, being in the right has its benefits and value. When our ideas win the support of others, we gain confidence in our thinking. Being right *a lot* gets the attention of those in command, so our influence and power increase. The right idea, if supported, can catalyze an effective implementation of a new strategy, boost the company's profits, and earn us public recognition. Being right can be good for us *and* for our organization.

So there is nothing wrong with being right. I am not always under the conditions of threat and embarrassment when I engage others in conversation. I don't enter every conversation with the goal of winning. But if the stakes are high, it is another ball game. When I perceive myself to be under threat, falsely accused, or doubted as adequate, there is a "must win" edge to my thinking. That "must win" edge is a unique expression of the unilateral quality of the model. When the refrain "I know I'm right" becomes a constant drumbeat in my head, I have dropped into the unilateral control mind-set.

The mind-set of "win, not lose" is reinforced by cultural norms that ordain holding one's position as a sign of strength. I hold my position ready to take the defensive or charge ahead. The point is to outmaneuver the other guy or at least block his ideas. Speaking confidently projects a message that I know what I'm doing. The communication equivalent of muscular strength is talking loud and fast. The louder I talk, the harder I press my point. When I talk fast, it is as though I am outrunning other people's thoughts, forcing them to keep up with my pace. I cram as many sentences as I can in a breath. I hit one bullet point after another without stopping. I'll admit that I am talking a lot, but no matter. I have something to say, and it should be clear and obvious to everyone.

Repetition is another common practice of the "win, not lose" mind-set. If someone responds with "I don't understand what you're saying," I assume that they have misheard or that I haven't been clear, so I repeat myself. Usually by the time I am on my third explanation, the noise in my head hits a fever pitch, screaming, "What is it that you don't get? If I say it again, will you get the obvious?" I don't have mental space left to explain my point any differently because I am consumed with the thought of how stupid the other person is. I usually end with a crescendo of "What is wrong with you?" and bring the curtain down on the conversation. For my listeners, my multiple explanations have only increased their level of frustration, further confusing the people who don't understand and boring the people who do.

When, in a point of conflict, two people adopt the same mind-set of "win, not lose," the results are predictable. Opinions are thrown back and forth until one person finally "caves." Outwardly, he or she accepts the other's proposal—while privately believing the proposal is worthless. The participants may give up on resolving their conflict themselves and call for an outside authority to make the decision for them. In both cases, the quality of decision making suffers.

The assumptions that accompany the socially supported position of "win, not lose" follow the one-sided nature of the thinking. I experience your view as utterly wrong. I have to get you to admit your errors. I want concession on your part. There is no room for differences. One of us has to win, and the other must lose. The assumption that I am on the winning side neglects the possibility that you may be thinking the same thing about me—namely, that you are right and I am wrong. Hence, the paradox is that for me to be effective, everyone else has to be ineffective. I ask of others what I would not want to do myself—to be ineffective. This assumption violates the justice of a fair exchange.

Another characteristic inherent to the "win, not lose" mind-set is the high degree of certainty to which we hold our point of view. A high level of confidence leaves no room for discovery of error. The folly of complete certainty is its belief in constancy. The odds are that we are not always right. Persisting in a position of "I know I'm right" can have repercussions.

The American satirist Will Rogers said, "You may be on the right track, but if you stay there long enough you are bound to get run over." Rogers twisted the idea of being right just enough to expose some of its vulnerabilities. The strategy of winning plays out in loud conversation, hammering a point, or imposing one's authority. Assuming you are right and embarking on the task of convincing others of that fact may not get you run over, but there is a greater likelihood that the conversation will be derailed.

More so now than in Will Rogers's time, the concept of the right idea has a short life span. Change is a reality in the business environment. What may be a good idea today won't work tomorrow because of changes in the business world. Staying ahead of change or, even better, leading change requires a high degree of flexibility, an acute ability to detect and correct error, and an uncanny sense of seeing what others miss. Staying with one idea, even the right one, for too long gives your competitor the opportunity to run you over and keep on going.

Adapting to change is not the work of any single individual within an organization. The expectation that a business leader can hold all the relevant facts and possess a single perspective on the complicated issues current in our business world today is unsound and unrealistic. More and more, business leaders have to rely on multiple perspectives in order to garner the information necessary to make informed choices. To gain the best possible thinking from the multiple perspectives found in team and individual exchanges, business leaders cannot afford to rely on the tactical strategies of wining or losing arguments.

Being Rational and Avoiding Upset

The aim of remaining rational is to avoid creating upset. Upsetting situations are breeding grounds for the conditions of threat and embarrassment. It is embarrassing to show too much emotion. Public displays of anger can be very intimidating to others. We suppress these negative feelings if they arise within us. In case studies of difficult conversations, there are often LHC comments like "There's that big smile as he worms his way out yet again. Stay cool, take a deep breath, and try one last time" or "I hope I am not letting on that this is getting really annoying. Take it easy." These are instructions for coaching ourselves to remain rational. Remaining rational is a way to get a grip on the situation. The appeal to rationality keeps things cool and away from emotions. We tell ourselves that bringing emotion into a situation where conflict already exists will only make matters worse.

Our desire not to upset others is highly valued as altruistic and caring. Getting upset is not a pleasant experience for anybody. Feelings of anger, sadness, and hurt are real, but ones we want to get past as soon as possible. Soothing another's feelings with calm assurances is caring as well as a subtle message to get a grip. We take whatever steps necessary not to hurt others' feelings or upset them. In the LHC of case studies, there are such comments as "I'd better encourage him, but I still want him to know that he has underperformed" or "I only agree because you are the boss." Each of these examples illustrates what Argyris identifies as two common strategies we use to remain rational and avoid upset.

The first is to support others by telling them what they want to hear; the second is to respect others' views by not challenging their thinking. These two common strategies belong to a heavily sanctioned set of social norms deemed virtuous by our society. Argyris refers to them as "social virtues." But here's the rub: as Argyris points out, these are virtues only in the sense that society ordains their value and prescribes behavior as socially appropriate or polite. Under the influence of the Unilateral Control Model, they are strategies that aid and abet a habitual pattern of thinking and behaving designed to protect us from conditions of threat and embarrassment. Let's consider three social virtues in turn.

Social Virtue: "Supporting Others"

We like to hear that others think we have the right idea. We feel good about ourselves when they tell us how great an idea it is; we feel supported. When we as listeners affirm another's idea, we often do it out of a sincere desire to be caring and helpful—even though we may think differently. We might say to someone, "That's a wonderful idea. Keep up the good thinking." What we think to ourselves is "She is off on a wild goose chase. That idea will never work." We want to encourage other people's ideas and not stifle their thinking.

Supporting others and their ideas is a wholesome custom of everyday civilization. We need people to be civil with one another. If I had to engage every disagreement I had with the people in my daily life, I wouldn't get anything done. I can let minor disagreements go or simply not consider an issue very important.

When our cherished values and firm beliefs clash against each other, we can quickly find ourselves in situations of threat and potential embarrassment. The social norms for showing support prevent prolonged exposure to such situations. They are the "nice" things to do when interacting with someone whom you would rather throttle or run away from. In our day-to-day business world, we get very busy making nice.

In my travels across the country, every company I have visited has made the claim that it suffers the effects of being too polite and nice. At a large company in Michigan, the management admitted that there were too many people being "Michigan nice." Employees at other companies have confessed, "We are killing each other with politeness." People indulge themselves in a "misguided politeness."

What I hear in these complaints is a fatigue from not being able to discuss the complicated issues that matter most. In the name of being nice and courteous, we don't engage the real issues. When we tell someone what we think he or she wants to hear—even if we don't agree with the idea or viewpoint—we do ourselves and the other person a disservice. We may do this out of a sincere desire to be caring, helpful, and respectful, and to help make the other person feel supported and good about himself or herself. To those ends, we don't challenge the person's thinking. Instead, we might say, "Let's agree to disagree" or "I respect your view." Meanwhile, we're saying to ourselves, "She's just wrong." Recall something you've recently said to another person's face. Then remember what you said about that same person to someone else. Chances are there's a distinct difference in the content of the two exchanges.

This strategy carries with it a not-so-charitable assumption: that others are too fragile to handle bad news or criticism. If a particular person is told something negative, he or she will break down in tears. It would be too upsetting and embarrassing for the person to handle. This may be true for a very small number of people, but when we generalize this thinking, we pay a high price because it prevents people from learning from their mistakes. Instead, we protect them from their own errors in the name of support and caring.

Social Virtue: "Respecting Others' Views"

Respecting another person's view is a valued standard of behavior in the workplace. Respect shows an attitude of high regard or esteem for another's character, thinking, or behavior. A secondary meaning for showing respect suggests that one should refrain from interfering with another's thinking or plans. In many cultures, a sign of respect is to leave another's point of view alone. Hear it, acknowledge it (with or without understanding it), and move on. If we disagree with someone's point of view, we do our best to disagree politely. We state our opinion and leave it standing next to the opposing view without engaging how we see it differently. It takes skill to show respect while privately thinking that the other person's thinking is wrong.

Respect has become associated with not disagreeing publicly. This meaning is particularly pronounced in our relationships with authority. I witnessed a president of a Saudi Arabian company make a passionate plea to his senior leadership team to air their disagreements with his point of view. After he sat down, I said to his team, "I can imagine that some of you may be thinking to yourself, 'Yeah, right, no way am I going to disagree with the president.'" One courageous senior leader stood up and responded, "That's right. You have to understand that we live in a culture with a ruling monarch. In this country, you don't disagree with the king." Pointing to the president, the man continued. "In this company, he is our king."

Although the president's personal reflection might include seeing what he has said or done that could have inhibited others' ability to disagree with him, the instance nevertheless demonstrated the power of this pervasive social norm to shape behavior in the company. In spite of people's good intentions, and even when they demonstrate the best communication skills, productive business conversations can be limited by the value of respect embedded in a company's cultural structures. At another Saudi Arabian company, I heard the Arabian idiom, "The king wants to go water skiing; start rowing." The cost of showing respect by not disagreeing with those in authority carries a heavy price. Inefficiencies are tolerated and accepted. Business meetings lack a robust discussion of diverse ideas. Ultimately, the quality of decision making suffers due to the lack of information flowing to the top of the organization.

Social Virtue: "Being Honest"

Often I hear from people that they don't act in these indirect or polite ways. They see it as a violation of another valued social norm. They embrace "Honesty is the best policy." Being direct is virtuous. Once, a woman stood up in a workshop and publicly declared to everyone that she didn't have an LHC. At first I thought that a rather odd thing to say. It is impossible not to have private thoughts. When awake, the mind is always chattering away.

Upon inquiry, I heard her meaning as essentially saying, "I don't censor my thinking. What you hear is what I think or feel." She admitted that not everyone likes what she says, but at least people know where she stands. She held the virtue of honesty and directness with great pride and confidence.

I wouldn't disagree with her about honesty being a worthy virtue. We all strive to be honest in our dealings with others. I do question whether blurting out whatever we are thinking or feeling is a practice of honesty. Honesty gives allegiance to truthfulness, not impulse. What we blurt out is spoken with the conviction of speaking our mind. The conviction carries with it the assumption that what we've said is the way it is, certain and obvious. What we are saying may be exactly how we are thinking and feeling in that moment, but it may not be completely true or valid. We may not be completely honest with ourselves. To take up honesty as a virtue entails a commitment to be as honest with ourselves as we are with others.

When we practice social virtues that support the Unilateral Control Model, we think we're being diplomatic and polite. But most people see through our posturing. Although these social virtues help us maintain an appropriate level of civility with each other in society, they do not serve us well when we're discussing important, complex business issues. They get in the way of learning, prolong decision making, and result eventually in lost productivity.

THE UNILATERAL CONTROL MODEL REVEALED: THREE COMMON REACTIONS

Whether presented in a lecture format, a presentation, or written material, the Unilateral Control Model and its accompanying social virtues are easily understood, but people's reactions to the model differ from person to person and across cultural lines. In my experience, I have seen three common reactions. The first reaction is often a simple denial: "Not me! But I know someone who is Model I." The second reaction is an honest admission of the person's own culpability, followed by a zealous resolve to "Get rid of it." The third is a backlash protest: "What's wrong with it?"

Not Me!

I learned about the Unilateral Control Model when I attended the first Action Design Institute at Babson College in 1993. The partners of Action Design had boiled it down to a few bullet points that fit neatly in a PowerPoint slide, and Chris Argyris himself talked the participants through its main features. I had a self-satisfied reaction. I thought to myself, "I don't do that. I take other people's viewpoints into account. I am willing to admit that I am wrong. I can hang out in upsetting situations. I can deal with mine and others' emotions. I don't just live in my rational head."

Fortunately, this initial assessment of myself didn't last long. As always at the Action Design Institutes, there are small group sessions in which the participants bring their LHC-RHC case study of a difficult conversation. There is the promise that the case writer will be able to "do something more effective" with the help of the faculty and group members. I was eager for them to help me deal with my absolute egomaniac idiot of a boss. I began with a robust description of his abode in a special corner of hell. I was confident that my vivid description would win the support of my group. I expected that they would support me entirely and tell me how to deal with this guy.

They didn't. As the first surge of heat swept over my face, I realized that I was in for a different experience. The group was focusing not on what my boss was like, but on what I had said to him. The coup de grace was my private thoughts in the LHC of the case study. They betrayed me. I was functioning in perfect accord with the Unilateral Control Model. Talk about embarrassing. As it turned out, I was a little demon myself, stoking the fires in that special corner of hell we had created for ourselves at work.

I couldn't think of a worse time for this to happen. I looked around the circle of strangers, colleagues, and a faculty member I wanted to impress. I had just made myself a shining example of what everyone wanted to avoid. I could feel my psyche freeze up. I was going into shut-down mode. To this day, I can recall only my awkward silence and fumbling utterances of "But wait, if you knew this guy. He is impossible to work with. I work to serve his ego." I remember that it was difficult to hear what others were saying. I wasn't quick to admit to anything, yet I was the one who provided the evidence.

After a bit of self-loathing and the thought that "I can't believe I actually behave that way," I settled down and listened to what others were observing. As much as I disliked my boss and thought poorly of him, we were no different from each other when it came to thinking who was right and who missed the obvious. We were never of one mind in our conversation, but we surely shared the same mind-set. It was now glaringly apparent to me that I was (and still am) capable of thinking and acting out of the Unilateral Control Model.

Get Rid of It!

A common reaction to the discovery that we are perfectly capable of thinking and acting in the ways of the Unilateral Control Model is to want to get rid of it as quickly as possible. The problem is that getting rid of the Unilateral Control Model is about as likely as getting your mind erased. The Unilateral Control Model has its place in our psyches. Whether the model is a master social program or an encoded relic from our prehistoric ancestors, our minds possess the capacity to think and act according to its precepts and assumptions.

The Unilateral Control Model is there and at our mind's service when conditions of threat and embarrassment occur. There will be future situations where our neuron pathways will light up with signals to activate the Unilateral Control Model. The real issue is whether we have any choice.

There is no evangelical call to rid ourselves of the Unilateral Control Model. Argyris's work is about offering another choice. The key to making a choice is awareness. A good first habit of practice is simply to be able to catch yourself when you find yourself fully operational in the Unilateral Control Model.

What's Wrong with Unilateral Control?

The third predominant reaction to the Unilateral Control Model comes in the form of "What's wrong with it?" Workshop participants think that the presenting practitioner is asking everyone to give up being right or being polite. I don't know whether this reaction indicates a mishearing or a tendency on the part of the presenter to communicate a negative value to the Unilateral Control Model. I do know that in my past experience of describing the model, I tended to place a stress on the "win, not lose" mind-set as a "Don't do it any longer." Understandably, there was a protest.

In every workshop, I heard a chorus of "What is wrong with being right?" and "But we have to be polite." When I first heard these comments, I just thought the participants were stuck in the Unilateral Control Model. Obviously they were unaware of how they were demonstrating the model by refusing to admit that they could be anything other than right. I could not have been more wrong myself. In my own mind, they were wrong for thinking that way. Once I was able to free myself from this view, I was able to listen to their stories about how much these social virtues influence our behavior.

I have learned to respect the power these norms and values exert in our respective cultures. Students from Asian cultures have provided me with firsthand knowledge. In my college courses, I have an average of three to five Asian students. They never speak up. It isn't always an issue of a language barrier. Most of them speak excellent English. Once I asked several of them, "I notice that you all remain quiet during the class. Is there anything I need to be aware of that is making it difficult for you to participate?" One student answered quickly, "In our culture, you don't interrupt the professor. It is disrespectful." Things got a little clearer then. They went on to say that their role was to take in the information the professor was providing. The professor was the expert. If they had any questions, they would approach the professor privately. That explained the long line of Asian students I always had at break time.

In every discussion of whether to be polite or direct, there is always one person who throws out the well-known phrase, "You have to pick your battles." This phrase announces the end of the discussion with a note of resignation. What is unspoken but understood is that the situation at hand is not worth fighting over and that the person should move on. The statement is often used as a justification not to engage or be direct with what you are thinking or feeling.

The recommendation to pick your battles suggests that the correct action is to say nothing or to adopt an indirect approach. Oddly enough, this ensures that one does lose even though the message carries an implied positive affirmation of victory. The person loses in the sense that the results offer no resolution. The suppressed thoughts and feelings promise a potential escalation of tension in the future. These negative results are mitigated by the implied message "I am being strategic in choosing not to fight this battle." In other words, you may have lost this battle, but you will win the war.

The phrase "Pick your battles" is a product of the unilateral control mind-set. It confirms the perception that every conversation is a contest. You win or lose. The tally of frustration and emotional tension from battles not picked continues to be counted. Finally, when the time comes to engage in battle, it has become all-out nuclear warfare with mutual destruction assured.

The social values of respecting and supporting others help us live together civilly. Although variants exist from culture to culture, every culture has norms and values that govern how people interact with each other in a civil manner. These norms and values are important to the functioning of a society where great diversity exists, but have limiting effects on our ability to engage differences when learning is a requirement. These limiting effects are particularly evident when the Unilateral Control Model is fully operational.

Exercise

Being in Control

Recall the exercise from the previous chapter, "To Defend, Serve, and Protect (Your Face)." The questions in that exercise were

What is the worst thing that could happen to me in an interaction with another person (or people) in a business situation?

In this real or imagined scenario, what is the other person saying to me?

What is my internal reaction?

What threat do I perceive? What is it about this threat that has such a strong effect on me?

For this exercise, consider your answers to the questions above, and ask yourself,

What do I find myself saying or doing in response?

It can be helpful simply to think about all these questions, answering them mentally. But it is generally more useful to write down your responses. If you only think about the answers to the questions, you can fall into a sort of mental shorthand. There is more to be gained if you let yourself create an actual scenario, including a full-sentence dialogue.

With the complete dialogue in hand, ask yourself these questions:

How would I describe my behavior in the face of threat and embarrassment?

How would I describe the statements I felt the other person would make?

In Chapter Five, Mark and Brenda illustrate how the Unilateral Control Model plays out in action. Reluctant to confront one another directly, fearful of losing control, and unwilling to "lose," Mark and Brenda attempt to get their messages across to one another via strategies that "bypass" the conditions of threat and embarrassment. They are polite; no one oversteps "socially acceptable" boundaries. But neither is fooled.

Bypass Tactics and Covering Up

FIX IT NOW OR FIX IT LATER, SCENE THREE: BEING NICE

Mark pushed back in his chair, rested his feet on an open file cabinet drawer, then punched in the familiar number on the phone pad. He'd tried calling Brenda at least a half dozen times in the past few days without any luck. He'd even begun wondering if she was avoiding his calls.

He straightened when he heard her voice. "Hey, Brenda, it's Mark."

"Hey, Mark. How are things going?"

She sounded cordial enough, thought Mark. He'd better keep things light for a bit. "Great, now that we're actually talking to each other. I don't know how you get anything done sending e-mails and leaving voice messages. Corporate must be keeping you pretty busy."

"No more than when I was working at the plant," she laughed. "Never enough time, you know? Like right now. I've got about ten minutes before my next meeting. How about if we put our heads together and see if we can't tackle this problem of yours?"

Mark bristled. Now it was *his* problem? "I'd appreciate that, Brenda," he said, ignoring her condescending tone. The sooner he could get her buy-in on extending the turnaround, the sooner he could put in the work order. "Have you got everything straightened out with your customers about the product delay?"

There was a pause. "No, I haven't," Brenda said, her voice brittle. "I'm hoping you and I can work something out so I don't have to."

Mark shook his head. He knew she was going to resist him on this one. It was going to be a fight, and he had to stay cool.

He leaned forward, pressing his elbows against the desktop. "I'd really appreciate your cooperation on this, Brenda. This failed exchanger was totally unexpected. You had some unexpected delays in your time too, remember?"

Brenda hesitated. She could hear Mark's attempts to connect with her over their shared past experience, but she wasn't about to let him off the hook. They were wasting time killing each other with niceties. She had to be firmer and more direct.

"We did have delays while I was at the plant," she said. "but none that caused customers dissatisfaction."

"I want to avoid that, too," said Mark. "A small delay couldn't possibly cause that much trouble, right?"

"It's a problem, Mark. Any delay is a potential problem."

"A potential problem," Mark said. "So nothing that you know of right now will cause a problem if we delay the turnaround?"

Brenda sighed. Mark was probing for a weakness in her position, trying to trap her. That wasn't going to happen.

"Look, I don't even want to go there," she said firmly. "It sends the wrong message to our customers if we even hint at the possibility of a delay. What about scheduling the repair later?"

Mark dropped his head into his hand. The woman clearly wasn't listening. If she didn't get the importance of fixing the problem now, he wasn't going to keep trying to explain it to her. Obviously she had no intention of changing her position.

"That's a thought," he said trying to remain polite. "I'll run it by my crew, but you know how things work around here. If it breaks, we fix it."

Brenda could tell by the tone of Mark's voice that he was blowing her off. He had no intention of running it by his crew. Even if he did, they would back him no matter what. He was right. She did know how things worked around there.

"I am not telling you don't fix it, Mark," she said. "Give me a break. I have been in your position."

"Then you understand that we need to delay the schedule."

"What I understand, Mark, is that there's too much at stake here. Sometimes you just have to look at the bigger picture."

"All right, take it easy," said Mark. "We need to make a decision here. I'm not going to run my operations on bad equipment."

Brenda gripped the phone. "And I'm not going to lose customers over this."

"Then we're going to have to agree to disagree on this one," Mark snapped.

Brenda's throat tightened as she laughed. "What's that supposed to mean? That doesn't get us any closer to a final decision."

"I don't think you have much choice on this one."

Brenda glanced at her watch. Her next meeting was supposed to start three minutes ago. She was going to have to kick this problem up a level. She knew that the plant manager, Walter Burton, would keep an eye on the bigger picture and not just focus on Mark's sliver of the pie.

"This really isn't your call, Mark," said Brenda. "Walt is going to have to weigh in on this."

"Not a problem. I'll schedule a meeting with him and a few of the crew who are up to speed on the equipment. Can you fly in by the end of the week?"

Brenda smiled. "I'll clear my calendar."

SUMMARY: KEEP ON KEEPING ON

The only thing Mark and Brenda have cleared the way for is a showdown of conflicting views and opposing solutions to the problem. Each has adopted the Unilateral Control Model of thinking and acting. They are so deep into a defensive routine that there is little hope that the meeting they scheduled will get to a solution. Typical of defensive routines, the situation is escalating. Mark sees himself as being right and Brenda as wrong. Brenda sees herself as being right and Mark as wrong. The task is to convince the other person of how wrong he or she is. Telling someone directly that he or she is wrong can be threatening and embarrassing. To avoid experiencing either threat or embarrassment, they both act in ways to protect each other. Their attempts are polite and diplomatic, but easily seen through by the other.

MARK AND BRENDA ASIDE: HOW DO WE KEEP DEFENSIVE ROUTINES IN PLACE?

Mark and Brenda's interchange is full of common strategies we use to keep defensive routines in place. They are ways to "bypass" or avoid the threat and embarrassment and are a part of our everyday social interactions. We all use them, and for the most part we feel good about using them. We don't see how limiting they are because they are socially sanctioned behaviors. In this chapter, we will look at these behaviors in detail and how they contribute to making things undiscussable. Chris Argyris identifies three socially sanctioned and common forms of bypassing: easing in, sending inconsistent messages, and saving face. They contribute to making things undiscussable because for the bypass strategies to work, we must cover them up.

Easing In

When an idea pops into my head that I think is valuable, I hope others will think the same. Their agreement affirms that my idea is the way to go. It feels good to have others agree with me. The only problem is that I have to put my idea out there in order to get agreement. I hesitate slightly before I speak. In this nanosecond, an assumption lurking under my thinking comes into play: my view might not be received well. Others could disagree with me.

It doesn't have to be a three-alarm bell that signals a full-scale threat to my thinking. I could just be uncertain of my colleague's response. Maybe I don't know the person well and want to appear cooperative. In that case, I might consider taking a softer approach. I will say something like, "Don't you think it would be a good idea if . . .?" I expect the other person to say, "Yes, it would be."

If I know the person well, I might anticipate a disagreement. In that case, I'll find all kinds of reasons for thinking the other party would not agree with me. It could be that he or she has voiced disapproval in the past. If there have been enough times in the past when I have put out my view and the other person's response has been less than enthusiastic, I'll enter the conversation with the thought, "Go slow. Don't be too blunt. Do a soft sell."

Whatever the reasons I anticipate for possible disagreement, I still want to convince the other party of my position. Using an indirect approach, I "ease into" my position. Easing in is a skillful strategy whereby I try to get the other person to come around to my point of view without my stating it directly. Both Mark and Brenda employed easing-in strategies. Brenda says to Mark, "How about if we put our heads together and see if we can't tackle this problem of yours?" Mark would find it hard to say no to wanting to work together with Brenda, but in saying "Yes, let's do it," he is agreeing to the hidden advocacy in her leading question—that it is *his* problem. Mark uses the same easing-in strategy a few sentences later when he says, "A small delay couldn't possibly cause that much trouble, right?" He is not asking a real question. He is expecting her to say, "You're right. A delay isn't that great of a problem. You win." The problem for Mark, as well as for us when we use leading questions, is that the strategy doesn't always work. People will say the opposite of what we hoped or, as is the case for Brenda, feel manipulated or trapped.

We typically use easing-in strategies whenever we anticipate a negative response and wish to avoid it. For example, in a casual conversation after a meeting, I might approach a team member and say to her, "So do you think we could have gotten more done in the meeting?" If she gives me a quick "I don't know; I think we accomplished a lot," then I have to up the ante. I expected agreement but didn't get it, so I hint at the deeper reasons for the meeting's ineffectiveness. "Really? Well yes, we got through the easy stuff, but on the tough issues, we just skimmed the surface; don't you agree?" She says in return, "Well, we couldn't get through the WI project because Sam wasn't there, and he is heading up the project."

Great, she took the bait. Now I am on to the real issue. I want her to make the same evaluation of the meeting as I have: that the problem lies with Sam. "That's it exactly," I say. "It doesn't make much sense to have a meeting without the proper leadership support, does it?" A simple yes from the team member will confirm in my mind that we have agreement on the lack of progress and the source of our ineffectiveness. I have succeeded in getting her to come around to my view without discussing the details or testing my thinking. (The DVD that accompanies this book includes a scene in which two actors role-play this scenario. To view it, go to the main menu, click on Bypass Strategies, then select Easing In.)

Two common business situations where an easing-in approach is used are requesting help and delivering bad news.

Requesting Help

This tactic is often employed when someone anticipates resistance after asking others to do something. Let's say I'm thinking that it's about time you took the lead on a few projects around the office. I think that you are lacking some core skills and that it's high time you learned them. I say to myself, "I can't be doing these things for you all the time anymore."

Let's say I start with a polite request: "No one is available right now; would you mind leading on this project?" You respond with, "No, I am not comfortable doing that. You need to lead it." Right away, I am going to start thinking that you are lazy and unwilling to try. Besides, it's your turn, and I am sick and tired of doing everything. I try again: "I think I led the last project. Wouldn't you like to give it a try?" I want you to say, "Yes, I will give it a try," but what I get is "No way, I am not doing it." Now I have a problem. You are not buying what I am selling.

My challenge is to get you to agree with me without your getting upset or defensive. If I am too direct, then there is a greater chance of your getting defensive. By adopting an indirect approach, I hope to bypass the potential conflict while also convincing you of my view. I put you in a position that if you don't agree, you will be disagreeing with something that is obviously the right thing to do. The difficulty is that my indirect approach doesn't always work. As in this case, it is just as easy for you to continue to say "No way." Now I'm stuck.

How can someone break this pattern? One way is to try asking for help in a more productive, specific, and empathic way. More specifically, when asking for help, consider these questions:

Is there anything in how you ask that might be interpreted as "demanding"?

What kind of help do you really need? Be specific. What would the help look like?

Have you made explicit what you are up against that necessitates help?

Does the other person have a clear idea of what you are specifically asking him or her to do?

Does the request for help exceed the limits of the other person's capacity?

What would be considered "finished"?

Sometimes it is easy to think that our request is manageable and should be greeted with willingness and cooperation. When that result doesn't follow, our (LHC) private thinking isn't so kind to the person who refused. Before heading too far down the road of attaching "obstacle" next to the person's name, stop and check to see what kind of concerns or difficulties your request creates for the other person.

Specifically, after making the request for help, ask,
Is my request doable, or does it create any difficulty for you?

Before you decline or accept my request for help, what do you hear me asking for?

Are you aware of any potential obstacles that might make it difficult to provide help?

Delivering Bad News

People often ease in when they find themselves in a bind trying to get someone to "fess up" to messing up. On one hand, we don't want the other person to take the negative evaluation of their performance personally and get defensive. On the other hand, we need to be firm and get the other person to see how he or she has messed up. So we start with an innocuous, "How do you think you did?" The hope is that the other person will admit that he or she blew it. If the admission is not forthcoming, our questions become more revealing, and can go something like, "Well, the numbers didn't add up exactly, did they?" or "You can't say that all the customers were exactly happy, can you?" The answers are implied and expected.

Like other bypass strategies, this "soft" approach to delivering bad news works in the short term, but eventually backfires. People will begin to suspect that there is a point of view lurking just under the surface. They may feel manipulated. Or they may think the person asking the questions is holding back information. They may also feel as though they are being interrogated. Ultimately they'll become defensive, which is the situation the person asking the leading question was trying to avoid in the first place!

It can sometimes take a while for people to break the habit of cloaking their point of view in vague or leading questions. The basic rule of thumb is that if you have a point of view, put it out there. Now, how you put your view out makes a difference. "You really blew it" may be a true statement, but it isn't helpful to the other person's learning. As with any high quality advocacy, showing the steps of your reasoning (the Ladder of Inference) is more productive. It's also more helpful to illustrate your point of view with an example. After you state what you think, you can then balance your view with an inquiry, such as, "Do you see it the same or differently?" or a more neutral "What is your reaction to what I said?"

Sending Inconsistent Messages

We use inconsistent messages to prevent people from responding negatively to our actions. We say one thing when in fact we feel or think the opposite. Then, not wanting to appear insincere, we act as if our message were consistent. Mark sends an inconsistent message to Brenda when he says "That's a thought" to her suggestion to schedule the repair at a later date. He tells her that he will run it by his crew. He sounds sincere, and in doing so is being polite, but Brenda knows that in reality Mark is going to blow off her suggestion. She can't call him on it, however, because he hasn't said so.

We employ inconsistent messages whenever we put on our best "I am listening" face, nod our heads at the right moments, and affirm the other's point with the ever popular phrase, "That's interesting." All the while, the thought that is screaming the loudest is, "That's the craziest idea I have ever heard. What am I? Flypaper for freaks?" The more the other person talks, the more time is a-wasting. An exit strategy becomes critical. Again, wanting to avoid any awkwardness, we reach for the easiest but maybe not the truest excuse: "That's great. Your idea is worth studying more. I'll pass it on to the subcommittee." We start to backpedal out of the conversation, thinking to ourselves, "The subcommittee will bury it." (For a look at an inconsistent message in practice, click on Bypass Strategies on the main menu, then select Inconsistent Messages.)

Inconsistent messages take several forms, but the most common are little white lies and interruptions.

Little White Lies

No one believes that you are purposefully being dishonest when you're telling a little white lie. A white lie is an unimportant fib told to maintain the appearance of being tactful or polite. You still believe in being honest, but you don't apply the principle of honesty blindly without consideration of the specifics of the situation. You feel that there are times when it is appropriate to level with people and others when it is best to keep quiet or remain polite.

Like the social virtues of supporting and respecting others, an inconsistent message in the form of a little white lie allows us to be civil and to exercise prudence in determining when and how much of the truth to tell in a given situation. In some cases, such a little white lie may be completely harmless. If, for example, you don't like a piece of artwork that someone has obviously taken pride in, there's no need to say flat out that you despise it. However, inconsistent messages can do damage in the long run. I would be giving someone false hopes if I indicated support of an idea, but actually thought poorly of it. My actions would eventually betray my true thoughts. People would begin to question my motives, and I would have to explain why I said one thing when in fact I believed another. How embarrassing.

For better or worse, telling little white lies is a common social practice of civility. Prudence dictates its use, as does a consideration for learning. If a white lie prevents learning from taking place, in particular with regard to something that could adversely affect business results, then it does all parties and the organization a disservice. When learning is a requirement, then a direct approach using the highest quality advocacy and inquiry skills serves as the best policy.

Interruptions

The most frequently used inconsistent message is "I don't mean to interrupt, but . . ." Imagine you are scrambling for airtime in a group discussion. Your coworker is rambling. In your head, the mounting backlog of commentary on what you have heard is deafening. You want to respond to something your coworker said ten minutes ago, but the rules of polite discourse dictated to you since early childhood cautions "Don't interrupt." Interrupting is rude.

It is disrespectful to stop someone from speaking midsentence because it sends the message "I can't listen to you any longer. Where you are going, I can't go any longer." Saying something like "Right now, I am visualizing duct tape over your mouth" is a bit too transparent and direct. Your coworker would surely respond negatively to such a frontal assault, yet you can't take it any longer. You have to interrupt. You figure out a way to jump in politely. You say, "I don't mean to interrupt, but . . ."

With the emphasis on "I don't mean to," you have inoculated yourself from any negative response. It is like saying, "Don't think of me as being bad for interrupting because it is not my intention. My intentions are good. I can take this conversation in a more productive direction. And as long as you don't think of me as bad, I can get away with interrupting."

Yet there is a fundamental inconsistency in your statement. You don't mean to, but you will. You say one thing and do another.

Like the other inconsistent message bypass strategies, interrupting as politely as possible is a civil action. There are times when you need to interrupt someone. The question is how. If the other person's train of thought has veered off track and left you wondering where he or she is heading, stop the conversation by saying, "I need to interrupt. I have lost the connection between point X that began our discussion and the point you are making now. Can you or others here help me make the connection?" In this case, I am using my own confusion as the explicit reason for interrupting. Similarly, if another person is rambling on and on and I can't keep up, I'll say, "I need to interrupt. You have made a number of points. Before you add another, I'd like to recap what you've said to make sure I got them and then give myself and others a chance to respond." In both instances, the alternative approach follows the spirit of high quality advocacy by being more explicit and intentional when you are about to interrupt someone.

Often, when I offer advice on how to avoid inconsistent messaging, people say, "I can't do that. I don't have time to engage in a debate!" That might be true. We can't engage every little difference we encounter with others. Unfortunately, people use this excuse more frequently than necessary. It does nothing toward developing the skill of engaging differences in a productive manner. It simply reinforces the legitimacy of using the bypass strategy.

It would be unrealistic to think that anyone could cease to use these bypass strategies altogether. But becoming aware of when and why we use them is a good step toward allowing us the running room to reflect on their effectiveness and to consider other options.

Saving Face

We typically use the face-saving strategy when confronting another's error or mistake. When someone messes up badly, common courtesy prevents us from saying, "I see the screwup fairy has come to visit you again." Instead, we rush to mitigate the impact of bad news or negative evaluation on someone.

For example, let's say that the word got out that a colleague's project failed miserably and cost the company plenty. I might, as a fellow project leader, approach her wanting to provide some support. I also know that the word is that the failure is her fault.

I open with a vague acknowledgment: "I heard the project didn't go well."

To my relief, she admits it: "I think the word is *bombed*."

Clearly she is aware of how bad it is, so it is time to show support. My strategy is first to criticize myself to ease her discomfort:

"Well, don't feel bad. It happens to everyone. I am embarrassed to tell you how many times I've blown it."

She comes back with, "It was an impossible project. The customer changed his mind a thousand times, and then there was my team."

I think to myself, "Oh boy, she is off blaming others and is absolutely clueless that her team was about to commit mutiny." But I still stay on the path of support, trying to drop hints in the hope that she'll get the message that she is part of the problem.

"Yeah, your team. Well, it is not easy to manage technical personnel. Have you ever done interpersonal skill- and team-building exercises with them?"

She doesn't take the bait. "No, I communicate with them clearly, but they just don't know how to get a job done right."

I hit the bailout button, thinking she is a hard nut to crack when it comes to being introspective. I walk away thinking I did my job of being supportive, but in reality, I failed to convey information that is possibly critical to my colleague's ability to rebound and learn from her experience. Instead, I "saved her face" by protecting her from an embarrassing situation. She and everyone else in the company knew how badly the project failed. It was the talk of the hallway for a month. I didn't want her to feel bad, but as in many face-saving situations, she became defensive. The more defensive the person becomes, the more likely the situation will become awkward. And the more apparent the awkwardness becomes, the less effective the face-saving maneuvers become.

(To view a role-play of this scenario, click on Bypass Strategies on the main menu, then select Saving Face.)

"Face," Defined

One's face is the visible, outward appearance one shows to others. Someone's face is what makes him or her unique and recognizable. Face, therefore, is a natural symbol for describing the presentation of the self vis-à-vis the other in social reality. Terms like *reputation, status, poise, prestige,* and *respect* are partial descriptors, but none alone capture the full meaning associated with face. In an excellent article, "On the Concept of Face," David Yau-fai Ho explores the distinct features of the Chinese social reality of saving face. Although the concept of face originated in China and remains dominant in Asian societies, its salient features are also detectable in Western societies, which value the individual over the collective.

We don't gain face. Face is what we have already, just as we are born with our own physical face. One of the Chinese words for saving face, *lien,* connotes entitlement. It is not something to be earned, but is granted to everyone as a member of society.

With entitlement come expectations. Just as I take care of my physical face, I also have to maintain my social face. There are cultural precepts I abide by in order to keep face. Business transactions are conducted in the good faith of full disclosure and mutual advantage. I honor what I say with what I do. I respect the social contracts of timeliness, dress, commitments, and obligations. I can lose face only if what is seen by others is deemed inappropriate, inadequate, or incompetent.

The expression "to lose face" refers to "a result of [one's] inability to measure up to expectations in [one's] social performance" (p. 872). The criteria for measurement and the exact nature of the expectations are the vital or essential requirements for proper conduct within a culture. If one's conduct falls below the minimal level of expectations, one loses face. There is no universal set of actions that incites a loss of face. Rather, a person's actions are judged according to a set of culturally specific, valued-based expectations and judgments.

Expectations and Judgments

The possibility of losing face is a social reality in situations where people hold expectations and make judgments about individual actions. If a person's actions don't measure up to a set of spoken or unspoken expectations, he or she loses face, regardless of whether or not the individual agrees with these expectations. His or her actions are still judged.

It is important to understand that the cultural norms for saving or losing face differ from country to country, and the nuances are not universally known. At a gathering of Saudi businessmen, for example, a manager said something to me that he later thought might have been offensive and caused me discomfort. When he was apologizing, he informed me that it was an Arabic custom to kiss the forehead of the person you offended as an acknowledgment of grievance and a gesture of apology. Then he approached me to place a kiss on my forehead. Because he was a good foot shorter than me, I bent my head forward. But as soon as I did that, he recoiled and stepped back from me. "Never do that. You never reach down to accept a kiss on the forehead. That is not a gracious reception, but a condescending gesture." He explained that my action was like pushing his mistake in his face. In Western society, we would call it "rubbing it in."

In that moment, my unfamiliarity with the custom nearly caused him further disgrace in front of his colleagues. To his credit, he approached me again, grabbed my head with both hands and brought my forehead to his lips. The Arabic term for saving face is *Hifz maa' al wajh,* which translates literally as "preserving the water of the face." The water of the face is sweat. For a moment, I was the one sweating, but in the end, all turned out fine.

Reciprocity

We work to save our own face and extend the same protective strategies to others who fall under the conditions of potential threat or embarrassment. We take great care in saving the face of others. Ho makes the point that "Reciprocity is the key to the understanding of face behavior: to extend face to others is no less important than to safeguard one's own" (p. 882).

Maybe it's an innate altruism of the human spirit or simply a need to avoid those awkward moments when we bring up an embarrassing incident, laugh nervously, and change the subject. We want to avoid feeling embarrassed by others' embarrassment. It is uncomfortable to see someone we care for and respect fumble so badly in public. There is an immediate reaction to run over and say, "It's not as bad as you think." On the surface, protecting ourselves and others from embarrassment can be a kind thing to do. Unfortunately, it also prevents us from learning from our mistakes.

I was on the receiving end of a collective face-saving strategy once without even knowing it. I was a guest lecturer in a colleague's class. I mistakenly kept referring to him during my presentation as Al when his name is actually Guy. During the break, his wife came up to me and said, "Do you know that you've been calling Guy, Al?" I said, "No, I'm not aware that I've been doing that."

When the class reconvened, I asked the students whether they knew I had been calling Guy by the wrong name. Many of them nodded. I asked them what had prevented them from pointing out my mistake. As it turned out, each person had an elaborate plan designed to protect me from the embarrassment of discovering my error. One student said that he had made sure when he spoke up in class that he slipped in a loud reference to Guy. Another student knew she would see me the next day and planned to tell me then. That would have been great; then I would have felt completely embarrassed the next day that I had spent the entire class calling my colleague Al. Guy himself thought I was talking about someone else, so it didn't matter to him. What did matter to me was that these "caring" strategies prevented me from discovering my mistake and rectifying it during class.

A Western Reaction

A final note on face-saving bypass strategies. Because of Western society's emphasis on individuality, I have often heard people say they don't care what others think of them. I'll admit that the degree to which one incorporates social norms and expectations into his or her frame of self varies from individual to individual. Just the same, the "essential requirements" around the loss or saving of face are based not on individual evaluation but on the social expectations of others. One loses face in the eyes of others. When the stakes are high and the issues complex, how our actions affect others and how they respond are out of our control.

Exercise

Preventing Learning in the Name of Being Nice and Courteous to Your Fellow Human Being

Here is a quick exercise designed to increase awareness of your preferred bypass strategy. First, write or review your own LHC-RHC case study. Identify the bypass strategies you used in the conversation.
Then ask yourself these questions:

What is my preferred strategy?

When do I tend to use the strategy the most?

What might I experience if I were on the receiving end of this strategy?

Covering Up

For any bypass strategy to work, it must be covered up. I can't say to you, "I think you did a lousy job, but I want to protect you from embarrassment, so I am going to save your face by telling you not to worry because we all make mistakes." If I said something like that, I'd be tipping you off to my intentions and defeating my purpose of protecting you from embarrassment. Instead, I cover up my actions with silence and turn the situation into what Argyris refers to as the undiscussable. I make an implicit agreement with you that we will not say anything, nor will we say anything about the fact that we have made the topic undiscussable. As Argyris says, "We make the undiscussable, undiscussable."

The cover-up is a quiet vow of complicity that holds the organizational defensive routine in place. We know what is really going on, but we are not going to talk about it. This is sometimes referred to as "the moose on the table" or "the elephant in the middle of the room." Everyone sees it, but no one talks about it. Why is that the case? There are a number of reasons, not the least of which is how our minds work; left to its own devices, the mind can create all kinds of problems.

MAKING THE "WAY THINGS WORK AROUND HERE" ROUTINE

Bypass strategies and their cover-up are only a few ways we keep defensive routines in place within our organizations. Characteristic ways of thinking reinforce the certainty with which we perceive others as problematic. The stories and histories we recite to our colleagues about how others have behaved badly help establish a predictable pattern of behavior that will become the routine "way things work around here." In the end, a collective cry of helplessness to change anything is a signal that the defensive routine has taken hold and will remain permanent, absent the awareness that we created the situation in the first place. The following ways of thinking and the organizational use of storytelling describe how the "way things work around here" becomes routine.

Inventing Motives

When we're in "win, not lose" mode, our own view seems immeasurably sensible and obvious, so we assume that others should see it as well and agree with us. When other people can't see the sense in our thinking, we think that there must be something wrong with *them;* perhaps they're simply unable to follow logic or think as clearly as we do. We reinforce our own reasonableness by remaining rational. We say to ourselves, "If I explain harder and overwhelm them with my logic, they'll get it." We repeat ourselves, but with a bit more emphasis and volume.

If our listeners still don't get it, then we are faced with the challenge of figuring out why. And in an effort to make sense of why others would do something that to us is so obviously wrong or stupid, we assume their intentions are bad. Why would they do something so crazy unless they were acting out of ill intent or had a serious character flaw? We make a dangerous assumption that we are able to determine the nature of another's intentions. This is quite a skill, given that intentions are highly internal and private to one's thinking. Yet with absolute confidence, we think to ourselves, "He is only looking out for himself," or "She is being very difficult, headstrong, and self-assured." Our reading of another's intentions may be accurate or not. It's hard to read what motivates another person without asking the person directly. For the most part we don't do this, because we are already convinced that we do know the other's intentions.

Do a quick test. Think of the person with whom you have the greatest difficulty dealing at work. Get a good picture of the person in your mind. Imagine that person with a reasonable point of view. Do you feel your cognitive gears grind a bit? A more difficult task is to think of that person as having the best of intentions when interacting with you. What happens now? Your mind can go into a complete "brain vapor lock" with the warning lights flashing, "No way, not a chance." "Approach with caution" is the *modus operandi* for the relationship.

Unless another person publicly confesses his or her ill intentions, we are left to our own devices to invent them. The invention is not solely a product of our devilish imagination. We base our thinking on how the words and actions of the other affected us. They had an impact or made an impression on us. We react to the impact by assigning negative intentions and motives.

We willingly assign negative intentions to others, but we rarely see ourselves as having them. We think of ourselves as basically good and having only the best motives. This is an ironic and all-too-common twist of human thinking. This is not a modern problem. As pointed out in the Christian scriptures, it has always been easier to see the mote in another's eye and miss noticing the beam in our own. When it comes to finding the source of the problem, it is always easier to blame the other person.

Holding Others Accountable

Even if we did ask others about their intentions, there is a good chance we wouldn't believe their answers, because we hold them accountable for the problem at hand. (We know this, so we often feel that "it's just not worth going there.") We might preface our statements with "I know I am part of the problem," but we finish those same statements with the "real" reason why there is a problem: the other person's behavior. Notice the next time you do this and take note of how much time you spend reflecting on the first part (I know I am part of the problem) compared to the time spent describing what the other person did.

You've probably experienced conversations in which someone else's ideas or actions create difficulties for you. Maybe someone else's "bad suggestion" has created more work for you. Perhaps the person's "attitude" makes him or her hard to work with. When reviewing case studies, case writers' LHCs are full of comments like these:

"What is so wrong with her that she has to make everyone's life a living hell?"

"He's a black and white guy and doesn't understand the business as much as he thinks."

"Okay, have it your way, but you can't escape the truth."

When someone disagrees with us or causes us difficulty, we try to find reasons for their opposition that puts the focus on *them*, not us. As a result, we tend to hold the other person responsible for the problems we're now saddled with. It is much easier (and less painful) to blame someone else for a difficult conversation or situation than it is to actively look for ways we might have contributed to the problem.

Inventing Causal Explanations

Often in an attempt to make sense of the other person's bad behavior, we spin causal explanations for his or her actions. Causal explanations are our theories of why someone did what he or she did. On the basis of the impact that the other person's behavior had on us, we posit a "theory" full of attributions and ill intentions that give an account of the other's actions. We even might share our explanations with trusted colleagues or other players involved in the situation.

When the word "because" is used in a sentence, a causal explanation will follow. "Do you know why John said what he did? I think it's because he was unprepared and didn't want to admit it." Often our theories of other people's behavior can get pretty elaborate. "You know, when Jane gets into her 'command and control' mode, it's a good indication that she is really threatened by you. You remind her of those times in her early childhood. She told me once that the schoolyard boys used to make fun of her because she wanted to play baseball with the guys. The problem was that she was good at the sport. She got a kick out of beating boys. Now, every time she directly competes with another male, she'll do her best to dominate the guy, especially the alpha males like yourself." Each causal link is added to another, creating a chain of psychobabble explanations that extend out into the stratosphere of strange and undocumented personality deformities.

Inside our own heads, these causal explanations make sense. They appear obvious and even factually based on our observations of the other person's actions. In reality, they may or may not be true. Because our causal explanations are rarely shared with the person about whom they are constructed, it is hard to determine their validity. Private explanations and negative attributions are usually too risky to share publicly. They reside in our LHC and remain untested, yet serve as a filter that selects behavior to confirm our original explanation. If you have ever heard or said the refrain, "There he [she] goes again," there is a good chance you have seen some behavior that fits your original explanation for the other person's difficult behavior. If you consider your boss to be Attila the Hun, anything he or she does that is "nice" might be discarded as incongruous or exceptional.

Even though we don't share our private explanations of behavior and judgments with the person involved, they do "leak out" in our behavior. As my colleague Phil McArthur says, "We are all wearing psychic Pampers, and they are leaking."

How we think of others influences our interactions. If I see you as a person "out for yourself," "carrying a hidden agenda," and "lacking intelligence," I will be less likely to share information, follow through on your requests for action, or, for that matter, give you the time of day. My actions will then influence the way you think and behave toward me, which most likely were the original triggers that set in motion my reaction in the first place.

This interpersonal dynamic plays out in the workplace. Everyone comes to expect certain behaviors from the problematic person or department. In reaction to the person or department, people will often respond in a way that reinforces the designated problematic behavior. A pattern of interaction is established. Soon this defensive routine takes on a life of its own as people share stories of what can be expected based on past experiences and offer advice on how to behave around the problematic person or department. These stories practically become legends that circulate around the organization. Eventually they take their place within the workplace culture. As part of the culture, they exert a powerful influence on how people act toward one another.

Storytelling

The stories or legends are never shared directly with the designated "problematic" person or department. Instead, we often narrate the full details of the story to a colleague or sympathetic listener. The person deemed "in the know" is awarded a little extra status. All ears are tuned to his or her story. The full version of the story becomes a joint publication when sympathetic listeners add supporting evidence and a chorus of "I can't believe he said that to you" or "Let me tell what I heard." The stories are broadcast in the hallways, in break rooms, and behind closed doors. The word has gotten out, and the stories are told as a factual rendition of what actually happened. They are the "gospel truth."

When I hear stories told with the confidence of being the absolute truth, I attempt to investigate the storyteller's role and contribution. The response is often "If you knew this guy like I do, you would think the same way." This is an example of self-referential logic. Essentially, the person offers no possibility for verification outside his or her perspective. If by chance or design I actually meet the "other person," I hear a different story than what is commonly told to me to be true.

In my practice, when I am called in for an intervention, I interview all parties involved. Typically, a team member or manager is identified as the "problem." I listen to story after story that builds the person up into Frankenstein proportions. Finally, when it comes time to interview the monster, none appears. Instead, I hear of the struggles of another person attempting to do his or her best, absolutely clueless about what others are saying and unaware as to how his or her actions are affecting others.

This is not to say that the person is completely innocent. I am able to pick up on the behaviors that contribute to others' perceptions. I also hear about the trials and tribulations of working for the same people who complain about him or her. There are "two sides" to the story, but the stories don't jibe with each other.

Claiming There's a History

Eventually the recitation of a story includes the words, "There's a history here." A history is a reference to the backlog of past errors, failed interactions, and repeated offenses. With a history comes a citation of conviction against the other or others for being on the wrong side of the interaction. There is little evidence of forgiveness and nothing forgotten. The complete history is never told, only the particular selection created by the offended party. The retelling of a history is a cautionary tale warning of future betrayals and recommending mistrust.

Such oral histories can be very convincing. And they not only play an important role in the propagation of organizational defensive routines but also can become self-fulfilling prophecies. What occurred in the past will come again. Any time you say to yourself, "Here we go again," a history is repeating itself. Broadcasting the history through a department, division, or entire organization contributes to a state of generalized helplessness. When people plead that they are helpless to change what has been, they are making a choice not to engage, and it is this choice that keeps the defensive routine in place.

Designing Helplessness

Every time I lead a discussion on organizational defensive routines, there is an across-the-board recognition of their existence and a final resignation that there is nothing that can be done to change them. The end point to the discussion is often the phrase, "It's office politics." The "it" in office politics is always something outside one's influence. Yet as long as the excuse for not taking action holds, the existence of defensive routines is assured. Inaction is an action that keeps perpetuating the defensive routine.

Inaction stems from a state of helplessness. Helplessness enshrines the defensive routine in a place of permanence. Everyone knows what is going on. It is the big open secret. You walk into a meeting ready to play charades. The spoken words are unnecessary because none deal with what is really going on. Silent communication is going on in the eyes and faces of all gathered. There are looks of agreement that hide the worry of failure. A set of eyes may roll upward and around in amazed disbelief. People take comfort in catching the glance of a colleague whose facial expression bears witness to the insanity that is taking place in room.

I don't doubt the strongly felt perception that organizational defensive routines are external to oneself and beyond one's control. I have felt it in organizations I have worked for as a consultant or employee. People are experiencing genuine helplessness and resignation about a situation that feels utterly beyond their control. People become quite disheartened, and as Argyris points out, a culture of malaise takes over. The work environment becomes toxic.

What we don't generally see is how the state of helplessness is a creation of our own design. We don't readily admit to designing our own helplessness. The nature of the state bestows the status of victim. We see ourselves as the recipients of others' cruel words, malicious intentions, and outrageous behavior. We fail to see how our experientially sound case for helplessness is a choice based on an interpretation of reality that may not accurately describe what is going on beyond our own perspective.

And we fail to see how we contribute to the situation. The most tenacious aspect of an organizational defensive routine is the perception that it is external to us and our range of influence. The perception that the problem is "out there" is a hard one to shake loose. An "aura of externality," to use another phrase coined by Argyris, inhabits an organizational defensive routine. It is the ultimate padlock that confirms with a visceral certainty that organizational defensive routines are beyond individual influence.

Interestingly, although we almost always bemoan the existence of organizational defensive routines, we are not always ready to let go of them, even when we realize that we can. Why is that the case? Put simply, defensive routines make for good human drama. There is always an audience of coworkers ready to share the newest story of the management's dastardly deeds. Managers console each other over the lack of team skill and competence. The mention of the latest news brings people together for a little bonding around the water cooler.

For the teller of the tale, there is always a little sympathy and consolation for how rough it must be. There is the rallying cry of "Unfair!" and gasps of "I can't believe it." Discovering that the one person we deemed malicious in intent and ruinous in action was perhaps unaware of his errors isn't so exciting. Thinking that the other person has a reasonable point of view takes some of the air out of the story. All the secondary gains of sympathy, attention, and self-satisfaction are hard to give up. To let go of the secondary gains received by participants in an organizational defensive routine requires them to step out of the limelight of the victim and take their place within the defensive routine. And that's difficult to do, particularly when the "rewards" of doing so seem intangible and far off.

Yet the rewards are worth the effort. In the next chapter, you will be asked to watch the meeting scene between Mark, Brenda, and Walt on the accompanying DVD. This scene illustrates defensive routines at their most destructive. Subsequently, we'll start to explore remedies and solutions, and show how Mark and Brenda can help foster a healthier and more productive atmosphere at work by "massaging the knot" and beginning to counter defensive routines with more effective behaviors.

⟿

The next chapter marks the beginning of Part Three of this book, in which we explore the ways people can begin to overcome defensive routines and use the skill set introduced in Chapter Two.

Before beginning Part Three, take out the accompanying DVD and click on Fix It Now or Fix It Later on the main menu, then select The Business Meeting and watch it. Chapter Six picks up with a discussion of that meeting.

NOTE

Ho, David Yau-fai. "On the Concept of Face." *American Journal of Sociology,* 1976, *81*(4), 867–884.

PART THREE

Discussing the Undiscussable

You may have picked up this book with the hope of learning how to raise the undiscussable in your workplace, with the aim of demonstrating how others' behaviors are problematic. If this was the case, then I hope Part Two of the book caused you to take a reflective pause and revealed how your version of the undiscussable may be part of the problem. Possibly it shed some light on how you have contributed to the cycle of defensive routines that are now cloaked in the shroud of the undiscussable.

Getting to a place where an organization's most important issues are undiscussable doesn't occur in a day. By now, you have seen how organizational defensive routines arise from the conditions of threat and embarrassment. Our defensive, reactive thinking sets in motion a predictable routine of behavior designed to protect all parties from threat and embarrassment. Over time, socially sanctioned virtues and bypass strategies help keep the defensive routines in place. We cover up these actions with an implicit agreement not to discuss what we are doing. Instead, we carry on with "open secrets" and make our peace with the "elephant in the room." The defensive routines morph into the "way things work around here," and a culture of malaise takes hold.

I would not be surprised if at this point you feel helpless to do anything, yet staying in that state won't help matters at all. Part Three offers a remedy for the helplessness. Chapter Six provides a method for diagnosing defensive routines that serves as a way for people to discuss the undiscussable in a safe manner. Chapter

Seven asks you to tune into the "Self-Discovery Channel" before venturing into any discussion of the undiscussable. Chapters Eight and Nine explore the ways in which you can apply the foundational skill set (first described in Chapter Two) to situations in which organizational defensive routines are running amok.

Before starting Part Three, you should click on Fix It Now or Fix It Later on the main menu on your DVD, then select The Business Meeting and view the scene in which Mark, Brenda, Walt, and the plant's team meet to decide whether they should fix the exchanger now or later. This scene illustrates how defensive routines eventually get played out and escalate on an interpersonal, team, and organizational level.

Strategic Interventions

INTERVIEWS AND MAPPING

Please watch "The Business Meeting" on the accompanying DVD before beginning this chapter. Click on Fix It Now or Fix It Later on the main menu, then select The Business Meeting.

Having watched the meeting with Mark, Brenda, and Walt, you can probably see that not much got done. Not much, that is, unless you count the various parties' making things a whole lot worse.

In their interactions with each other, Mark and Brenda have exhibited all the classic dynamics of an organizational defensive routine. In response to threat and potential embarrassment, they exhibited defensive reasoning typical of the Unilateral Control Model. Throughout their interactions with each other, they employed protective strategies. Against a backdrop of large-scale assumptions about each other's respective division, they engaged each other in habitual, interlocking patterns of defensive behavior. As a result, relations between Operations and Sales are strained. Walt has to play the heavy and make a decision without the benefit of good information.

That's not the worst news, though. What's worse is that although Mark and Brenda are fictional characters, they are not exactly *caricatures*. The meeting scene was not exaggerated to make a point. In fact, during the many times I have shown the business meeting with Mark and Brenda to clients and workshop participants, I have seen the familiar nod of recognition with the exclamation, "Been there, done that meeting before." One story begets another, and soon participants have populated the discussion with examples of similar defensive routines in their own organizations.

So Mark, Brenda, and Walt are on familiar ground. Now the question becomes, How can they begin to turn things around? How can we do the same in our own organizations? A good place to begin is to change the way we think about defensive routines altogether.

MASSAGING THE KNOT

Imagine organizational defensive routines as a massive knot created by entangled lines of personal relationships, tightly wrapped perceptions, and restrictive cultural norms. From a distance, it seems impossible to figure out where one line begins and the other ends. Any attempt to pull tighter on one end or another only makes matters worse.

But what if you didn't attempt to isolate and deal with just one line? What if instead you started to gently work the entire knot at once?

My grandfather taught me that about knots. I'd get a firm grip on both ends of the string and pull hard. He would stop me. "That's not the way to do it," he would say gently. "It only makes it harder to undo." He'd take the knot in his big hands and began to massage the bundle of crisscrossed cords with his fingers. His gentle tugs and pulls began to loosen the core of the knot. Soon little loops would appear, giving way to opportunities for disentangling the whole mess. The same approach can work with untangling the knot of organizational defensive routines.

When you are tangled up in a defensive routine, your "stuckness" makes it difficult for you to see your own contribution, therefore limiting your ability to be the helper or facilitator who can alter the defensive routine. A third party who is outside the defensive routine stands a better chance of being objective or is at least less hooked by it.

In the following sections, I'll introduce the elementary components of an intervention strategy conducted by a third party. The best candidate for a third party is someone proficient in the Mutual Learning Model skill set. This may be an external consultant or facilitator, or a staff member from an internal consulting or Human Resources department. The minimum requirement is that he or she is not directly involved in the situation.

There are three components to the intervention strategy: the interview, analyzing and organizing the information from the interview into maps, and the facilitated dialogue. The first and second components are presented here in Chapter Six. Appendix A covers the process for the facilitated dialogue and provides the templates for constructing maps.

The first component consists of interviews conducted by the third party with each of the people involved in the defensive routine. Throughout the interviews, the third party puts into practice the skill set introduced in Chapter Two. During the interview, the third party listens to everyone's version of the story. By using high quality inquiries, he or she explores the individuals' private thinking (LHC) and helps them move down their ladders to observable data. As the stories unfold, the practitioner should be able to see how everyone is interacting together to create the problem at hand.

The second component is the organization of the information from the interview and the construction of a map of the defensive routines. Mapping is a visual technique that tells the story of how all parties contribute to the maintenance of a defensive routine through their thinking and actions. The map illustrates the strategic trigger points that reinforce the predictable and cyclical nature of the routine. Mapping is used primarily as a diagnostic tool, but it is also the access point for a safe, learning-focused discussion among all the participants. In combination with the prerequisite mutual learning skills, this strategy offers the best hope of altering a defensive routine. Using the "Fix It Now or Fix It Later" scenario, this chapter will present three maps depicting individual, team, and organization-wide defensive routines respectively.

The third component is the actual intervention when the practitioner meets with the parties involved in the defensive routine. In the meeting, the map is presented or constructed and the issues discussed. Although the following sections present an intervention strategy used by a third party, the strategy's main component, the technique of mapping, is available and useful to all. Understanding the methodology and purpose of mapping will help even those who are in the midst of a defensive routine gain a perspective on how their actions and thinking are contributing to a result no one desires or intends. The basic cautionary advice is not to rely solely on your own thinking; you will need the aid of others to fully understand and reflect on the impact your actions have on those you are trying to help.

THE INTERVIEW

Conducting private interviews with individuals is the preferred starting point for loosening the knot of defensive routines. If participants haven't been prepared or built any skills, large group discussions can quickly get out of hand and result in the repetition and reinforcement of the existing defensive routines. But working one-on-one with the third party in a private session, an individual is free to vent toxic feelings, nasty accusations, wild attributions, and outrageous theories about what is going on in the workplace. This initial venting helps relieve some of the pressure. Through active listening, the practitioner acknowledges the individual's version of the story, gaining important insights into his or her LHC and Ladder of Inference. This gentle approach builds a relationship of confidentiality, trust, and safety.

What to Listen For

When I am the third-party interviewer, I am primarily a listener while the person tells his or her story. I refrain from "Oh my God, how awful" statements and rely more on "Tell me more." I make use of the highest quality inquiries possible. My inquiries are designed to elicit two critical pieces of information needed to help untangle the knot: the concrete, observable data that serves as the basis for his or her conclusions, and the person's frame of mind.

Concrete, Observable Data

During an interview, people report events at a fairly high level of abstraction. Comments like "He always attacks me in meetings" or "She ignores what I have to say" are conclusions the person has drawn about what happened. They are not data. The data is the actual dialogue. Conversational data is a more reliable indicator of what happened than are abstract conclusions. I ask certain questions in order to recreate dialogue—for example, "Thinking back to the last time he chastised you in a meeting, what did he say to you exactly?" or "What does she do or say that you read as ignoring you?" If the interviewee is able to produce the dialogue, then I can make a better determination of the possible impacts and how the person arrived at his or her conclusion.

Usually people find it difficult to recall the actual dialogue. Instead they remember the end result of the encounter and report it later as if it were factual. For example, a person will insist that he was attacked in a meeting by a coworker, but not remember exactly what was said. As the interviewer, I can help jog his memory by asking, "Set the scene for me. What took place right before he attacked you?" This question helps him pull back from the critical moment and provide the details that led up to the event. Telling the background story stimulates more memories and triggers the recall of the actual dialogue.

Eventually, with some coaching he can recreate a paraphrased version of the dialogue. I follow up each line of the reported dialogue with another question, such as "So, he said that, and you responded how?" or "When you said that, what did he say in return?" With the dialogue recreated, I can get a better picture of the exchange between the two of them. I will be able to hear what he said that elicited the other person's reaction. Often after hearing what he said, it becomes more readily apparent to me than to the storyteller how the two coworkers triggered each other.

At this point, I can help identify the triggers by placing myself in the coworker's shoes and imagining the impact the interviewee's words would have on me. I say something like "If I were your coworker, I could imagine myself reacting defensively to what you said." I then go on to describe the impact. Through this feedback, the interviewee often realizes how he contributed to the problematic conversation. The coworker may now appear a little less "unreasonable."

During the course of the interview, I am also testing to see how certain the individual is about his or her version of what happened. By asking questions like "How might others interpret what was said?" or "What could the person do or say that might alter your view?" I am testing the firmness of the individual's belief. I am checking to see if there is any room for doubt. A softening signals a willingness to explore an alternative interpretation. Any movement toward a wider perspective helps loosen the knot.

If the interviewee holds tight to his or her version of the story, then I will proceed to investigate what gives him or her such a high level of confidence. This investigation inevitably leads to a deeper exploration of the person's frame of mind.

The Individual's Frame of Mind

The second line of inquiry teases out the individual's frame of mind during the problematic conversation. Frames are the thinking behind the action. They are most easily detected in what people were thinking or feeling but not saying in the conversation—in other words, their LHC. An individual's frame of mind tells him or her what to do in any given situation. Our frames are spontaneously generated when our mental models interact with the immediate context. For example, if I walk into a meeting and sense conflict, my mental model for how to deal with conflict is activated. I have had years of practice dealing with conflict in a certain way. My way may be effective, outdated, or ineffective, but the point is that I have one.

Like a picture frame, our mental frames direct our focus to what we consider important and what we pay attention to. They help us size up a situation quickly in order to act.

Because a frame of mind appears so natural and spontaneous, it is not readily apparent. We can gain access to our own frames through a review of our private thoughts. When it comes to determining another person's frames, that person must be present in order to reveal his or her thinking.

Too often, we try to infer someone's thinking based solely on his or her actions. This is a dangerous endeavor. Our guess as to what another person is thinking is too easily tainted with our own inferences. When describing another person's frame of mind, we must base the description on a reliable source for ascertaining his or her thinking. If the person is not directly available for questioning, then LHC material from a LHC-RHC case study offers the best access to his or her private thinking.

The partners at Action Design developed a convenient way to describe a person's frame. They organize the LHC comments into the categories of Self, Other, and Task. The category of Self gets at how the person sees himself or herself in the situation. This category takes into consideration the individual's view of role, responsibility, and intentions. It also includes emotional states or conditions, such as perceived helplessness and dilemmas. The category of Other covers how the person sees others' roles, responsibility, and intentions. The category of Task is what should be done in the situation. There is a direct correlation between the task and how the person sees himself or herself and the other. The following frame is a simple example: I see myself as right and you as wrong, so my task is to convince you that I am right and you are wrong.

The case here illustrates how to reconstruct a person's frame using the three categories of Self, Other, and Task, and neutral terms to describe the person's thinking so as to avoid extraneous inferences. This case comes from a department manager who is responsible for providing analytical information to the organization. The manager goes into a meeting of department heads with the hopes of limiting the number of requests for information from other departments that in his opinion are not useful or worth the investment of time and resources. On the left side of the chart are his private thoughts taken from the LHC of his case study. The other side is my translation of his thoughts into a neutral description of how he sees himself, the other person in the case study, and his task.

Private thoughts (in reaction to what others in the meeting said)	Frame
I'm tired of working so many hours digging up information that doesn't get reviewed or that no one cares about.	(Self) Is working hard on retrieving information that isn't used or important.
Yeah, right, you just don't want someone to ask any questions that you can't answer. You feel you might look bad.	(Other) Needs to know all the answers and doesn't want to look bad.
I would really like to get them to reduce the number of their requests.	(Task) To propose a limit of requests in order to reduce department workload.
Come on, let's be realistic. If no one really cares about the information, give those doing the grunt work a break.	(Self) Is being realistic. (Task) To convince those at the meeting to reduce workload.

The manager sees himself as being realistic, therefore correct in asking for a limit to the number of requests for information and the appropriate allocation of his department's resources. He sees other department managers as self-interested and protecting their own reputations. He believes that they request information because they don't want to be caught without an answer to a question and therefore look bad. On the basis of this attribution, he judges their requests to be unreasonable. Seeing himself as in possession of the sensible perspective and others as an obstacle to overcome, he sees his task as one of convincing them to reduce the number of requests.

The manager's frame provides him with "instructions" for action. In the meeting, he advocates for reducing the workload, but covers up his interpretation or theory for why the other managers are making so many requests—that they are self-interested and protecting their reputations. He proposes a solution to reduce the workload by simply stating, "I would really like for us to consider setting a cap on requests." Not surprisingly, he gets push-back from the other departmental managers because they see value in the requested information. The conversation never gets past "That won't work" versus "Yes, it will."

Often, how someone thinks about the problem can itself be problematic. The way the person frames the situation can be very limiting. In the example here, the manager's frame prevents him from investigating what leads other departments to make the requests they do. Because he is so sure of his own perspective, he does not feel the need to share his thinking about the impact the requests are having on his department. His attributions about other department managers' self-interest and self-protection are too toxic to share publicly, yet by covering them up he is unable to determine whether they are accurate or not. Because he believes them to be true, he acts accordingly. He pushes his view at an abstract level and creates the very result he wanted to avoid—no support for reducing the workload on his department.

Capturing the conversational data, testing the firmness of belief, and exploring the frame of mind during the interview process are the gentle strokes used to massage the knot of a defensive routine. These techniques elicit critical information important to tracking the pattern of unproductive behavior and thinking. In addition, through the use of high quality inquiries, the practitioner establishes a bond of understanding with all parties involved in the defensive routine.

ORGANIZING THE INFORMATION

After interviewing all of those involved, the practitioner has a tremendous amount of information available to use for demonstrating how all the parties involved are interacting in a way that none intended or desired. The next step is to organize the information in a way that everyone involved can see how he or she is interacting together to produce unintended consequences. Helping others see their interconnectivity is a matter of identifying loops—the basic dynamic of human interactions in which one person's response becomes a stimulus for another's response. The loops of human interaction occur when people with different views and contexts meet and form interpersonal working relationships. There is always a good chance that one person's actions will trigger a negative response from one or many people. If there are potentially embarrassing or threatening issues discussed, the chances increase that participants will exhibit defensive reasoning and actions. Analogous to undoing a physical knot, disentangling a defensive routine begins by detecting the loops of human interaction. Thinking in loops is a prerequisite skill for any practitioner who plans on intervening in an organizational defensive routine. Ultimately, it is also the way individuals themselves can detect and monitor their own defensive routines.

Recently, I bought a touring bike whose pedals lock on to my shoes. After many miles and a few falls, I got used to being locked in, and discovered the result of a more efficient motion that uses the pedal stroke up as well as the stroke down. Now I ride exerting equal pressure up and down as I make the circle around. The same principle applies to thinking in loops. As a practitioner, I look for how the upward and downward strokes of human interaction propel the players around a predictable pattern of thoughts and behaviors.

Each stroke represents the interpersonal force of action on thinking. Your thinking exerts a direct influence on your actions, which in turn have an impact on my thinking. My thinking shapes my actions. In turn, my actions have an impact on your thinking, and the loop repeats itself for the duration of our ride together. In this analogy, the pressure is equal and accounts for the dynamic motion of interpersonal relationships. Your reaction to what I say has an impact on me, as my actions have on you. Our manner of expression may be different, but an impact is made.

This is important to keep in mind when tracking the thinking and behavior around a defensive loop. As a facilitator or consultant, I have to guard against taking sides. My words may inadvertently trigger a reaction of favoritism. My focus needs to be on how all parties contribute to the cycle of defensive routines through their thinking and actions. Each interaction consists of a cycle of thought and action that contributes to the negative results of the conversation.

In that spirit, I must also keep in mind that organizational defensive routines exist at multiple levels. As in Brenda and Mark's case, there is an interpersonal defensive routine occurring between the two of them. Their conversation takes place within the context of a business meeting where the manager, Walt, and other team members are present. The team dynamic represents another defensive routine in which the collective thinking of a group suffers a lost of productivity due to their action of withdrawal.

None of these players come to the table without large-scale assumptions about their respective roles and responsibilities in their various divisions. These assumptions reflect the larger organizational defensive routines played out between their respective divisions within the organization. Organizational defensive routines comprise interpersonal, team, and interdivisional loops of interaction. They could be viewed as concentric circles, but it is more accurate to think of them as connecting to form a spiral that spins the organization as a whole in a downward path.

It's a daunting task to track the multiple layers of loops. There is so much going on that it is hard to sort it all out. The challenge of raising the undiscussables makes matters worse. When the stakes are high and issues complex, talking about undiscussables can activate the very conditions of threat and embarrassment that create defensive reasoning. A public discussion about organizational defensive routines can quickly deteriorate into fault-finding and assigning blame. People need a way to safely approach defensive routines so that they can mutually acknowledge the interdependent nature of their interactions.

Which brings me to mapping. When it comes to safely navigating an unfamiliar terrain, maps help us gain perspective. A good map of a defensive routine offers a neutral and balanced description of what is happening, helping us track the tangled loops of participants' thoughts and actions. When used effectively, it can reduce the tendency to blame and makes the undiscussable, discussable.

MAPPING

A map attempts to describe a territory from an outside perspective, enabling the user to see where the routes of connection exist between two points. Although maps can help us find our way, they are not to be confused or identified with the territory they describe. They leave material out or don't provide enough detail. They can become outdated or just be plain inaccurate. Yet without them, we run the risk of getting lost.

Argyris uses maps in many of his books to illustrate the connection between governing values, thinking, action, and consequences. The partners of Action Design have refined the map-making process to clarify even more exactly how an interconnecting pattern of interactions plays out in defensive routines. Specifically, their maps, Thinking-Action and Action-Impact, which I will use here, simplifies the process of understanding how reinforced patterns of behavior create predictable cycles and how our thinking and actions create unintended impacts on others. Altering defensive routines stands the best chance for success when through the use of mapping all parties can see how their own actions contribute to the problem.

Mapping "Fix It Now or Fix It Later"

In the following sections, I'll use maps to depict the cycles of defensive behavior at the interpersonal, team, and organizational level in "Fix It Now or Fix It Later."

Each map attempts to describe in neutral terms the interconnectivity between the thinking and actions of all parties. (At this point, seeing the interconnectivity is more important than knowing how to construct the map. Techniques and templates for constructing maps are in Appendix A.)

The first step is to pin down a narrative description of what has transpired and attempt to identify and describe the loops therein. A concise narrative description of the interactions between Mark and Brenda would be the following: after the perfunctory niceties are exchanged, Mark starts by stating what he believes is the obvious. The present turnaround is the best time to replace the exchanger. He asserts his position unilaterally and as if it were a fact. Brenda immediately objects to Mark's proposal by stating unilaterally and equally as factual and obvious that any delay will result in the loss of the customer. In the first loop around, there has been an equal exchange of "This is what we have to do" versus "That won't work." Their interchange follows Newton's third law of motion: for every action there is an equal and opposite reaction.

They are off toward a typical point-counterpoint conversation, trading abstract conclusions from atop their respective Ladders of Inference. Another turn around the loop begins when Mark counters Brenda's objection by employing a face-saving strategy, saying she is being customer-centric. This polite move is transparent because his view is that she should buy the product from someone else. Brenda dismisses Mark's proposal with an "I've done that," and switches to an easing-in strategy by asking a leading question: "Are you sure we have to replace the exchanger now?" Neither the face-saving nor easing-in strategy is effective in getting the other to give up his or her respective position.

In the third loop, Mark makes an appeal to the "expert authority" and directs Brenda to Josh. Brenda asks Josh for time parameters to support her position for planning a future delay. Josh restates Mark's position and dismisses Brenda's request for a future delay as impossible. He can't predict failure.

Before looking at the fourth loop of interaction between Mark and Brenda, go to the DVD, click on Fix It Now or Fix It Later on the main menu, then select Thinking Behind the Scenes. In this scene, you will be able to hear Mark's and Brenda's private thoughts (LHC). With the LHC material accessible, it is easier to see how each person's words affect the other's thinking and to identify both Mark's and Brenda's trigger points.

Mark gives his own meaning to time parameters by asserting that the exchanger is a "time bomb" and "could blow at any time." Brenda selects these words and interprets them as Mark being dramatic. She attributes negative motives to Mark and selectively focuses on the eighteen months as a safe harbor for repair. Brenda restates her position and faults Operations for past supply problems without giving an example.

The thinking behind Mark's and Brenda's established positions is filled with untested attributions, judgment, and accusations about each other. Mark's private thoughts exhibit the common features of assigning negative motives and holding opinions as factual. Mark argues that the customer has "no choice" and that delays are the "way things work around here." At this point, the toxicity level of Brenda's LHC increases. She faults any future loss of customers to the likes of people like Mark.

From this point on in the conversation, both Mark's and Brenda's private thoughts become more transparent. They start blurting them out uncensored. Brenda goes for the jugular by stating Mark's attitude toward customers is from the Dark Ages. If he had his way, customers would be burned at the stake. In kind, Mark returns the metaphor by placing the salespeople in the heat of the fire for making unrealistic promises in order to bag a sale. As his private thinking reveals, Sales is the problem, not a bad exchanger.

The heat of the conversation now ignites a final loop of accusations as each holds the other responsible for being the obstacle in the way of doing good business. Brenda defends her position by unilaterally asserting her view of competition. She asks Mark to share the risk without specifying what the risks are. Mark defends himself by claiming that Brenda is asking him to take on an unfair burden of the risks. He blames Brenda for making an unreasonable request. Brenda qualifies her risk as one that would ultimately affect the refinery and their salaries. Her implicit reasoning shows her view of the risk as greater and therefore more important than Mark's.

Mark and Brenda are acting very similarly toward each other. Both push their views by arguing harder, louder, and at a high level of abstraction. No attempt is made to inquire into each other's perspective. As their conversation heats up, they blurt out more emotionally charged assessments. Their actions are a classic example of Unilateral Control Model behavior.

Although they take opposing views, how Mark and Brenda see themselves and each other is very similar. Each sees the other as being wrong and as an obstacle to overcome. Each sees his or her own view as reasonable and obvious. Mark is looking out for his crew, and Brenda shares an equal concern for her sales staff and customers. Both are protecting the company's interests, yet each one questions the other's motives. They share the same mind-set: the Unilateral Control Model. They even think the same thought at the conclusion of the business meeting, as we hear their thoughts in unison on the DVD: "Well, I am not backing down." Whether it is Mark and Brenda or any two people engaging each other with this pattern of thinking and acting, negative results are predictable.

How Mark and Brenda triggered each other is mapped out in Exhibit 6.1. Using neutral and more generic terminology helps show how each of them is essentially thinking and acting toward the other in similar ways.

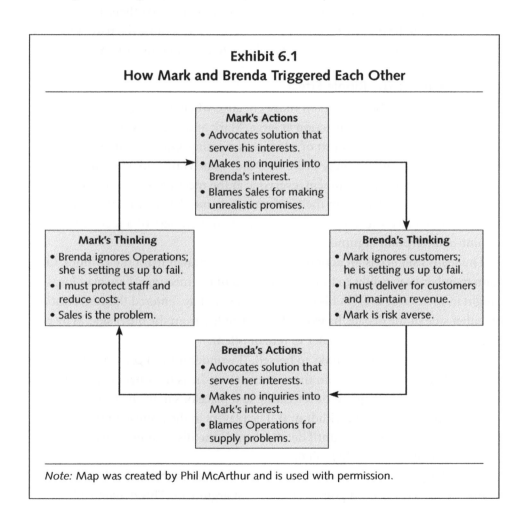

Exhibit 6.1
How Mark and Brenda Triggered Each Other

Mark's Actions
- Advocates solution that serves his interests.
- Makes no inquiries into Brenda's interest.
- Blames Sales for making unrealistic promises.

Brenda's Thinking
- Mark ignores customers; he is setting us up to fail.
- I must deliver for customers and maintain revenue.
- Mark is risk averse.

Brenda's Actions
- Advocates solution that serves her interests.
- Makes no inquiries into Mark's interest.
- Blames Operations for supply problems.

Mark's Thinking
- Brenda ignores Operations; she is setting us up to fail.
- I must protect staff and reduce costs.
- Sales is the problem.

Note: Map was created by Phil McArthur and is used with permission.

When people are caught in a defensive routine of this kind, the results are predictable. Mark and Brenda's working relationship suffers, the issue remains unresolved, and there is a delay in decision making. Although the specific content of their views is unique to them and their business issue, the pattern of their thinking and behavior mirrors a generic defensive routine found in any point-counterpoint conversation.

The map makes it clear that the participants are thinking and acting toward each other in the same manner. Looking at it presents a basic puzzle to each person involved in the defensive routine: I am doing to the other person the very thing I accuse the other person of doing to me. It isn't fair to act toward others in ways I myself don't want to be treated. Confronting this injustice can cause the participants to take a reflective pause and can stimulate a desire to do something different.

Team Dynamics: The Ripple Effect

The reflective pause becomes even more effective when we factor in the implications for the team and organization at large. Mark and Brenda were not acting in isolation, but within the context of a business meeting. Other team members and Walt, the plant manager, were present. Other than Walt's opening and closing remarks and Josh's brief comment, everyone at the meeting remained silent while Mark and Brenda got stuck in their defensive routine. The team's silence is also a common defensive routine that exists when two members of a team engage in a point-counterpoint argument.

The team's silence is an action. They have withdrawn from the conflict. One team member even thinks to himself at the end of the meeting, "I am glad I wasn't caught in their cross fire." In his mind, if he were to have entered the conversation on either side of the debate, he would have taken fire from the other side. Why risk it? From his perspective, it is safer to remain silent.

Another team member thinks to herself, "I wonder if I can get out early." Having completely withdrawn from the conversation, she is no longer even a spectator. Whether by checking out or retreating to a place of safety, the team members are taking the same action: withdrawal. The players in the point-counterpoint argument continue unabated until deadlock ends the discussion. The dynamic in map form is illustrated in Exhibit 6.2.

In this loop, the withdrawal by team members creates a void that is easily filled by the parties engaged in a point-counterpoint argument. This dynamic plays out

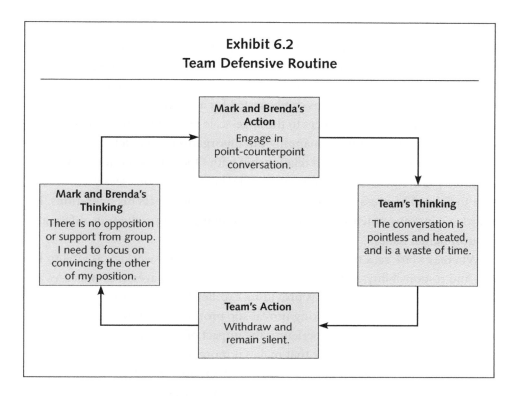

Exhibit 6.2
Team Defensive Routine

Mark and Brenda's Action

Engage in point-counterpoint conversation.

Team's Thinking

The conversation is pointless and heated, and is a waste of time.

Team's Action

Withdraw and remain silent.

Mark and Brenda's Thinking

There is no opposition or support from group. I need to focus on convincing the other of my position.

countless times in business meetings, resulting in poor decision making and hours of lost productivity.

On the Organizational Level

In the meeting, Brenda's and Mark's personal views reflect the concerns, interests, and governing values of their respective departments. These commonly held beliefs and values are steeped in the company's cultural history.

This brings us to the organizational implications of the defensive routines that are in play. Each division is dedicated to the pursuit of excellence in its respective areas of expertise. Divisions and departments make decisions that serve their own self-interest. When self-interests conflict, there is a good chance that one party will do something that causes difficulty for another department or division in the company. At that point, all the nasty intentions, whopping inferences, and damning judgments familiar to interpersonal interactions are attributed to whole classes of people labeled only as "Corporate," "management," or "the team."

By mapping an organizational defensive routine, members can see how the general, tacitly shared assumptions influence their individual actions. Decisions thought to be the best at the time are displayed in a way that enables participants to see the unintended consequences of those decisions. Once brought to the surface, the large-scale assumptions can be tested for accuracy.

Brenda's and Mark's references to the large-scale perceptions of each other's divisions is a starting point for mapping out an organizational defensive routine. How Sales thinks of its role and relationship with Operations reinforces Brenda's position. Mark's position is also reinforced by how Operations sees itself in relation to Sales. The pressure to keep to a tight schedule affects his operations. He guards against any potential risk to safety by looking after production, safety, and environmental issues.

Whereas Mark sees minimizing risk to equipment and workers as vital to his role and responsibility, Brenda experiences it as being risk averse. Brenda sees accommodating a client's needs as providing excellent customer service, yet Mark interprets Sales' efforts as "making unrealistic promises" that eventually create a supply crunch. Each person experiences the impact of one department's decisions on another as an inconvenience that makes it more difficult to get his or her own job done. With each participant focusing only on how the other is creating the problem, the cycle of defensive reasoning takes hold, as shown in Exhibit 6.3.

In a competitive market, Sales signs contracts with clients who rely on a regular flow of product. As this customer segment grows, there is increased pressure on Operations to maintain a tighter schedule. Tighter schedules require higher plant reliability in order to ensure the regular delivery of product. Tighter schedules are less flexible and don't tolerate unexpected events well.

When unexpected events do occur, there is a greater disruption to the schedule. Operations minimizes risk to equipment and crew by delaying the schedule. From Operations' perspective, delays in the schedule increase plant reliability. From Sales' perspective, the more the schedule is delayed, the greater the chance of losing customers. Wishing to avoid losing customers, Sales puts more pressure on Operations to keep on schedule.

If too many disruptive events occur that delay the schedule, the system will break down. As the system approaches breakdown, Sales blames Operations for the potential loss of customers, and Operations blames Sales for creating the time crunches.

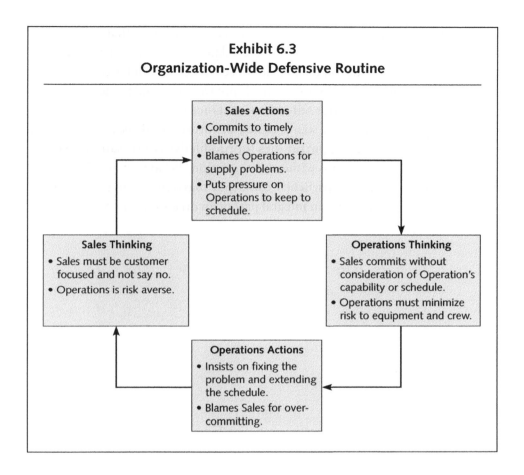

Exhibit 6.3
Organization-Wide Defensive Routine

Sales Actions
- Commits to timely delivery to customer.
- Blames Operations for supply problems.
- Puts pressure on Operations to keep to schedule.

Operations Thinking
- Sales commits without consideration of Operation's capability or schedule.
- Operations must minimize risk to equipment and crew.

Operations Actions
- Insists on fixing the problem and extending the schedule.
- Blames Sales for over-committing.

Sales Thinking
- Sales must be customer focused and not say no.
- Operations is risk averse.

Not addressing the problem systematically results in an increasingly strained working relationship between Sales and Operations. While the issue remains unresolved, blame abounds. This dynamic will continue to repeat itself as long as the members of the organization are unable to discuss the large-scale assumptions, theories, and causal explanations that inhibit their thinking and influence their actions.

These large-scale assumptions and beliefs can change. The change occurs when organizations publicly test their operating assumptions, detect and correct errors, and sustain their commitment to reflection. These actions are required of any organization desirous of de-escalating organization-wide defensive routines.

In the next chapter, I'll explore the personal commitment that individuals, teams, and organizations must make to de-escalate defensive routines. The commitment begins with a step on the journey of self-reflection. In the same spirit as the words of Socrates, "An unexamined life is not worth living," no defensive routine is worth engaging without self-reflection. Once we are on the road of self-reflection, mistakes become the source of new discovery. Conflicts, disagreements, and dilemmas are worthy opportunities for productive conversations. No encounter with another person is without the question "What's my part?" It is one thing to be able to describe a particular conflict by massaging a knot. It is another to make double-loop learning an integral part of an organization's culture. That's the ultimate aspiration.

The De-Escalation

FIX IT NOW OR FIX IT LATER: MARK AND BRENDA REFLECT

Brenda settled into her seat and waited for the rest of the passengers to board the plane. She flipped through the in-flight magazine, then gave up, unable to shake her early meeting with Mark from her mind. Walt's call for a cooling-off period hadn't lasted long. They had gone a few more rounds, less heated but still with the same result—no decision. Finally, Walt had ended the fiasco by saying he would consider his options and get back to them.

"Brenda?"

She looked up to see Jim Laughlin, a colleague from her department, standing in the aisle.

"Hey, Jim. Small world. You heading back to Houston?"

He shook his head. "Just starting out. I'm on my way to London. You?"

"Flew in this morning for a meeting. I'm headed back to the mother ship."

He glanced at his boarding pass and then down the aisle. "Mind if I join you?"

After clearing an exchange of seats with the stewardess, Brenda slid over to the window and let him take the aisle seat. With the hours he was facing, he could use all the leg room he could get.

Once his carry-on was stowed and seatbelt snapped, Jim turned to her.

"So this is familiar stomping ground for you, isn't it? Did you see any of your old colleagues from the plant while you were here?"

"Yes, I did. I don't think they'll be asking me back anytime soon."

"Meeting didn't go well?"

Brenda wrinkled her nose. "I'd say it rated up there with a fire at the refinery."

Jim laughed. "In damage-control mode now, are you?"

She nodded, then ran through a few of the meeting's highlights for him. "I guess I didn't help matters when I told Mark that his view of customer service was from the Dark Ages and that maybe we should burn a few customers at the stake."

Jim's eyes widened. "You said that? I can't imagine Mark responding too well."

Brenda closed her eyes, then opened them again, but the scene in her mind was just as dismal as before. "He came right back at me. Back and forth, back and forth. That's all we did the entire meeting."

Jim shrugged. "It's hard to listen to someone's point when you think he is wrong."

Her colleague's comment and nonchalant manner brought Brenda's thoughts to a halt. He was right, of course. Because she had considered Mark's solution to delay the schedule so obviously wrong, she had written off everything he said as having no merit. Even if he had expressed some legitimate concerns, she'd missed them because she wasn't listening.

"Brenda, where did you go?" Jim was staring at her.

"Sorry. I was composing a text message to Mark in my head. I'm going to propose another go at the problem, but this time, I'll do some listening."

After the plane landed, Brenda walked to the waiting area and pulled her cell phone from her purse. She typed in, "Mark, I didn't do enough to understand where you are coming from. Can we talk again?" then pushed the send button. A few seconds later her phone let out a single ring, indicating that she had a voice message. It was from Mark.

Shortly after Brenda left, Walt and the rest of the team scattered back to their offices, leaving Mark alone. He looked over the empty conference room like a soldier surveying the aftermath of a battle. He and Brenda had knocked each other around pretty good; there was no covering that up now. Word would spread quickly in the hallways that the battle lines had been drawn and that both of them had put on quite a fight.

Unfortunately, there had been no winner. There still was no decision about when to fix the exchanger, and now there was even more strain between Operations and Sales. Mark felt a sudden surge of anger, wanting to blast Brenda again for being so stubborn. He hated to admit it, but he had gotten hooked. It happened every time he sensed that someone was attacking his view. He had immediately launched a counterattack, fortifying his position with every argument he could muster and guarding his flank by garnering additional support from Josh. He had had no more intention of backing down than Brenda had.

Mark shook his head imagining what it must be like to have been on the other side of that conversation. Wouldn't be pleasant, he thought. And he didn't take any satisfaction in that thought.

Mark collected his notes and headed back to his office. He checked his watch, then picked up his phone and dialed Brenda's cell. She'd still be en route to Houston, but would get the message once her plane landed. He waited for the beep.

"Hi Brenda, this is Mark. I guess that seminar I took at the Genghis Khan School of Communication hasn't served me well. I'd like to try a different approach. Give me a call."

SUMMARY: SEARCHING INSIDE

Mark and Brenda have begun to see their own actions and reactions for the defensive behaviors that they are. Even though Brenda prized listening as a value she expected others to afford her, she herself had not offered it to Mark. She made a stark realization that she had violated her own value of listening. She espoused listening, but had not practiced it. For Mark, he took measure of the result and saw that arguing to win did not yield any clear-cut winners but only continued tension. A different result would require something of him outside his tried-and-true ways of doing business.

However informally, Mark and Brenda have begun to "map" the situation they're in. They both realize that their respective actions served as a trigger point for the other. Neither treated each other as they would have wanted to be treated themselves. The end result was one that neither desired, yet their own actions had contributed to it. They know now that a "win-lose" situation won't help either of them in the long run, so each began the journey toward self-reflection with a commitment to do something different.

In the previous chapter, I explored ways in which a third party can begin to diagnosis a defensive routine within the safe environment of private interviews and to construct a map that allows all parties to see how everyone contributes to the routine's cycle of behavior and thinking. In this chapter, I lay out what it takes for every individual, team, and organization, absent a third party, to make the commitment to embark on the journey of reflection.

BRENDA AND MARK ASIDE: IT'S NOT ABOUT FIXING SOMETHING

The first step on the journey is to fully understand that we, as individuals, are both a part of the solution and a part of the problem. When people in my workshops learn about mapping, they quickly realize that the technique facilitates the detection and diagnosis of organizational defensive routines, but doesn't provide instructions for how to ameliorate their effects. The logical next question is, "What can we *do* about organizational defensive routines?" Generally, when people ask me that question, I make my speech about the practice of Mutual Learning Model thinking and acting. Everyone then nods their heads in agreement with the self-assurance that they would follow that path. But their next reaction comes in the form of "I am game, but there is no chance that others in my organization will ever admit to their part in a defensive routine and talk about it." That response summarizes one of the biggest challenges for making progress toward preventing or minimizing defensive routines.

If people are thinking, "What about the other guy?" it means that they are still viewing defensive routines as being "out there." The question implies an assumption that other people's behavior needs to change or needs to be fixed. But thinking of an organizational defensive routine as something to be "fixed" is problematic and, over time, only contributes to a greater sense of helplessness.

The Limits of the Fixing Metaphor

Fixing implies mechanical control. Machines are fixed. Damaged parts are removed and replaced with more efficient ones. Fixing is a methodical process of external manipulation that offers a guarantee of a successful outcome. Fixing is a metaphor that reflects the sights and sounds of the exuberant productivity occurring during the Industrial Revolution. The reality of machines, assembly lines, and engines shaped the images of organizations and, in turn, organizational behavior.

There are still vestiges of these images in the way we think of organizations today. We "reengineer." Departments are "restructured" or "downsized." We "drive" change. As long as we think of organizations in mechanical images, the dominant imagery of fixing will foster the mentality and actions associated with the command-and-control style of management. When the exercise of control is used to mitigate the negative effects of organizational defensive routines, the results are at best limited. In its worst form, the exercise of control is destructive.

Consider what happens when leaders attempt to "fix" organizational defensive routines by commanding employees to "get everything out on the table." At one company, this practice was institutionalized as part of a "change the culture" training program. In one regular exercise, the trainers made the participants write down on a slip of paper a short description of an undiscussable in their team, division, or company. Next they were instructed to drop them all in a bag. From the bag, a volunteer would draw a slip and read it aloud. The employees were then told to discuss the undiscussable.

Fortunately, the exercise was dropped within a few months. When I asked the company's corporate trainer why, he said, "Every time we ran it, the conversation blew up. People were yelling and screaming at each other." The exercise set people up to express their emotionally charged assessments and judgments of each other. Mostly likely, there was little genuine inquiry into conflicting perspectives. There is a good chance the conversation took place at a high level of abstraction. Facts were not verified independent of interpretation. Nor is it likely that many people invited challenge to their own thinking. This exercise only perpetuated the organization's defensive routines.

It is irresponsible on the part of practitioners to tell people to have a courageous, crucial, or difficult conversation with others without demonstrating how to have one. This is the basic criticism Argyris levels against change agents in his book *Flawed Advice.* Advice given by change agents often fails to prescribe what kind of behavior is required to perform the action. The advice is thus neither helpful nor actionable. Although well intended, the simple advice to deal directly and honestly with an organizational defensive routine is short on actionable knowledge. In other words, it is one thing to say it and another thing to do it. The "doing it" entails knowing how.

One "change agent" consultant a few years ago confidently assured me that her program prevented the rise of organizational defensive routines by keeping the focus on the positive. From my observations, I saw that a continual redirection to the positive only created a pink cloud of euphoria and served to bypass and cover up the conditions of threat and embarrassment. I still find it difficult to imagine how one could focus on the positive if experiencing a real or perceived threat to one's competency. Programs designed to circumvent defensive routines only cover them up by providing abstract advice and careless exercises that give false assurances of control.

Control Versus Influence

Organizational defensive routines exist outside the realm of personal control. As one individual, I can no more get rid of an organization's defensive routines than I can change the color of the moon. In many cases, I don't have control over the decisions that are made in an organization. The bottom line is that I don't have any control over how other people think and act. If I do attempt to control others' actions, the results are usually poor. People cannot simply be told to stop behaving badly. The mechanisms of control, such as instituting policy changes, commanding others to have courageous conversations, and offering abstract advice, do not work. A more powerful and effective way to deal with defensive routines is through influence.

The Greek Stoics knew the difference between control and influence. They knew that events external to oneself are outside the realm of personal control. Attempts to control people, places, or things create misery or insanity. Their advice was to accept what happens. According to the Stoics, wisdom comes from knowing the difference between what can be changed and what cannot.

When it comes to that which is beyond our control, the Stoics recommend letting go, acceptance, and vigilance for the unexpected. One of the immediate benefits of giving up trying to control what is not yours to control is a newfound ability to focus on what you can *influence*.

Influencing is taking action with the hope of changing the outcome, but never with the expectation of certain success.

Organizational defensive routines can be influenced. The greatest leverage for influence is one's own behavior. I can control my own behavior, and I am responsible for the consequences of my actions. To the degree that I can model the skills that help untangle defensive routines, I can influence others to do the same.

This means that mutual learning is a program of attraction. When I can ask a question that helps turn around a conversation by bringing more information to the surface, others want to know how to do that. Once blaming stops, mutual accountability can take hold in the organization. Altering interpersonal, team, and organizational defensive routines requires an internal commitment to changing how one thinks and acts in the workplace. At all three of those levels of organizational life, there is different demand for what it takes to make the change.

THE POWER OF REFLECTION

Change begins by taking the initiative to do something different. The initiative starts with changing my own thinking and behavior and not that of the other person, people, or departments. Of course, this advice appears too simple, especially when considering a protracted history of dysfunctional relationships existing in a culture of malaise. The scale appears too big and the task too daunting for a handful of willing souls. Yet no Herculean effort is required.

The key is to take small steps and "chunk down" the situation at hand. I learned this lesson while working my way through graduate school as a part-time painter. Taking it one brush stroke at a time was the only way to get the job done. The same process occurs for de-escalation of organizational defensive routines. The little choices made in a mutual learning mode can over time make a significant difference.

Each choice involves critically examining what we are thinking, what we say and do. It's important to note that "critically" in this sense does not mean casting an unfavorable light on ourselves or another person. Self-reflection uses the critical thinking skills of reasoned judgment. For example, we can shop critically or uncritically. Uncritical shoppers buy what they don't need and pay too much money. Critical shoppers think about how to shop. They evaluate impulses, discern between want and need, and compare quality and price. They use their critical thinking skills to make their decisions about shopping. Applied to human behavior, self-reflection is the ability to step back from our actions to evaluate their effectiveness and then, if needed, to redesign our thoughts and actions.

Making a commitment to self-reflection thus means questioning everything, not taking anything for granted, and keeping a vigil for mistaken assumptions and erroneous thinking. With critical thinking, we make reasoned judgments about our effectiveness. How well did our intentions match our desired results? What unintended consequences might we have produced? What impacts did our actions have on others? Critical thinking examines the multitude of assumptions, values, and beliefs influencing our actions at any give time and allows us to determine their relevance and accuracy.

The Mutual Learning Model utilizes critical thinking in the search for valid information and better, more informed decisions. The model's claim rests on the practice of its skill set. Each skill is a critical thinking tool. For example, when we filter out the toxicity of our private thinking, we are better able to discern what useful information can be shared publicly. The Ladder of Inference is a quintessential critical thinking tool that helps us trace the steps in our thinking and makes our advocacies more compelling, precise, and clear. The use of high quality inquiries helps elicit additional information and the reasoning of others. This foundational skill set is the basis for more effective action capable of leading us to more productive results. What makes Mutual Learning Model actions possible is the different mind-set that creates them.

The mind-set of "I am right and you are wrong" produces the actions consistent with the Unilateral Control Model. Views are pushed hard, and there is minimal inquiry. Win-lose leaves no room for ties. Insisting that others see what is clear and obvious in my mind without disclosing my view clearly and explicitly only leaves good ideas within the confines of my mind, and other people in the dark. Escalating error and poor communication and decision making are the results of the Unilateral Control Model. Its mind-set can not generate actions that lead to mutual learning. As Albert Einstein said, "You can't solve a problem from the same consciousness that created it." Different results can be achieved only by a concerted effort to think in a different way.

A change of thinking allows for new action. When I think to myself, "What am I missing?" I want to know more. Consequently, I ask good questions that bring more information to light and achieve greater understanding. Discovering new information is a positive result. Inviting challenge to my way of thinking keeps my mind agile. I am ready to shape and mold ideas that address multiple concerns and issues. In doing so, I can make better, more informed decisions. Better decisions increase the chances of effective implementation.

Although these results are desirable, making the necessary shift from one mind-set to another doesn't happen automatically, quickly, or easily. Changing one's habits of thought is just as grueling an enterprise as discovering what thoughts and actions haven't been effective. Because reflection requires a lot of work on the part of individuals, teams, and organizations, a legitimate question to ask is "Why bother?"

WHY BOTHER?

When I teach philosophy, I tell my students that if we find ourselves discussing a ponderous, learned philosophy that doesn't help them make better sense of this world and live with greater sense of purpose and meaning, they can yell out, "SO WHAT?" I propose a similar offer for self-reflection. Rather than "So what?" a better question to the invitation for self-reflection is "Why bother?" After all, it is much easier to wash your hands of the whole mess and get back to your own little corner of the universe.

The problem is similar to the plight of the mobster in the movie *The Godfather* who has a desire to leave organized crime, but in the end says, "Every time I think I've gotten out, they pull me back in." No matter where you go, you will find yourself in situations of potential embarrassment or threat. Your and others' reactions will give rise to defensive routines. Avoiding any interaction with others around difficult and complicated issues is an option, but the result will always be the same. In time, the continued existence of defensive routines will become intolerable. The pain in your life and in the lives of others and the organization will become so great, it will force a course of action. In too many cases, the course of action is to remove the people involved in the defensive routine through termination, resignation, or relocation. This action provides temporary relief, but eventually new or similar defensive routines arise. Long-term, productive change depends on the ability to think and do something different.

Pain as an Incentive

Pain is one incentive to "bother" to do things differently. I was once facilitating a meeting with a corporation's top executives, who had a bad habit of getting into heated discussions in which two or more executives would talk over the top of each other. I began to count the number of times it happened. In a thirty-minute period, they talked over each other twenty-two times.

After the first morning of the meeting, the pain of getting nowhere became too much. After continual return trips to the same old tired dynamics, there was finally a collective throwing up of hands. Their cry was "We will do anything." I drew a map of the dynamic and pointed to it every time they started to talk over each other. They considered the day a success when later in the afternoon they were able to catch themselves in the act, stop the pattern of talking over each other, and slow down the conversation so that each speaker could be heard.

Pain may be the incentive for changing the culture of today's business world. In his article "Taking Personal Change Seriously: The Impact of Organizational Learning on Management Practice," Peter Senge reviews the impact of twenty-five years of Argyris's work in the field of learning organizations. He pays tribute to Argyris's work and like many others shares the commonsense desire to see a shift in the culture of the business world toward the adoption of the Mutual Learning Model. He questions how it is that Argyris's work can be so attractive and hold so much promise for a more productive work environment, yet not have been put into practice more than it has.

Senge reminds us that twenty-five years is still a brief period of time to transform a culture. His conjecture is that the transformation will continue to be slow because "so long as people feel that their conventional ways of handling their affairs can work, they are not yet motivated to really break out of their habitual ways of doing things." He predicts that the learning advocated by Argyris and Schön's work will increase when the current way of doing business will no longer suffice. In other words, when the pain gets too great, change will occur.

Spotting the Gap

Milder forms of pain can work to motivate someone to make personal change. The discovery of the gap between what I profess to believe and value (espoused theory) and what I actually *do* (theory in practice) usually generates enough dissonance for me to "bother" to engage in reflection.

Argyris uses a technique called unfreezing the LHC to make the gap apparent. Action Design and I have adapted this technique in my workshops and classes. Here's how it works:

I break the participants up into groups of six. They have done either a full LHC-RHC case study or a mini case study in which they have written two lines of dialogue and a corresponding LHC comment. To protect confidentiality, the cases have no personal names on them. I collect the cases and exchange them with another group.

The members of the small group read another group's LHC comments. The task of the exercise is to characterize the kind of thinking found in the LHC. Each group writes their list on flip charts. The list always includes items like "making judgments," "blaming," "attributing negative intentions," "I am right, the other is wrong," and other common characteristics of LHC thinking. Once all the lists are posted on flip charts, the groups see very quickly that the lists are the same.

This technique validates the extent to which the Unilateral Control Model is shared among people across gender, age, and cultural differences. It also stimulates self-reflection. Participants are often shocked to see how judgmental and negative their private thinking is. This realization is inconsistent with how people generally see themselves as being honest and fair.

The exercise continues with an examination of the dialogue in the RHC of their case study. Participants compare the LHC with the RHC to see what strategy was used to communicate the censored information without blurting it out directly. They see the various strategies of being polite and diplomatic, showing respect, and supporting others. By the end of the exercise, they are able to see that the strategies of action yield at best short-term gains and are quite ineffective in the long term.

At the conclusion of the exercise, group members express a desire for change. They want to know how to express their inner thoughts more productively. By stimulating self-reflection and inducing mild discomfort, the reflective exercise led them to make an important discovery that had previously been outside their personal awareness. They realized how their private thinking influences their actions.

The Limits of Human Awareness

On a basic level, the limits of human awareness account for many of the difficulties we get into when it comes to organizational defensive routines. Simply put, we are not aware of everything that goes on around us. We miss a lot of stuff. These are not senior moments, but a general state of the human condition. Philosophers call it "subjectivity." I call it just plain being blind.

Once I befriended a woman born blind. Not knowing how to be a good friend, I asked her, "What could I do that would be helpful and what would not be helpful?" Her response has always stayed with me. She said, "Once you get to know me you will realize that being blind is the least of my problems." She turned out to be right, but what turned out to be true for her was the exact opposite for me.

Being blind is one of the worst of my problems. I am blind to all sorts of things. I am blind to information outside of what I consider important. I can't see others' intentions. I am blinded by my assumptions. I am unaware of how my actions affect others. Conversely, others are blind to my intentions and how their actions affect me. We are born blind to anything beyond our own perspective. These limits of human awareness darken our ability to see different perspectives. Only the light of self-reflection helps us see our shortcomings.

An admission of blindness may help stimulate a need for reflection, but the challenge to be self-reflective always remains personal. An organization can not program insight, write a policy for reflection, or develop a procedure for self-discovery. Each of us must make our own journey of self-discovery. The invitation for self-reflection is accepted by our own will to do so.

AN INVITATION TO REFLECT

One of my initial mistakes early in my career as a counselor was to think that I could get another person to be self-reflective. At the time, I was a counselor for a hospice and was ennobled by the vision of helping people come to a peaceful acceptance of their death. I got off to a rough start when I was fired by my first patient.

Before my first visit, I was told that she was dying of cancer but was in denial about her death. I got ready to bust down denial with the latest psychological judo maneuver. During my first visit with her, I continued to bring up in our conversation the reality that she was going to die soon. When I called to make our second appointment, she told me not to come. I asked, "Why not?" and she said, "You are too depressing. All you want to talk about is death." She was right. I was pushing my agenda for when and how she was going to deal with her own death.

In that moment, I learned that even if I am helping another person reflect on his or her words, actions, or course in life, I cannot engineer that individual's reflection simply through my desire for him or her to do so. The invitation must come by way of an offer and not a demand. In dealing with clients, I make the offer to reflect together on the thinking and behavior that troubles the organization. If the offer is refused outright, I respect their decision. I will call attention to the limitations of the decision and its consequences, but not push. When the offer for reflection is accepted, but the person's reflection yields insights only into how others are the problem, I point that out and bring the reflection back to that individual's own contribution. A full commitment to self-reflection begins the journey of self-discovery. The discovery is a continual process of unlearning and learning anew.

What Does It Take for an Individual?

A main premise of Argyris's research and theory is that before we can learn something new, we must unlearn what it is we are doing that results in error. Simply, if we don't stop what we are doing that generates error, then the error will persist. One of the challenges of self-reflection is that it is very difficult to unlearn something that is outside our conscious awareness. We are not always aware of what we are doing that generates the error.

As I've mentioned elsewhere, because what we have learned is so deeply ingrained, our actions appear spontaneous and natural to us. Argyris points out that these actions are experienced as natural because they are so skillful. Anything done skillfully looks easy and natural, but it has come about through much practice. This is true for our own actions, so self-reflective thinkers need to find ways to observe their own behavior and examine the thinking behind their actions.

One way to overcome the limits of awareness and the difficulty of catching errors in the moment of live action is to retrieve artifacts from the past. This is especially important for reflecting on our thoughts and actions when we have been under the influence of the Unilateral Control Model. We are not usually aware that we are in the unilateral control mode until we see it play out in retrospect. Reflecting on a past conversation provides sufficient distance, and an ounce of regret usually motivates us to examine what went wrong.

Capturing Action

For us to reflect on our actions, we need reliable, observable examples of our behavior. A few years ago, I took a masters swimming class with Matt Biondi, the 1988 Olympic gold medalist. He brought with him a videotape of himself swimming. The camera was under water, so we could observe his stroke technique. He talked about the hours he watched himself on video noting the subtle differences in his stroke and how it affected his performance. He was able to see a gap between two fingers where water passed through. A more efficient stroke is with a closed hand. When winning times are determined by few hundredths of a second, a small alteration like that can make the difference between first and second place. I left the masters swimming clinic deeply impressed with how athletes diligently learn from their mistakes through the practice of critical observation. Watching replays of their actions is the staple of their learning. In the world of business, this is not the case.

Recording meetings for the purpose of playing them back and analyzing the course of human interactions is not a regular practice in most companies. In the litigious society we live in, the practice of recording meetings would most likely inhibit communication. Yet it is a missed opportunity. By not applying the consistent discipline of critical observation with the same dedication to performance as exhibited in Olympic and professional sports, business leaders run the risk of repeating the same mistakes in the arena of human relationships over and over again.

When we take the opportunity to step back and observe our actions, we notice more than what our ordinary self-awareness allows us to. We have a rare chance to see ourselves as others might experience us. Stepping back and observing is very difficult to do. We can't stand outside ourselves and watch unless what we have said or done has been either taped or video-recorded. If that is the case, then critical observation can reach its full benefit for self-reflection.

A recorded conversation relieves me of a faulty memory. Although it may be the best tool for reflection, a recording is hard to listen to. I am subjected to the indisputable reality of my own actions. After listening to what I actually said, I fall into a state of disbelief. "What was I thinking?" is no longer a sufficient plea of ignorance. I know now that there is a design to my actions. The tape or video has now become an artifact, and I have to begin to do my work of reflection.

An alternative avenue into reflection is case study writing. Transcribing a recorded conversation into a LHC-RHC case study format is a labor-intensive exercise, but immensely valuable. You have to hear all of what someone says in order to write it down. You can hear what was missed the first time around. Best of all, the record is indisputable. It is what was said. The action is captured in its entirety.

In lieu of a tape or video recording, the simple act of writing out the case from memory generates insight. It is not necessary to write out the entire conversation. The critical moment when the conversation went south or hit an emotional peak of frustration is usually sufficient. First-time writers often select a case with an eye on how to win the other person over to their perspective or to solicit help on how to deal with such a difficult person. By the second or third round of writing cases, writers shift their focus to what they might have done to contribute to the problem or to how they got stuck and want to do something different.

Once a case study has been written, the best forum for its presentation is a study group of like-minded learners. The case writer receives benefits from the group's reflection and modeling of the skills, and each case yields learning applicable to all members of the group. There are a number of different strategies for working on case studies that deepen everyone's knowledge of the concepts and tools, as well as provide a field of practice. Appendix B describes four strategies that you can use to structure a study group session.

I have heard students and workshop participants praise the merits of writing LHC-RHC case studies, but I rarely hear about people continuing the practice much past the initial workshop. Study groups are formed with the best of intentions, but the ones I know of rarely sustain themselves for more than a few months. This is not due to a lack of desire, but to the general busyness of work and life, which takes its toll on a commitment to regular meetings. As practitioners, we don't write cases as often as we should when we get stuck. I have come to see the LHC-RHC case study as a rare but excellent opportunity for learning. Whenever a group or skilled practitioner is available, we should take advantage of presenting a case.

Although writing an LHC-RHC case study may be valuable, its benefits are limited if I am the only person doing the reflection. I always need to enlist the help of others. Such help is amply available in study groups, but even more important, it is available in real-time situations.

Enlisting the Help of Others

We can reflect on our actions in the moment with the help of others. I make it a regular practice to contract for learning. If I wish to explore another person's point of view, I might say, "I want to ask a few questions to learn more about your view. If at any point you begin to feel interrogated, stop me." In classrooms and workshops, I always reserve time at the end to ask two questions: "What did I do to promote your learning?" and "What did I do that might have inhibited your learning?" The participants' responses over the years have led me to improve my instructional design and presentation style.

On occasion I give the participants permission during the evaluation to blurt out their LHC comments about my presentation or the design of the workshop, with the promise that I will help them help me. If I get a "Yeah, the day dragged," I can take the opportunity to model the skills with a "That may be true, but not helpful. What part of the day dragged, and what do you recall my doing or saying at the time?" With a little work, I am able to identify the part of the day that dragged and then check with others to see if they experienced it the same or differently.

Learning in the moment is always preferable, but I am not always on top of my game. When I get hooked or triggered emotionally by someone, I enlist others' help by asking them to allow me to vent first and then reflect on my trigger points. If I have walked away dissatisfied with the outcome of a conversation, I always know that restarting it is an option. I return to the person and take the initiative to inquire into what I might have said or done that contributed to the negative outcome.

The rigors of self-reflection demand a tremendous amount of mental work. Monitoring our actions requires constant vigilance. We are on alert for false assumptions, errors, and mistaken thinking. We must realistically appraise our limitations and keep them foremost in our mind. In any human interaction, the mind needs to remain agile and curious. It takes a lot to be self-reflective.

What Does It Take for a Team?

What does it take for a team to talk about how a defensive routine exists within its own membership? First, everyone must be willing to engage in a tough conversation. This is not to say that everyone is at the same level of commitment or skill. I would expect various degrees of skill within a team. There is always a chance that the lid will come off, and the conversation will get hot.

When the temperature rises in the group, there is a good chance that everyone's defenses have been engaged. This doesn't mean that all hope of a productive discussion has evaporated. I have found it helpful to see defensiveness not as something to be resisted or eliminated. I reached a comfort level with public displays of defensiveness largely because of my experience of sitting at the bedside of the dying.

From the dying, I learned to respect defensiveness. I have often heard the phrase "I am not afraid of death." Most of us can deal with the *thought* of death, the general concept. But the impending reality of one's own death is a different story. When they first hear the news that their death is imminent, most people have a natural defensive reaction. Many move to a place of acceptance. There are a lot of other feelings and thoughts in between.

I apply the same lesson learned in hospice to interventions with teams. Defensiveness is something to be expected, especially when difficult, embarrassing, or threatening issues are discussed. I not only expect defensiveness but also anticipate seeing every aspect of the Unilateral Control Model play out before me. If a fully engaged defensive routine is in place and operating full throttle, it plays itself out in my presence. I have found that a team can get there very quickly, but like the dying, they don't have to stay defended all the time.

A team's defensiveness can be reduced dramatically as members learn how to disagree with each other productively. They need to be willing to engage their differences in views. In theory, no one is against the idea of disagreement. Disagreement is healthy. Yet many people find disagreeing unpleasant, uncomfortable, and threatening. I hear comments such as these all the time: "If I disagreed, he'd snap my head off" or "It is very difficult to disagree with her. I have seen over the years what happens to people when they have disagreed with her." There are perceived and real negative consequences that follow from disagreement.

A prevalent assumption is that open disagreement or conflict is bad or destructive. People formulate "theories" around why it is important not to disagree publicly, especially with the boss. Some examples of what I have heard are "Don't disagree with him in public; to do so would be to challenge his authority" and "I avoid raising issues because I don't want to take on the executive officer and embarrass him in front of my peers." The candor of these examples explicitly spells out the conditions of threat or embarrassment.

In the effort to protect the boss from the threat and embarrassment of being challenged publicly with a different point of view, employees censor valuable information. The information might be critical to an important decision, but no one will ever know because it is not mentioned. People go on to justify their cover-up by telling themselves something like "Sometimes it is best to ignore it, because it is a little thing. I can get away with it. I don't do this regularly. Sometimes it's better to use your best judgment. I have worked with him long enough to know where the line is."

Or, in the name of efficiency, someone might think, "In a sense I am doing things without him really being aware. I am doing this to facilitate the process or making sure we get a good result. You do certain things to get the process done."

These ways of "justifying" withdrawal from disagreement ultimately do a disservice to the organization. Learning is inhibited, and information is lost. Withdrawing from conflict helps maintain the very pattern that causes inefficiency and discouragement.

As we begin to explore how conflict can be raised and resolved productively, we lessen the need to cover it up. Indeed, we may find ourselves beginning to see conflict in a fundamentally new light. Instead of finding a way of disagreeing "that will not cause friction," we might get to the point where we see conflict the same way that Mary Parker Follett did in 1924: "Instead of condemning conflict, we should set it to work for us. Why not? The friction between the driving wheel of the locomotive and the track is necessary to haul the train. All polishing is done by friction. The music of the violin we get by friction. . . . So in business too we have to know when to try to eliminate friction and when to capitalize on it. . . . whether we can set conflict to work and make it do something for us."

Friction can work more effectively for teams as they begin to practice ways of challenging and disagreeing openly.

What Does It Take for Organizations?

At an organizational level, there needs to be a full-scale commitment to reflect on the company's thinking and actions. On this level, it is vital that senior leadership participates. Conversation between a company's leaders and teams can spark a movement toward the reduction of organizational defensive routines.

Senior leaders must commit themselves to the challenge of having tough conversations. Instead of cramming a meeting with an agenda designed to truncate any possibility for reflection and deep dialogue on complex issues, they need to set aside large blocks of time dedicated to a thorough exchange of views and issues.

I have heard many senior leaders complain that they are unable to have tough and difficult conversations because of the "egos" around the table. Of course, the conflict exhibited in organizational defensive routines is a result of people's coming together with different views and contexts to discuss complex issues. Yet the excuse of big egos as a justification for not engaging the conflict is not a satisfactory explanation. Phrases like "There is a personality conflict" or "It's all about egos" are more examples of causal explanations used to sanction the feeling of helplessness and to justify taking no action. It is too easy to write off defensive routines as personality conflicts and leave them alone. This is a surface explanation, and it fails to explore the deeper perennial tensions inherent to organizational life.

Organizations need to appreciate that as they grow, determine direction, foster creativity, and establish alignment, inextricable dilemmas will arise. Argyris said it best in this short statement: "Organizations are social devices that turn dilemmas into inter-group conflict."

This is a critical insight. By their nature, dilemmas prevent two rival perspectives from reaching an outcome completely satisfactory to either view. In the end, there is a need to balance the rival perspectives in untidy circumstances. Crucial to successful business results is finding a way to manage organizational dilemmas in ways that minimize risks and maximize advantages.

For example, an organization's alignment to its mission and vision is a necessity for success. In order to accomplish the organization's goals, all members must think and act in similar enough ways to achieve the goals. Problems occur when each division or department, clear in how its business area needs to function to accomplish the company's goal, sets out on its own path to get there. As a business leader told me once, "Unfortunately, we are not all on the same road. We're not even headed in the same direction. Each of us is pretty strong in our own areas, and we're driving our own areas of business in separate ways."

Misalignment comes about when departments go their separate ways and end up running into each other, creating conflict, mishaps, and error. Misalignment is common to organizational life. Inherent to the work of alignment is the development of shared meaning and action. Creating shared meaning and action entails raising concerns and interests that often pull a group apart, especially in an organization that deliberately chooses business leaders with the diversity of knowledge, background, and expertise necessary to compete in the market. On one hand, alignment does not mean thinking and acting exactly the same. On the other hand, if organization members think and act differently, they often work at cross purposes. This is the heart of the dilemma. We are people who think and act differently from each other who must work together toward a common goal.

Whether it is alignment, development, accountability, or autonomy, every business issue contains inherent dilemmas that make their appearance as intergroup conflicts. There are two guiding principles that will help you find a way to productively manage these dilemmas:

- Look for reasonableness in how others are thinking and acting, without necessarily agreeing.
- Seek to understand what leads to the behavior you find problematic. Are people caught in dilemmas? Are you contributing? If so, how?

By focusing on the intergroup conflict, members of an organization miss the underlying dilemma. Dilemmas occur all the time as different people try to work together to get things done. They are tensions that will never resolve themselves completely, but must be managed. When people frame these tensions as a dilemma, they will have a greater understanding and compassion for how they find themselves and others caught in interlocking patterns of behavior.

⟿

When it comes to de-escalating defensive routines, the commitment to self-reflection and the willingness to engage differences and discuss the dilemmas inherent in organization life are what it takes to step up to the plate; getting into the game calls for skill, endurance, and daily practice. In the next chapter, you will see Mark, Brenda, and their team hold conversations with each other as if they had practiced the skill set over a period of time. In a sense, Chapter Eight fast-forwards the scenario to a productive time and place where all the players have made the commitment to self-reflection and have become fairly accomplished in the practice of the skill set. The chapter will also give you the chance to get there yourself through its exercises and practical suggestions.

NOTES

Follett, Mary Parker. *Creative Experience.* New York: Peter Smith. (Originally published 1924.)

Senge, Peter M. "Taking Personal Change Seriously: The Impact of Organizational Learning on Management Practice." *Academy of Executive Management*, 2003, *17*(2), 47–51.

Engaging Differences

F aced with a situation in which you feel threatened, embarrassed, or potentially both, what will you do? The instant and readied defensive reaction will be there, but now you know you have a choice. You can go the defensive route or take an alternative path toward mutual learning.

In this chapter and the next, you will be directed once again to the accompanying DVD. You will watch Mark and Brenda demonstrate an alternative to the thinking and behavior that originally propelled them into the vicious cycle of defensive routines. Specifically, Mark and Brenda's awareness of the Ladder of Inference and their productive use of their LHC and of high quality advocacy and inquiry serve them both very well. In the scenes that accompany these two chapters, Mark and Brenda are in fact modeling double-loop learning, or the Mutual Learning Model. Their actions will serve as a teaching tool for helping you move from theory to practice.

In other words, even though Mark and Brenda are fictional characters, what you read or watch is a demonstration of a reproducible skill set. You can hone your ability to reproduce the skills by completing the exercises offered in this chapter. Like Mark and Brenda, we all can use high quality advocacy and inquiry to understand our different points of view, test our assumptions, and create mind-sets capable of moving our conversations forward. Communicating more effectively is the counterbalance to the negative effects of defensive routines.

ALTERNATIVE ACTION BEGINS WITH CURIOSITY

Throughout this chapter, as you watch Mark and Brenda reengage, this time much more productively, step back and think about how you might describe what they're doing. One word that comes to mind to describe these new interactions is "curiosity." Becoming curious about differences is a fundamental shift in thinking vital to unlocking organizational defensive routines and generating productive business conversations. Curiosity leads people to engage the differences between their views, instead of avoiding them. The ability to engage differences is key to averting the rise of defensive routines.

Anytime I'm having a conversation where complex issues give rise to the conditions of threat and embarrassment, I find myself at a critical juncture. I can choose to defend my position. I can persist in my view of the other as "mistaken," an "idiot," and "plain crazy." This road will lead to the further polarization of ideas and ultimately the deterioration of the working relationship.

Or I can get curious. Curiosity poses these questions:

How is it that we see this issue differently?

What does the other person see that I may be missing?

What can I learn from others' perspectives?

How can I discover the reasonableness of another's perspective?

What does it take to be curious? Basically, it takes an appetite for learning—not from books, but from others. Curiosity takes a willingness to see your own perspective as partial and limited. Once you assume partiality, you will feel a greater drive to seek out perspectives different than your own. Curiosity seeks out differences. When differences are found, curiosity tunes our ears to pick up how we are diverging in our thinking from each other.

Curiosity is what compels someone to "come down" from the top of his or her ladder and examine the rungs climbed to the conclusion. Curiosity also entices a person to think about the ladders that other people might be on and how they arrived at their conclusions. In other words, curiosity uses the Ladder of Inference as a tuning device to draw out more information from others, explore our own reasoning process, and identify where our views differ from those of others.

ACTION DESIGN'S ADVANCED VERSION
OF THE LADDER OF INFERENCE

To use the Ladder of Inference in service of curiosity, we need a more precise and advanced version. As presented in Chapter Two, the simpler and more popular version of the ladder shows three rungs: select data, interpret data and add meaning, and draw conclusions. That version of the ladder covers the basic ideas that observable data forms the basis of our inferred conclusions and that moving from data to conclusion is an interpretative process. For introductory purposes, this version is easy to understand, but it's limited in its application to actual dialogue and a productive facilitation of differences.

Action Design developed a version of the Ladder of Inference that is more versatile and precise in its use for facilitation and interventions than the simpler version in Chapter Two. I'll introduce that more complex version here, because it shows more clearly the kinds of thinking or spoken statements that exist on the three rungs: select data, interpret data and add meaning, and draw conclusions. For example, at the top rung of the Ladder of Inference, rather than the simple label "conclusion," Action Design has been able to delineate what I call variations on the theme of a conclusion. If one listens carefully to the types of conclusions people make on top of the ladder, one can discern three varieties: proposing action, explaining, and evaluating. At the interpret data and add meaning rung, there are two distinct types: naming what is happening and paraphrasing. The select data rung is the same as in the simpler version.

Although the Action Design version is more complicated than the basic definition of the ladder offered in Chapter Two, it offers a great advantage to the practitioner who wants to use more precise inquiries to identify and explore the points of divergence. The following sections will examine the variations on the theme of a conclusion, naming, selecting data, and paraphrasing. Along the way, you will find a set of exercises you can use to become more familiar with the "Advanced" Ladder of Inference.

Proposing Action

When we use such language as "We should do . . . ," "Let's not do that," or "The way to go on this is . . . ," we are proposing action. This is different from *taking* action. We are privately thinking or publicly suggesting what we should or should not do.

Explaining

A second variation on the theme of a conclusion consists of explanations. When someone says, "This happened because . . . ," the person goes on to give a causal explanation or theory for what happened. It is the answer to the question "Why?" For example, someone says in a meeting, "The project failed because it lacked upper management support." The causal explanation may be true, but the statement offers no data for what management did or did not do to support the project.

Causal explanations or theories are rarely testable. This is especially true when it comes to explaining someone's behavior. People spout off causal explanations containing psychological conjectures usually reserved for the psychiatrist's couch. They serve to account for why the person did something that appears obviously wrong or stupid. These casual explanations are the common currency of defensive routine. They circulate around everywhere except with the person who is the object of the explanation.

Discovering why something happened the way that it did has an important place in our reasoning process. Explanations tend to be interesting, but if they remain at a high level of abstraction, their accuracy or truth claim becomes difficult to verify. Conversations get bogged down under the weight of too many competing, often lengthy explanations for why something is happening. Eventually the conversation concludes on the note of "interesting opinions" without any deep understanding of the problem or progress on what to do differently.

Evaluating

The third variation of conclusion found on the top rung of the Ladder of Inference is the evaluation. Evaluations focus on whether something is good or bad, wrong or right, better or worse. We hear evaluations when someone uses such language as, "It's totally unethical," "That's a bad idea," or "That's the right thing to do." Our evaluations are tossed back and forth at a high level of abstraction. The abstract quality of "It will be good for the company" is added to any proposed action as a further justification for its adoption. What are often lacking are the criteria used to make these evaluations. Specific values and beliefs are embedded in our evaluations, but we are not always consciously aware of using them. We do not make these values and beliefs explicit and thus available for public discussion. Instead, they remain tacit and abstract, with everyone making the dangerous assumption that everyone else shares the same meaning of good, bad, right, or wrong.

The Hazards of Arguing from Atop Our Ladders

In many of the early narratives, particularly in the meeting scene, our characters Brenda and Mark have been proposing different actions for what to do. They have been arguing solutions: "We should do this . . . No, we should do this." A lot of discussion during meetings takes place with everyone on top of their respective ladders trading proposals for action back and forth. After all, we are people of action, and business is about getting things done. If there is a problem, we jump into action to fix it and move on to the next item. We must and do commit ourselves to action, but often we do so at the cost of not having a shared understanding of the problem. When the meeting ends, people go off with the privately held assessment, "This will never work." To no one's surprise, the plan doesn't work, and people scratch their heads wondering how their best-laid plans went awry.

Another scenario is the slinging of solutions back and forth until someone in a position of authority steps in, makes a unilateral choice, and declares one party the victor and the other the loser. Another end to the same scenario is the "stalemate" or a "dead heat match" where no decision is made during the meeting, but people spend countless hours in "behind the scenes" lobbying of the authoritative decision maker to take one side over another. The final results are delayed decisions, reduced team efficiency, polarization of team members, and limited problem solving.

These are the hazards of arguing solutions. This is not to say we should not propose solutions, but we must be aware that when we are proposing action, we are on top of our ladder. Others may agree with the course of action, and things move along. When there is disagreement, however, it is time to get curious and discover the various objections, concerns, and needs behind the proposals for action.

Similar dynamics play out when we trade positive and negative evaluations back and forth. Arguing conclusions at the level of proposing action or trading causal explanations and evaluations is a common place where people get stuck. The difficulty usually lies either in participants' having different understandings of the problem or in making proposals for action that don't adequately address the concerns and needs of others. Getting unstuck is as simple as asking the right question.

People propose a course of action based on their understanding of the problem, but the connection between the two is not always made explicit. By asking for their understanding of the problem, we can make the connection. A high quality inquiry like "What do you see going on in the organization that suggests that taking your course of action would be beneficial?" The question helps the other person "down the ladder." We are asking the other person to provide a more detailed description of the problem, what he or she is selecting as important, and any observable data. Once we establish a shared understanding of the problem, then the proposed courses for action have a better chance of being adopted.

If proposed solutions or actions are met with resistance, it usually means that they haven't addressed an underlying issue or lingering concern. By making an inquiry into the objections to the proposal, we can bring the unaddressed concerns and needs to the surface for discussion. For example, "What difficulties might this course of action create for others?" or "What obstacles might we anticipate?" are two general inquiries that invite challenge to the proposed action by seeking out potential difficulties or concerns. Incorporating ways to address those concerns and needs increases the chances of finding a solution that all can buy into and implement more effectively.

With both of the strategies I've described here, inquiry is being used to help people down their ladder to either the interpret data and add meaning rung or the select data rung.

Exercise

What Would Walt Say?

Take on the role of Walt, the plant manager. As Walt, you have heard Mark and Brenda trade different conclusions back and forth. Your challenge is to stay on task with the business issue. Your goal is to focus on the issue at hand and obtain the information you need to make an informed decision.

As Walt, write down (don't just think about) what would you say after Brenda ends with "I have to deal with lost customers, which means lost production for the plant. Let's not forget that customers pay all of the salaries."

After you have written down what you would say, go to the DVD, click on the screen titled Engaging Differences, and choose What Would Walt Say? to play. Watch and compare your intervention with what Walt says.

Exercise

Inquiry—Exercise I

In this exercise, we return to the conversation with a focus on how Mark and Brenda traded proposals for action back and forth. You will sharpen your inquiry skills by designing an intervention that will help Mark surface additional information.

Take on the role of Brenda and write down (don't just think about) what question you would ask after Mark says, "Well, we discovered a bad exchanger during turnaround. This is the best time to replace it. It'll only extend the turnaround by a week."

After writing down your inquiry, go to the DVD, click on the screen titled Engaging Differences, and choose Inquiry—Exercise I. Watch the scene and compare your inquiry with the one Brenda makes into Mark's thinking.

Naming

Even if you avoid getting stuck at trading proposed actions back and forth, you are not always free of a point-counterpoint argument. You can still get stuck at the level of naming what is going on. You know you are there when you feel as though you are in the old Miller Lite commercial in which the characters are arguing about the two distinctive features of the same beer. In the commercial, one man says, "Tastes great," and the other responds, "No—less filling." They go back and forth saying, "Tastes great," "No—less filling" for the entire commercial. Our conversations can sound like this when we have interpreted the same observable data differently.

When you listen to how people describe an experience they all commonly shared, you can hear statements rich in personal meaning and informed by values and assumptions. Such language as "What is going on here is . . ." or "The problem is . . ." is a cue that the person is describing what he or she has seen. For example, phrases like "He is mad" or "She is worried" are statements describing states of mind or emotion. A person's attributing anger to someone whose face is red and voice is loud is drawing on a commonly shared meaning associated with this set of characteristics and behavior. These statements are lower on the ladder than the conclusion rung in the sense that they are less abstract than the conclusions on top of the ladder and closer to the observable data that serves as the basis for the reasoning process.

Metaphors and images also provide a window into how someone is describing a situation. The common reference to "shuffling the chairs on the Titanic" communicates clearly the speaker's meaning associated with the futility of action in the face of an impending disaster. The values and assumptions we hold shape how we describe something. Because these factors are unique to an individual's experience, shared events can generate a variety of meanings and an assortment of evaluations.

Exercise

Inquiry—Exercise II

Although our images, metaphors, and descriptions can enhance shared meaning, we also can find ourselves using different words to refer to the same event. We can get ourselves into "apples and oranges" conversations all the time, using different terms to describe the same thing. The reverse can be true as well. We use the same word, but the word means something completely different to those having a conversation. In either case, we are stuck on the naming level of the Ladder of Inference. The skill of inquiry helps people stuck on the rung of naming to climb down to the select data rung.

In this exercise, take the role of David, a team member at the plant. In the meeting, you hear Mark and Brenda using the same word, "risk," but each uses it with a different sense of its meaning. Craft an intervention that states your understanding of what you see happening (an advocacy at the naming rung) balanced with a question that helps Brenda be more concrete about what she means by risk (an inquiry to elicit more information at the select data rung).

Brenda: You have to take some risks in this business. I'm asking you to share the risks with me.

> **Mark:** It sounds like you're asking me to take all the risks—risking a failure, environmental problems, damage to other equipment and my budget.
>
> **David:** [For most effective practice of the skills, be sure to write down your response.]
>
> After you have written down what you would say, go to the DVD, click on the screen titled Engaging Differences, and choose Inquiry—Exercise II to play. Watch the scene and compare your intervention with what David says.

Selecting Data

If there is any area where people get confused about the Ladder of Inference, it is the select data rung. As my colleague Phil McArthur says, "It may look like data, smell like data, but it ain't data." How do you know if something is data? It must be observable. You and I can mutually agree that it exists independent of our interpretations.

Our conversations can become more efficient if we focus on what people are selecting from the data pool, what they choose to ignore, and the underlying assumptions and values that determine their choice.

Exercise

Inquiry—Exercise III

The purpose of this exercise is to craft an inquiry capable of surfacing reliable and verifiable data that will help make an informed choice. Josh recommends replacing the exchanger, but does not make his thinking explicit. Take on the role of Brenda and ask Josh a question that will help her identify data that can be verified and observed by all parties independent of anyone's conclusions.

Brenda: Josh?

Josh: The exchanger has serious problems. I'm recommending that we replace it.

Brenda: [For most effective practice of the skills, be sure to write down your response.]

After you have written down what you would say, go to the DVD, click on the screen titled Engaging Differences, and choose Inquiry—Exercise III to play. Watch the scene and compare your intervention with what Brenda says.

Paraphrasing: Low-Level Inference

We are not always aware of what data we are selecting, especially when we are listening to another person's words. When we are listening, we are going through a selective process. We hear some words and miss others. We begin the interpretative process by paraphrasing the other person's words in our minds. A paraphrase puts into our own words another person's thought or view. In this way, paraphrasing is an example of a low level of inference because its construction consists of many of the actual words used by the other person, but rearranged, edited, or modified slightly by our own interpretation.

Paraphrasing others' thinking is a excellent skill to practice. Essentially, a paraphrase is an advocacy statement. You are advocating your understanding of another person's thinking at a low level of inference. The art and craft of paraphrasing involves capturing the fullness of the other person's thinking without adding your own inferences. To do it well means listening attentively and bracketing your own reaction to what the other person is saying.

Quite likely, you will have a reaction. Although there is an appropriate time to share it, if you pay too much attention to your own reaction up front, you will lose your concentration on what the other person is saying, and your paraphrase will be your interpretation of his or her words based on your reaction. Bracketing one's personal reaction puts a pause on the inner voice that constantly interprets, judges, and evaluates what is being said.

With your personal reaction set aside, you can listen intently to what another person says. Listening deeply makes paraphrasing what the other person said easier and more accurate. When listening intently to the other person, you can easily identify the information and meanings he or she is selecting as important. In other words, a good paraphrase makes explicit another person's Ladder of Inference. If you are able to succinctly paraphrase another person's Ladder of Inference, you have captured the fullness of his or her thinking.

The other important element to paraphrasing is brevity. Paraphrasing is not parroting back the exact words that you heard, but staying close to the meanings of the words used. A good paraphrase highlights key meanings and sums up in two to three sentences what is really important to the speaker.

When using paraphrasing, you can increase its quality by following it with an inquiry—for example, "Have I heard you correctly, or is there anything you would add or change?" This inquiry invites challenge to how you have captured the other's thinking. A poor-quality inquiry would be, "I got it, right?" You know you have it right when the other person says, "You said it better than I did."

Exercises

Paraphrasing Exercise

Suppose you were to jump into the conversation after the following exchange:

Mark: They create these crunches. They make unrealistic delivery promises just to bag a sale.

Brenda: That's how you compete out there, Mark. You try to meet the customer's needs. You have to take some risks in this business. I'm asking you to share the risks with me.

Using your own words, write down how you would paraphrase back to Brenda what you understand to be her key points.

"Brenda, what I hear you saying is . . .

After you have written down what you would say, go to the DVD, click on Engaging Differences on the main menu, then select Paraphrasing Exercise to play. Watch the scene and compare your intervention with how Mark paraphrases Brenda's position.

Paraphrasing Practice

1. Contract with a friend, spouse, or trusted colleague to practice paraphrasing. Practicing with someone you trust will give you honest feedback on whether your paraphrasing is accurate and concise.

2. Ask your paraphrasing partner to select a topic that is important to him or her and to talk about it for a few minutes.

3. After two to three minutes, stop your partner and paraphrase his or her position. When you've finished, ask "Did I get it or miss it?"

4. Listen to your partner's feedback. You hope to hear "You said it better than I did." If your paraphrase was inaccurate, identify what part of your partner's thinking you missed or where you added your own inferences.

Group Paraphrasing Activity

1. Select a printed quotation from someone addressing an important business issue. It can be a memo from your boss, an e-mail from your division, or a quotation from a magazine. Make sure the printed text is at least one paragraph long and that its content has a certain degree of complexity or controversy.

2. Ask your team or study group to paraphrase, using their own words, what they hear the person quoted saying. Have them write it down.

3. Have everyone read his or her paraphrase aloud, one after another, without discussion between each reading. The group should be able to hear the differences in interpretation.

4. Ask the group participants to select which paraphrases captured the fullness of the person's thought without additional inferences. Discuss what it is about each paraphrase that either hit or missed the fullness of the quoted passage.

A LEARNING STANCE TOWARD DIFFERENCES

A common dynamic in conversations where opposing views exist is for both parties to argue harder, louder, or better in order to convince the other of the "rightness" of their respective positions. There is an alternative. Instead of hurling conclusions back and forth, stop and ask a question. Making a high quality inquiry into another person's view promotes learning and fosters a deeper understanding of how the person arrived at his or her conclusion.

The suggestion to adopt this strategy often raises a concern that the other person will think you are caving in and that he or she has won the argument. When people bring up this concern, I am reminded of the wonderful cartoon "Calvin and Hobbes." Calvin tells his imaginary tiger friend, Hobbes, that you can score points in a conversation by interrupting the other person and opposing his or her idea by taking the idea in a different direction. Hobbes simply replies, "Conversations aren't contests." Calvin quickly retorts, "Okay, a point for you, but I am still ahead." Interchanges like this one occur when someone who wishes to initiate a collaborative conversation in which both parties can learn from each other's perspective is met with an "argue to win" mind-set.

There is a good chance that this scenario will occur, and with some frequency. I have come to expect it. I can confidently continue the conversation because I have shifted my thinking to a learning mind-set and have experienced success in the use of these skills in the past. You can too; it just takes practice and more practice.

The slight shift in thinking comes with the recognition that understanding another's position doesn't mean that I have to agree with it or give up my view. As Argyris said, "You must be simultaneously aggressive and vulnerable with your point of view." I will put out my view, but in a way that remains open to what I might be missing. What I may be missing can often be found in another person's perspective.

Getting positive results after practicing the skill set builds confidence. When you find yourself in a conversation with someone with opposing views, you know that you have a choice. You can either argue to win or take a learning stance. The result of two people's trying to convince each other that one is right and the other is wrong is fairly predictable. In my experience, if I take a learning stance and ask a question, the other person usually reciprocates by attempting to understand my position better.

This doesn't happen automatically. I have found it helpful to use a three-step strategy toward adopting a learning stance.

1. Become aware. I begin by acknowledging that I am in a conversation with someone who has a different view. This may sound simplistic, but it is an important step in stopping the conversation from sliding into a point-counterpoint argument. I name the difference publicly by saying something like, "We have different views on this issue" or "Based on our exchanges of 'Yes, but,' I suspect that each of us sees our respective view as being right."

2. Signal my intentions. I want to interrupt the dynamic of trying to convince each other of our respective "rightness." I might say something like, "I want to back off trying to convince you of my position. Instead, I am curious as to how we see things so differently. In the end I still may disagree with you, but I want a better understanding of how you arrived at your position."

3. Ask a good question. I take the initiative in breaking the pattern of exchanging statements by asking a question helps me understand what the other person is seeing that I may be missing. I might say something like, "What is an example that might illustrate your view?" or "When you said x, what would you see taking place that gives merit to your concern?"

Even with the best of intentions, this approach may not work. The other person may be stuck in his or her position. I don't know if that is the case unless I ask certain questions that test whether or not the other person can be influenced. I might ask these questions:

Is there anything that could be said that might change your mind?

What could take place or what would you need to see that would give merit to my concern?

If the person responds in a way which signals that nothing can change his or her view, then I know to back off trying to convince him or her of my view.

If you find the conversation moving forward rather than getting stuck in a point-counterpoint argument, invite the other person after the conversation is completed to reflect with you on your mutual learning experience. Ask questions like these:

What was the turning point in our conversation?

What did I say that was helpful? (Share with the other person what he or she said that was helpful to you.)

What did I say that was not helpful to our mutual learning?

A FOUR-STEP PROCESS FOR ENGAGING DIFFERENCES

When in the heat of a point-counterpoint debate, it is not easy to pull out and change directions. I have a mnemonic device that helps me turn the conversation around. STEP consolidates the major tips, techniques, and concepts of this chapter into a four-step process.

STEP

Stop the action.

Try getting curious.

Engage the difference.

Pursue a line of inquiry.

First Step: Stop the Action

Stop as soon as you realize that you are trading abstract conclusions back and forth with another person. Your chances of stopping the action improve if you are able to detect the mental and physical cues that tell you that you are stuck in a point-counterpoint argument. By taking a moment to reflect on the argument's probable results, you will consider doing something different.

Second Step: Try Getting Curious

It is time to adopt a different mind-set by getting curious about the differences. Shift to curiosity with a mnemonic device like "What may be obvious to the other person may not be to me" or "What may be obvious to me may not be to the other person."

Third Step: Engage the Difference

Acknowledge the difference by publicly naming it. Paraphrase the other person's position in a way that captures the fullness of his or her thinking and underlying concerns. Refrain from adding your own inferences. Let curiosity drive the discovery of what you don't know about the other's perspective or what is missing in your thinking.

Fourth Step: Pursue a Line of Inquiry

Ask well-crafted questions that help bring the other person down his or her Ladder of Inference, surface additional information, solicit examples, and invite challenge to your way of thinking.

~

Chapter Eight has taken the basic skill set of Argyris's Ladder of Inference, advocacy, and inquiry to a deeper level and demonstrated how they can be used to promote learning and productive conversation. In the DVD case scenario, Mark, Brenda, and their team members have modeled ways in which to put the skill set into action. The chapter's exercises, guidelines, and suggestions are all aids to help you further your practice of the skills. From here on out, it is a matter of practice, practice, and more practice. Exercising these tips, techniques, and observations is critical to making the skills your own. Yet skill building is not a matter of parroting stock phrases. The mind-set behind the actions is what drives the perfecting of any skill or craft. How one thinks differently is the creative pulse behind new actions. Chapter Nine explores the thinking that enabled the action Mark and Brenda took in Chapter Eight.

Key Thought Enablers

After raising an undiscussable topic during a difficult time in their organization, a manager said to me, "It's all just people, so no matter where we work, we've got to find a way to get along with the people around us." That's easy to say, but as we all know, it's not always easy to do.

We know intellectually that asking questions that help us learn from others' perspectives goes a long ways toward getting along. We know that listening deeply in order to paraphrase another's point of view fosters understanding. Being more transparent in our thinking by making high quality advocacies clears the air of hidden agendas and misguided assumptions. All of those behaviors make plain common sense for getting along with others, yet in the heat of the moment, they are difficult to put into action.

Why is that the case? One piece of the answer is simply lack of practice. These productive behaviors are skills, and as is true of any skill, they need to be practiced for a while to be done well. But to practice these skills, a person has to have the right mind-set. So that's the bigger piece of the answer: to model double-loop learning in real-life situations, people need to think in ways that make the desirable actions easy. New actions come from a different way of thinking. New thought comes about from a conversion of old.

INSTANT CHANGE OF THINKING

Sometimes a conversion of thought from less productive to more productive can happen quite suddenly. I have had a couple of experiences where my thinking was changed suddenly or, more precisely, turned upside down. One of these experiences was an encounter with Chris Argyris. Chris always came midweek during the Advanced Action Design Institute for a chance to spend a day with the participants and the faculty during evening dinner. It was customary for one of the faculty members to come with a case for Chris to work on. That year, I was the candidate.

I remember looking around the room and seeing everyone who I knew to be smarter and more skilled than I. Feeling a little vulnerable, I began my introduction by saying, "I look around the room and I see Ph.D.s from Harvard, professors at Yale, Diane Argyris, and then me. I can't believe I am here. I got here because I know Diana Smith. I am living large as a lowlife."

Chris, who was sitting next to me said, "How arrogant."

I was so stunned that my mind came to a complete halt. I heard someone say in the background, "What do you mean by that?" I thought that was a good question, so I managed to whisper under my breath, "Yes, I would like to know the answer to that question."

"You think everyone in this room is stupid," he responded simply. "That's arrogant of you."

Now I was completely perplexed, but also curious to know what in the heck he was saying. I could only get out, "I think these people are stupid."

"Yes," Chris said, "you think they are so stupid that they would risk their consulting business by hiring a person of no real value only because he is a friend of Diana's."

It made sense in a strange sort of way. I looked around the room until my gaze met Phil McArthur. He was there smiling and slowly nodding his head up and down. "Yes, you think we are stupid."

My face-saving strategy had completely backfired. Believing that the impending analysis of my case study would reveal a host of errors and blunders, I wanted to avoid any potential embarrassment from having my mistakes exposed in front of skilled practitioners. I preempted the criticism by announcing my inexperience first. By attacking myself, I hoped that they would tread softly. I appealed to the social virtue of support—don't attack someone who is already down. A show of support would be to go easy on me.

I combined my plea for support with a declaration that my admission to the group was based on the merits of friendship instead of personal value. There existed in this declaration an implicit assumption: that the partners of Action Design would foolishly risk their business on someone who had no value to them. Not only did I call them stupid, I accused them of cronyism. My arrogance was in thinking that the partners of Action Design would sacrifice their reputation and clients' needs to help me out. Their world doesn't revolve around me.

With two words, "How arrogant," Chris Argyris disrupted my thinking of "I am not good enough, I don't belong here, and I will be found out." Through his challenge to my thinking, I was able to hear a different message. I realized that I was included not because of a friendship, but because they saw a value and skill capacity worth developing in me. This realization reframed how I saw myself within the group. In that moment, I acknowledged my own value, began to feel more comfortable, and found my place in the Action Design community. Since that day, I don't feel the need to demean myself in order to barter some protection from any impending threat or embarrassment.

GRADUAL CHANGE OF THINKING

My experience that day caused me to have a sudden change in thought. Although the dazzling moment of having an "Aha" insight is wonderful, it doesn't happen as frequently as many of us would like. Fortunately, with the help of a few important "cues" and some discipline, a change of thinking can also take place gradually.

This chapter introduces four such cues, which I refer to as *thought enablers:*

1. Granting legitimacy to another's perspective

2. Assuming partiality

3. Attributing positive intentions

4. Acknowledging unintended impacts and consequences

We can train our minds to think differently through the regular use of these devices. When called to mind, they trigger the new way of thinking. Reduced to their essentials, these thought enablers reflect the values and aims of the Mutual Learning Model, which is the alternative to the Unilateral Control Model. They are the thinking necessary for breaking down defensive routines. Each one acts like a mantra that helps you shift your thinking and enables new action. And although you may find it difficult to summon them at first, with regular use, the thinking they trigger begins to come more naturally.

Of course, in the heat of the moment, even people in possession of all these thought enablers will sometimes have a hard time drawing on them to guide their behaviors. When under stress, we have an increased tendency to rely on skill sets we've learned in the past and to revert to a "default" response, however unproductive it was and is. In a crisis, we use first what is most deeply ingrained in our learning, mindless of its ineffectiveness. It is what we know how to do when in a state of being out of control. Over time, however, we can change the default, or at least alter it enough to allow the thought enablers "equal time" when we're faced with conditions of threat or embarrassment.

In the previous chapter, the DVD vignettes showed Mark, Brenda, and their team having a productive conversation using high quality advocacy and inquiry. Their new actions were possible because they used the four key thought enablers I discuss in this chapter.

The following sections present the four key thought enablers with a corresponding DVD vignette. Each vignette replays the sequence of actions seen in Chapter Eight, but with the addition of the private thinking that demonstrates a key thought enabler. Start each section by watching its corresponding "Key Thought Enablers" scene first. After viewing the scene, return to the text to read the characteristics of the key thought enabler, the required shifts in thinking, and the mnemonic devices that aid the transformation of thinking.

KEY THOUGHT ENABLER I: GRANTING LEGITIMACY

In "Key Thought Enablers—Scene I," Walt is the first to see Mark and Brenda heading toward a point-counterpoint argument. His first thought is, "They both have legitimate points of view." This key thought enabler prevents him from taking sides and helps him focus on the business issues. If in his role as a manager he were to give any indication of preference for Mark or Brenda, it would only support an attribution of playing favorites.

Granting legitimacy allows him to level the playing field. Knowing that each team member has a legitimate set of concerns, he wants to get at the risks and trade-offs in both proposals. It is not a matter of who can out-argue whom. By taking this approach, he begins to address the difficulties each proposal raises for the other. The conversation can continue on a track focusing on how to manage the risks by minimizing their impact, negotiating interests, and clarifying the trade-offs.

Granting legitimacy to another person's perspective is your acknowledgment that the other person's view appears as reasonable and sensible to him or her as your own view appears to you. Granting legitimacy is easier to do if you are not in vehement disagreement with the other person. If that is the case, you will need a little extra effort in transforming your thinking. The place to begin is with how you experience your own thinking.

Granting legitimacy to the reasonableness of others' thinking is based on the claim that we all use the same reasoning process described by the Ladder of Inference. Our conclusions make sense given the meaning we have attached to data we have selected as important. As our reasoning process moves from the bottom of the Ladder of Inference to the top in a nanosecond, we experience a sensation of internal cohesion and sensibility in our thinking. When the steps of our Ladder of Inference are visible, the reasonableness of our thinking is evident.

Shifts in Thinking

Granting legitimacy to another person's perspective is not an admission of agreement, but an acknowledgment of reasonableness. The move from viewing another person's thinking as stupid to considering it reasonable is a full 180-degree turn. Getting from one end of the spectrum to the other is accomplished through two mental shifts.

The first shift rests on a simple axiom: what is true for me is true for you. If my reasoning appears sensible and reasonable to me, then there is no reason to believe that others experience their own reasoning any differently. This assumption is a bit more reliable than thinking the other is crazy.

The assumption of reasonableness is grounded in the virtue of justice. I grant equality and fairness of belief to those who think differently than me. I would want the same standards of fairness applied to me. In a case where I see my own thinking as clear and another person claims it to be unreasonable, I would call it "unfair." If that is so, then it would be unfair of me to turn around and treat others in the same way I prefer not to be treated myself. Justice requires the same standards of fairness to be applied equally to all people regardless of differences.

A second shift in thinking questions the expectation that others should see the obviousness of my own thinking. There is a good chance that they do not see the obviousness of my thinking, because I haven't made my thinking explicit. It is an unfair assumption to expect others to know what is in my mind without my telling them.

So I work to drop that expectation by thinking to myself, "What is obvious to me may not be obvious to others." Chanting this thought in my head, I prepare to present my view by using a high quality advocacy that makes visible the steps in my thinking.

Practical Examples

The key thought enabler of granting legitimacy comes in handy when teaching. In the past, when students appeared confused by what I said, I would think to myself, "They don't get it." Now, I short-circuit that phrase by thinking, "They are hearing something different than I intend." This mnemonic phrase also serves to protect me from the self-deprecating thought that I had presented an idea ineffectively.

Early in my teaching career, if a participant or student said that he or she didn't understand a concept I had just finished presenting, I assumed that the student's lack of understanding was my fault. My course of corrective action was to repeat myself. Yet saying the same thing over again didn't seem to help the student, and it bored the rest of the participants. After a number of failed attempts, I began to attribute stupidity or resistance to the person.

When I changed my thinking from "They don't get it" or "I'm not doing an adequate job of explaining" to "They are hearing or interpreting what I said in a different way," I was able to ask the person, "What is your understanding of the concept?" This gave me an opportunity to hear how he or she was interpreting the material and locate the exact point of disconnection or misunderstanding. Once I heard how the person interpreted their selection of the word or phrase I used, I was able to see the reasonableness of his or her conclusion.

Often, when a misunderstanding occurs, it is because a person picked up something that I said that was vague in nature and gave it a different interpretation than I had intended. For this reason, I keep in my mind the phrase, "I may not have been clear in presenting my thoughts." A quick review of what I said makes it understandable how someone could interpret my words differently. When this occurs, it is a good reminder to return to the Ladder of Inference and use it to trace the steps in my thinking.

KEY THOUGHT ENABLER II: ASSUMING PARTIALITY

From the onset, Mark thought that replacing the exchanger during the turnaround was the obvious course of action. He believed that his reasoning should also be obvious to Brenda and others. In "Key Thought Enablers—Scene II," Mark assumes partiality. Assuming partiality is Mark's acknowledgment that he doesn't see the complete picture. He now sees Brenda as having different concerns than she had when she was in Operations. Realizing that her concerns may not be apparent to him, he thinks to himself, "Replacing the exchanger may not be as obvious as I thought." By assuming partiality, he can ask Brenda a high quality inquiry: "What are your customers up against that makes a delayed shipment a problem?" Her response yields information that leads him to modify his thinking.

The Limits of Our Thinking

Assuming partiality is a realistic, humble acknowledgment of the limits of our thinking. When it comes to the accuracy of our thinking, we can be right and we can be wrong. A good reminder of the fallibility of our thinking is the Alcoholics Anonymous (AA) slogan: "Remember that your mind is like a dangerous neighborhood. You are not to go in there alone or unarmed." This slogan reminds us that we can be "mugged" by false assumptions. Our thinking becomes dangerous when we don't acknowledge any difference between our view and outside reality. The extreme of "I am right and you are wrong" holds no space for differences. There is no distinction between "having a perspective" and the way it actually is. It is a declaration of omniscience.

I grew up listening to Walt Cronkite report the news. He always ended his broadcasts with "And that's the way it is." When Cronkite retired, Dan Rather took the helm of the evening news. He had to come up with a signature sign-off. His was "And that is part of our world tonight." His sign-off lacked the confidence of Cronkite's firm assurance that we had seen the way it truly is. Yet Dan Rather's sign-off reflected the current times, when no complex issue could be contained in a single perspective. There was an implicit acknowledgment that the news media itself was limited and was providing only a partial view of what was going on.

I use these two sign-off signatures as mental descriptions of two states of mind. When I am in unilateral control mode, I am in the telling mode of broadcasting what I think as "that's the way it is." When I get into mutual learning mode, I am able to think to myself, "My thinking is one part of the world."

Assuming partiality and getting into the mode of mutual learning requires an interjection of doubt or mistrust of your inferences. Recognize your conclusions for what they are: inferences. Your inferences could be right, or they could be wrong. Your inferences are to be tested against others for validity. If this is too much of a leap to make, then don't give up "being right." Assume partiality and ask yourself, "What may I be missing?"

One great thing about assuming partiality is that it fosters curiosity. Curiosity takes seriously what you don't know. Curiosity sends you on missions of discovery. Curiosity pushes past the limits of your own way of thinking. Ultimately, by discovering additional information, you may modify your inferences.

The Virtue of Humility

Assuming partiality also allows you to practice real humility. The phrase "I may be wrong" or "I don't know everything" is commonly used as a preface to a point of view. Sometimes the phrase is used to execute the inconsistent message bypass strategy (discussed in Chapter Five). I admit that I might be wrong, but still believe I am right and act accordingly. The disclaimer inoculates me against any potential negative response by allowing me to assume a false humility. Genuine humility is more productive. Humility is an honest, realistic appraisal of my abilities, character, and ideas. There is an appreciation of limits and a valuing of what is possible.

When I am curious and able to practice genuine humility, I am also keeping my thinking agile. I tell my students in philosophy class, "Don't hold on to your beliefs so tightly that they hold on to you." Ideas have no room when held in a tight fist. The discovery of error is less likely, and the chance of imposing the ideas on others greatly increases. An agility of mind keeps thoughts open and limber. The ideas are more flexible and can be molded by other ideas or new information. They can be experimented with and improved.

Ultimately, I see Argyris's view of advocacy as applying the scientific principles of experimentation to our thinking. Experimentation starts with a hypothesis. The validation of the hypothesis is established by attempts to disprove it. If the hypothesis can stand the tests of disconfirmation, it is more likely to be adopted as reliable, good information and as a basis for action. The same principles can apply to thinking. I think of my ideas as a hypothesis. I am just as vigilant about seeking out disconfirming information as I am hoping to find confirmation of my view. My inquiries, such as "Does anyone see it differently?" or "What have I missed?" actively encourage challenge to my thinking.

Help from Others

Assuming partiality necessitates a reliance on others for help. Left to my own devices, I am capable of saying or doing things that I regret later. I am referring to those times when I wish I could roll back the tape and record something different. The AA slogan I mentioned earlier is a cautionary tale warning me that if I enter my mind alone and unarmed, I could get into trouble. The analogy advises all of us to seek the help of others and arm ourselves with the critical thinking skills that can save us from self-deception.

When it comes to my thinking, I need the help of others to see what I don't see—new information, a different perspective, or a mirrored reflection of my own behavior. As Phil McArthur of Action Design is fond of saying, "Reflection is a team sport." Aided by an honest interaction with another person, we can see ourselves through the eyes of another who brings honesty and compassion to the encounter.

Understanding Others' Resistance

Finally, by assuming partiality, I'm able to understand others' behaviors more clearly. I can now mentally turn the tables and think, "What is obvious to them is not to me." This mantra puts on the brakes when I experience someone as being resistant to influence or just plain stubborn.

If I'm not in mutual learning mode, seeing someone as not open to being influenced is a frame that usually signals either a retreat or a more concerted effort to push my own view. I end up exhibiting an equal degree of stubbornness. However, the other person may not be as hard to influence as I suspect, but more caught up in the obviousness of his or her own thinking. The assumption of obviousness may be preventing both of us from sharing the steps in our thinking. Remaining on an abstract and vague level of communication reinforces the mutual perception that the other is not subject to being influenced. Underlying the obviousness of our thinking is a reasonableness waiting to be discovered through inquiry.

KEY THOUGHT ENABLER III: ATTRIBUTING POSITIVE INTENT

In the scenes where Mark and Brenda demonstrate more productive conversation skills, each assigns positive intentions to the other. In "Key Thought Enablers—Scene II," Mark understands that Brenda's position in Sales has brought a new set of concerns that differ from those of Operations. He attributes positive intentions to her concerns about sales and the timely delivery of product to her customers. In "Key Thought Enablers—Scene III," Brenda attributes positive intentions to Mark for looking after his crew. Once Mark and Brenda are able to attribute positive intentions to each other, they are more willing to incorporate each other's concerns and interests into any future proposal.

Attributing positive intentions to others can be a stickler for many of us. When people do or say things that cause us difficulty, we are hard pressed to come up with anything less than a negative motive or intention for justifying their actions. Why would they do something so awful unless they meant to do it? What they did may have been experienced by you as being awful, but they also may not have intended it to be so. They may have been unaware of how their actions affected you and others.

We are quick to think others have negative intentions, especially when their actions or words cause us difficulty. Yet we are often wrong, because motives and intentions are complex and always private. We cannot see into others' minds.

This is a hard key thought enabler to put into practice. I'll admit that there are a few people in my life with whom I can't do it. No matter how hard I try, it is impossible for me to see them as having good intentions. They are more appropriate candidates for forgiveness and mercy.

For the vast majority of people with whom I interact, I can safely say that they have good intentions. When I get into a difficult conversation, I assume the other person has positive intentions, but is unaware of the impact his or her actions have on me. It becomes my responsibility to talk about the impact of another's actions on me in a way that helps both of us mutually learn from our interaction.

The shift in thinking required for attributing positive intent rests on the same axiom as the first key thought enabler: what is true for me is true for you. I intend to do well. I desire to succeed. I don't get up in the morning and say to myself, "What can I do today to screw up the team's project?" I want to be competent and achieve the desired results I set out to accomplish. If I find this true for me, it is reasonable to assume that others experience the same.

What is also true for each of us is that we don't always do what we intend to do. St. Paul mused about this human condition centuries ago when he said, "What happens is that I do, not the good I will to do, but the evil I do not intend" (Romans 7:19). There is a gap between what we intend to do and what we do. A contributing factor toward creating the gap is the limit of human awareness—in other words, a blindness as to how our actions affect others.

Personally, I remind myself of this shift by calling to mind the image of that friend of mine who is literally blind. I remind myself that I am blind as well. And this simple phrase is the mental cue that keeps me in check and reminds me that I cannot "see" other's intentions. Similarly, I find it helpful to think of the other person as being unaware of how his or her actions affected me. If I say to myself, "She is clueless" or "He is unaware," it is enough to hold off any negative attribution of intention. Instead, I focus on the impact of their actions on me.

KEY THOUGHT ENABLER IV: ACKNOWLEDGING IMPACT AND CONTRIBUTION

In "Key Thought Enablers—Scene IV," Brenda puts the conversation with Josh on pause and then restarts it in a different direction. She realizes that the way she is asking her question could be having an impact on Josh that she had not intended. She keeps an ear open for what those unintended impacts might be. Suspecting that Josh may be hearing her questions as soliciting a guarantee of how long the exchanger would work, she stops the conversation. She acknowledges the possible unintended impact and signals to him her intentions. She wants to discover what is specifically wrong with the exchanger that warrants its replacement now. Acknowledging impact and contribution is a key thought enabler that prevents conversations from derailing and allows for the correction of error.

There is more to acknowledging our contribution than just saying, "I know I have a part in it too" or "This problem may be more about me than you." No one hangs out in that reflective space very long. A few short sentences later we can be off to a full-blown description of the offense the other person committed against us. Nor am I suggesting that we should all beat our breasts and say "Mea culpa" (Latin for "my fault") for our part in a defensive routine without hearing the additional voices of the others in the organization. A true acknowledgment of contribution means that everyone understands and appreciates how his or her actions affect the others with whom he or she is involved.

Our actions have an impact on others. An impact is the impression left by a force of one thing upon another. It is a collision of sorts. The impression is made by the force of the action, but the surface with which the force makes contact also determines the degree of impact. If the material is hard, there is very little impact. Deeper impacts are made in softer surfaces.

In human interactions, when someone does or says something that creates difficulty, we feel the force of his or her action immediately. The impact of action also says as much about the person on the receiving end of the action as it does about the person who initiated it. Understanding the impact of our actions upon each other requires attention to both parties' contribution: what is said or done and how it was received.

When we acknowledge mutual contribution, we are admitting to the simple truth of the phrase, "It takes two to tango." A virtuous first step in the dance of reflection and mutual learning is discovering one's own involvement in the defensive routine before focusing on the behavior of the other person. The first step is asking, "How am I contributing to the defensive routine?"

I never like to admit my own contribution to a defensive routine. There is a sinking feeling in my gut that says, "Face it: I didn't help matters much by what I said." I wrestle with the feeling because any further investigation will only heighten the sense of embarrassment. Even if I invite the scrutiny, I feel that I am opening the door for the other person to confirm my bad behavior and keep the focus on me. I am always ready to shift the focus back and ask, "What about you? What is your part?" The only thing that helps me resist the temptation to shift the focus back to the person is an admission of blindness on my part and a commitment to detect error.

Often I am not aware of what I may be doing that is contributing to a result I neither intend nor desire. Because I am blind to how my actions have an impact on others, I have to rely on others for help. By acknowledging my blindness, I am in a better position to ask for that help. By bringing the impact of my actions to my attention, I can discover any possible error on my part and try again to realign my actions with my intentions.

A New State of Alertness

Seeking our own contribution is an exercise in humility. I know that I am perfectly capable of saying and doing things that cause difficulty for others. My past track record makes it difficult for me to deny it. This acknowledgment does not need to become an occasion for me to beat myself up for past mistakes, but it can help me become more vigilant for errors in the future. If I am in error, I want to know it. Persisting in error is not something that I want to do for very long. I must remain open to hearing what I did or said that generated error. A vigilant state of alertness for the detection and correction of error keeps my focus on my thinking and actions.

This state of alertness allows me to take the initiative in the conversation and ask, "What kind of impact did my words or actions have on you?" I get ready to listen. I don't always like what I hear. Sometimes I get triggered by what the other person says, and I have to work a little harder listening to him or her describe the impact of my actions. I'll admit it is a bit of white-knuckle ride. I have to bracket my own personal reaction, recite my mantra "acknowledge contribution," and listen to what is sometimes very uncomfortable to hear—all in the span of a few minutes.

I am listening for the reasonableness of the other person's response, given what I said or did. I want to hear what words or actions of mine the person selected and how he or she interpreted them. By taking this initiative, I can hear how my actions made an impact and contributed to the difficulty at hand. I acknowledge the impact by saying something like, "I can see how you heard my words in the way you did, given what I said." The acknowledgment piece is important. If I merely respond with something like, "That is not what I was trying to say," I am encouraging further defensiveness because I am implying that the other person is wrong for interpreting my words the way he or she did. I always need to remember that even though I didn't intend my words or actions to have their reported impact, my words or actions did contribute to the difficulty.

When I acknowledge the impact of my words or actions on another, I gain an opportunity for correction. I can choose other words or be more explicit. Even better, I can avoid making the same unintentional impact in the future by asking, "What can I say or do differently in the future that would have a less adverse impact?" I have always found others to be very helpful in making suggestions in response to this question.

On the Receiving End

When on the receiving end of others' actions, I am sorely tempted to place all the blame on the person for what was said or done to me. I can resist this temptation if I pay attention to what is getting triggered in me. For example, I still get a little wigged out when people interpret what I say or do differently than what I had intended. My initial internal reaction is to punish them. How dare they think I would have less than noble intentions? When I can't hold back my internal reaction, I get mad and accuse the offending party of doing me an injustice. On occasion, I will return the injustice by attributing bad intent, stupidity, and meanness to the other.

By practicing the key thought enabler of acknowledging impact and contribution, I refrain from jumping down the other person's throat. I have come to expect others to interpret my words differently than what I might intend. I no longer consider them malicious in their intent. It is their interpretation of what I said or did. Using the Ladder of Inference, I ask, "When you heard me say *x*, how did you make sense of it?" The other person's response then helps me discover what specifically she selected from our conversation that she then took to the top of her Ladder of Inference.

There are other times when my focus is not on what triggers me but on the clear impact someone's words or actions had on me that created difficulty. In those cases, I register the impact of his or her actions upon me without bestowing blame.

Registering the impact of another's action upon yourself requires a skillful use of advocacy and inquiry. This means that you make statements that are at a low level of inference and that are balanced by an inquiry that allows the other to challenge the statements. The crafting of a high quality advocacy begins with the paraphrase of what the other person said or did that created the impact: "When you said *x*, . . ." Your paraphrase is on the select data rung. You are referring to the conversational data you have selected that is the cause of the impact.

Next, you describe the effect of the impact using the second rung of the Ladder of Inference: interpret the data and add meaning. Your description of the impact can begin with something like, "I found myself reacting . . ." or "I took it to mean . . ." You balance the advocacy with an inquiry like, "Is that what you were intending, or something different?" This gives the other person a chance to modify what he or she had hoped to express.

The conversation can move forward sounding something like this: "I can see now that when I said *x*, you heard it as . . . , which led you to respond in the way you did." From there, the two of you can explore the impact of each other's words and actions. The conversation yields a mutual understanding as to how two or more people got into a dance with each other that created a result that neither intended.

Verbal and Physical Cues

I usually don't have the mnemonic phrase "acknowledge contribution" in my mind. Instead, I am on alert for the physical and verbal cues the other person sends which indicate that my words or actions have had an impact. Those verbal and physical cues are like trip wires. When I stumble across them, I know it is time to seek my contribution to the difficulty. In some cases, it is very easy to tell when I have tripped one. I know exactly the look on my wife's face when what I have said has made an impact I hadn't anticipated. Others let you know with a slight emotional flare-up or a strong reaction that gives you some indication that you have hit a bump in the conversation.

A bump usually calls for a stop in the action. The pause is used to gain a moment for reflection. The reflective space allows for curiosity to take over, and you can find an answer to the question, "How did we get here?" especially if it is a place that neither party intended or desired.

PUTTING THE ENABLERS TO WORK

The thinking represented in the four key thought enablers makes it possible to act in ways consistent with the Mutual Learning Model. This thinking doesn't come automatically, but through a disciplined change of mind. In the beginning, people hold a reasonable suspicion that these thought enablers may not work with those who are not aware of them or who do not endorse the same mind-set.

I have found that the virtuous behavior of the Mutual Learning Model is as contagious as the bad behavior. As I mentioned in Chapter Seven, the aims, values, and actions of the Mutual Learning Model are a program of attraction. For example, I continue to find myself in point-counterpoint arguments. The difference now is that I can catch myself sooner in the act of "Yes, but." I gain enough of a reflective moment to get curious and ask a question. Once others can see that I am making an attempt to understand their point of view, I can sense a softening on their side. In return, my actions are reciprocated, and questions start coming my way.

I can't claim that this happens every time, but it happens now more frequently than not. I never have control over how another person is going to react, but I can influence his or her reaction by my actions. When I have taken the initiative, I have found reciprocity. Reciprocity doesn't always occur at the first initiative, but it does happen. When it does, things change.

Reciprocity may be more difficult to come by when there is an established history of dysfunctional behavior. In these situations, it is far too easy to see only the behavior that confirms the original frame. Trying the key thought enablers requires you to go against your instincts that tell you they won't work. When experimenting with a new frame of mind, you need to shift away from your current spontaneous, intuitive reactions and act *as if* the alternative frame of mind were true. By acting *as if* another assumption or frame of mind were true, the experiment allows you to test for different results. If you get different results, then you will find it easier to adopt this way of thinking the next time. Soon it will become a natural, skilled part of your thinking. You will notice an internal shift, such that whereas before you might have been thinking, "I am right; it is so obvious," you are now thinking, "I could be missing something."

Exercise

Strategy for Making the Shift in Thinking

The following list is in part an exercise and in part a set of guidelines for bringing new thought into play at critical times. To use this list as an exercise, you can review it in light of a recent situation in which, on reflection, you realize you were in Unilateral Control Mode. To use it as a set of guidelines, keep them in mind when you sense you are in a situation conducive to the rise of a defensive routine.

1. **Catch yourself in the act.** If you find yourself thinking, "Why did she do that? She is just looking out for herself," or "He is on his power trip again," then you know you are attributing negative intentions.

2. **Acknowledge your blindness.** Although your reaction feels clear and certain, the reality is that you cannot know another person's intention without directly asking him or her.

3. **Make the switch.** Make an alternative assumption that you are blind to the other's true intentions.

   a. Assume others have positive intentions. If you have difficulty making the leap from negative to good intentions, then ask yourself, "If the tables were turned and the other person assumed I had negative intentions, how would I like it?" If you would not like it, then it is only fair that you treat others the way you would like to be treated.

    b. If making the jump to positive intentions is just too difficult, then make the neutral assumption that the other person is clueless about the impact his or her behavior had on you.

4. Separate intent from impact. Assuming positive intent does not mean brushing off what the other said or did and excusing him from his actions. His behavior had an impact on you. The impact is what you want to raise with him in conversation.

5. Register the impact. Start with the observable behavior that had an impact on you; that is, paraphrase what the other person said or did. Keep your paraphrase free of inference. Then describe the impact it had on you. The following is an example of the language for registering impact: "I am unsure as to what your intentions were, but when you said . . . , I had x reaction. Did I mishear you, or did you intend something different than what I heard?"

⌐

    Chapters Eight and Nine set up something of a chicken-and-egg question. What comes first? Alter the action, and with new results comes a change of thinking. Change the thinking, and new action comes more easily. Both of these statements are true. When it comes to implementing the skill set of the Mutual Learning Model, we are simultaneously trying new behavior to see if we get better results and employing new ways of thinking in order to act differently. Over time and with practice, the skill set and its accompanying mind-set become integrated into our personal style of communicating and interacting with others. But this is not the end of the story. The pursuit of learning is lifelong. We cannot stop or rest on our journey of self-reflection. We take up the banner of vigilance, ready to detect and correct any errors and mistakes we are bound to make in the future. In Part Four, Chapters Ten and Eleven look ahead to what can be expected for those who continue on the learning pathway and take up the challenge of teaching this mind-set and these skills and concepts to others.

PART FOUR

Staying on the Path of Learning

Committing to self-reflection, taking up the skill set of the Mutual Learning Model, and integrating the key thought enablers are the essential elements needed to reduce the incidence of defensive routines in the workplace and to mitigate their negative effects when they do occur. When you put these elements into practice, what can you expect along the way? Part Four describes what lays ahead for those who have taken up the commitment to and practice of the Mutual Learning Model. As you will see, it is not a case of practice makes perfect; instead, it is a case of practice makes better, through failure, experimentation, and more practice.

Mistakes, Continuous Learning, and Progress

Learning occurs when we detect and correct error," Argyris wrote in his book *Knowledge for Action.* "Error is any mismatch between what we intend an action to produce and what actually happens when we implement that action. It is a mismatch between intentions and results."

It is easy to think of examples of how learning occurs when we detect an error because we've performed a task incorrectly or when we've experienced a mechanical failure. For instance, if I turn the screwdriver the wrong way, I know immediately that I am not getting my desired result.

When it comes to human interactions, however, detecting an error so that we can learn from it isn't so simple. In situations of threat and embarrassment, errors and mistakes aren't so easily identified. In fact, it's often nearly impossible for individuals to spot an error in their own judgment or behavior until much later on when they have time to reflect. And sometimes, by then they're mired with other individuals in a defensive routine. What's more, even though people often recite the mantra "It's okay to make mistakes" in meeting rooms, they don't always believe it—or mean it. Even though no organization would explicitly make a policy of punishing mistakes, too often that is what is carried out in practice. People end up paying lip service to the value of making mistakes. After a particularly embarrassing situation has passed, they are quick to say, "There is a lot to learn from this."

The resolve is there, but the reflection doesn't always occur. "Moving on" is the more likely exit strategy for dealing with mistakes.

And yet learning from our mistakes is key to sustaining any progress we make in dealing with defensive routines. Failure to learn from our mistakes is a recipe for insanity, as defined by a familiar quotation from Alcoholics Anonymous: "Insanity is doing the same thing over and over again and expecting different results." The price of not detecting and correcting our mistakes is repeating them.

This chapter addresses the ongoing commitment individuals, teams, and organizations must make to remain in a mode of learning and to interrupt the vicious cycle of defensive routines. Essentially, it is a commitment to learning through the detection and correction of error. The goal is not the complete elimination of error, which is not humanly possible, but an increase in the speed of recovery. As individuals, teams, and organizations improve their competence in the practice of the skills set out in this book, they will be able to detect error sooner and recover more quickly from it.

OBSTACLES TO LEARNING FROM OUR MISTAKES

Learning from our mistakes is hampered by three prevalent factors: the skill with which we make errors, the way we view mistakes, and a proverbial Catch-22 when it comes to learning from mistakes. The next three sections will explore each of these obstacles in turn. Following that, I'll offer another way of looking at mistakes and managing them.

"Skilled Incompetence"

Our common, day-to-day errors often go unnoticed. They frequently occur in our conversations with others. I will go into a conversation with a particular intent or desired result in mind, but then things don't go the way I would like them to. I emerge later on, thinking that I would have preferred a different result than the loud argument, lingering tension, or bruised ego. But I don't know why things unfolded as they did.

For example, I want to be helpful and point out something in your behavior that would be in your best interest to change. Not too far into the conversation, you get defensive. I abandon my hope of getting you to agree with what I see, and I back off. At that point, the excuse of "I was only trying to be helpful" doesn't erase the action of not being helpful. More important, I don't see my failure in presenting the feedback in a way that is truly helpful to your learning. I am blaming the failure to achieve my desired result on you for getting defensive.

Our failure to see our own errors and mistakes has to do with the fact that we are so good at making them—good as in very skillful. Argyris refers to this phenomenon as "skilled incompetence." These are unlikely words to string together, but they work to communicate how ingenious we are in not being effective. The ingenuity is not measured in brilliance, but in our efficient use of thinking to help us act quickly. The skill is evident in how our thinking appears almost automatic.

As when we master a craft, our actions appear effortless, second natured, and easy. Our behavior is actually the result of many years of practice. We are well practiced at making mistakes in that we continue to act with the same thinking that we have grown accustomed to. It may have been effective some time in the past, but it now fails us in our current transactions with others.

Consider this example. With the best of intentions, I want to be a good team player. In my mind, this translates as "Don't say no to requests for help." Very soon, I have taken on more work that I can do. Some of the work requires a steep learning curve, and I quickly reach the outer limits of what I feel capable of doing. I start feeling resentful that others are not pulling their weight. People are getting mad at me because I am missing deadlines or dropping off half-baked deliverables. I am now saying yes when I really mean no. My internal voice is throbbing with the incantation, "Don't do it," but I can't say no, so I say yes. I am making the same mistake over and over again. My error is in thinking that being a team player always means saying yes to every request. I habitually operate on the basis of this assumption without testing it publicly. One way for me to recognize my error will be to look at the final result: in the end, I am not being effective and am feeling like the only team player and not part of the team.

How We View Mistakes

Making a mistake or an error is clearly an uncomfortable experience, and the Western cultural meaning attached to making a mistake only exacerbates the discomfort. Making mistakes is bad. To be in error is to fall short. From our school days, the goal of getting it all right was held out as desirous and expected. Anything wrong was counted as points off. We were no longer on the top. Those who got it all right were rewarded. No one with a C average got a star. Anyone with a D or F was seen as stupid. It is no wonder that when we as adults make mistakes, we find it difficult to learn from them. With this kind of social training, it is not surprising that we view mistakes as crimes to be punished. The punishment can be both self-inflicted or applied to those whose mistakes cause us difficulty.

When I Make a Mistake

I don't like making mistakes. Disconnects, misunderstandings, and crossed signals are all mental mishaps that lead to results I neither intend nor desire. Any time I make a mistake (read "do not do it perfectly") I am ready to march myself before a firing squad to get my brains blown out.

I am my own worst critic, capable of heaping mountains of punishment upon myself. There is plenty of punishing self-talk, as I chastise myself for errors, failed expectations, and poor interactions with others. The mental message "I blew it" scrolls across my mind like those endless digital news headlines at the bottom of the TV screen. No matter what may be going on in the main picture, my eye keeps getting drawn down to the bottom of the screen.

In dealing with my own errors and mistakes, I often feel as though I have reached the outer limits of my intelligence. I can't figure out what went wrong. I am stuck. I am aware enough to know that the result didn't match my intention, but unaware of how I got there and what to do differently. If there is not movement in solving this initial quandary, my mind can quickly and easily slip into a downward spiral of deflation, depression, and dejection.

One of the more difficult aspects of dealing with a mistake is the emotions surrounding its discovery. There are the feelings of embarrassment that others may see me as truly as incompetent as I feel at the moment. It is easy to feel depressed. The wind gets knocked out of me, and I can't get up off the mat. The particular danger here is how the emotions color the thinking. The pervasive feeling turns one incident into a global statement of incompetence. To extrapolate from one event in which I clearly made mistakes to hitting the bailout button and thinking "I am no good at this" can be an unhealthy generalization that provides no value for learning. The dispirited emotions tend to wipe out past successes and blow the error out of proportion.

Failing erodes my sense of competence. It feels like a stain that can't be removed. The past has set it into the fabric of my life. I enter into the game of "if only I had done" or "if only I had said . . ." This kind of thinking doesn't serve learning from the mistake but only gives an illusory sense of a different result. In the fantasy, I emerge victorious in the conversation, and my opponent is humbled. An honest reckoning of the error would entail examining how my own thinking and actions contributed to the mess.

When Others Make a Mistake

One of my favorite quotations from the "Peanuts" cartoons comes from Linus, who said, "I love mankind, it's just the people I can't stand." When listening to people talk about their jobs and workplace, Linus's words come to mind with a little twist: "I love my job, it's just the people I can't stand." Occasionally I will hear the honest admission that the person believes he is working with absolutely complete idiots. If the conversation digs deeper into the person's own sense of competence, he will sometimes confess that he has been fooling everyone else. Funny how that works. We possess both the ability to see stupid people all around us and the confidence that we can hide our own incompetence from others.

When others make mistakes, I am quick to get on their case. The first words in my mind are, "How could you have done that? What were you thinking?" Needless to say, these are leading questions. My view is that the other person was wrong and should have avoided the error in the first place. My list of "should haves" is an indictment against the guilty who go without a public trial. His or her mistake is a crime to be punished. The punishment is an immediate declaration of wrongdoing. The sentence is doubled by a series of "should have known better" pronouncements. The person is wrong for being wrong.

I am not proud that I can easily punish others for their mistakes, but I do it. When someone's words or actions cause me difficulty, either I am quick to let him or her know or I steam inside with anger and disgust. I don't think of myself as a malicious or mean judge, but I act as though I were one when I am quick to blame.

Blaming

When errors are made, blaming others is the first level of protection against the conditions of threat and embarrassment to oneself. Blaming keeps the focus of the problem on the other guy and avoids one's own contribution. When failure occurs, members of an organization think linearly and react by pointing a finger and saying, "It is your fault." As one workshop participant reflected about her company, "There is an unwillingness to forgive people for having made a mistake, for having challenged them, or for having insulted them. They are not willing to forget about anything. Those are the kind of indicators that I tell me that the attitude is not yet right."

What is "not yet right" is a conducive environment where people can discuss mistakes. Talking about mistakes can create the conditions of threat and embarrassment that trigger defensive reasoning. The defensive reasoning sees mistakes as crimes to be punished, further reducing the chances of learning. And finally, to avoid any punishment, we cover up our mistakes, thereby preventing any possibility of learning.

The Catch-22

In dealing with mistakes and failure, we run into a basic Catch-22, or emotional bind, that makes it difficult for us to learn from them. No matter how often we are told that it is okay to make mistakes, it rarely *feels* okay when we make one. Talking about mistakes can be upsetting. Our sense of competency or self-esteem may be threatened, or a general sense of embarrassment may overtake us. In reaction, we use defensive reasoning and strategies to protect ourselves from these conditions of threat and embarrassment. We end up getting more defended, and thus shut down any possibility for learning. Our defensive reaction is not unreasonable or unnatural given our attitude toward mistakes. To overcome this prevalent attitude and extricate ourselves from this Catch-22, we need another way of looking at and managing mistakes.

THINKING OF MISTAKES AS PUZZLES

Detecting and correcting our mistakes is a fundamental, creative source of learning. Artists over the centuries have attested to the value of making mistakes. The famous composer Igor Stravinsky said, "I have learned throughout my life as a composer chiefly through my mistakes and pursuits of false assumptions, not my exposure to founts of wisdom and knowledge." For Stravinsky and other artists, a mistake becomes the royal road to new invention. Mistakes are, as James Joyce said, "portals of discovery." Mistakes yield the information necessary for corrective action.

Taking the corrective action ensures improvement, growth, and future success, yet turning off the inner critic or holding back a punishing response to another's mistake is not an easy thing to do. A different approach was suggested to me by my friend and colleague Diana Smith, from Action Design. Her suggestion is to think of mistakes as puzzles, not as crimes to be punished. When all the pieces of a puzzle lie on the floor, it is hard to see how they might fit together as a whole. One would not yell at the puzzle for not being complete, but rather would begin to piece it together. We can apply the same strategy to mistakes. We try to figure out how all the parts interlock: How did we think and act together to create a problem or difficulty that no one intended or desired?

First, Ask Some Questions

To begin putting the pieces together, it's important to discover the reasonableness of the other person's action. So when someone does or says something that creates difficulty, ask yourself,

> What was the person up against that would lead him or her to act in that way?
>
> What was the person thinking that made it reasonable to behave as he or she did?
>
> How might I have contributed to the problem?
>
> How would I wish to be treated when others think I have made a mistake?
>
> Am I extending to the other person the same consideration I wish he or she would extend to me?

These questions, of course, reflect a fundamental change in thinking. Thinking of mistakes as puzzles takes a different path than finding who is to blame and what went wrong. Thus it's useful to draw on the same key thought enablers I introduced in Chapter Nine. Here they can help navigate a productive discovery of errors.

Assume partiality. First, I acknowledge that I may not have all the information. My view is partial, therefore I need to seek more information through inquiry. Partiality presumes that neither party is wrong, only limited in perspective.

Grant legitimacy. Granting legitimacy to another person's thinking helps me make the connection between his or her thinking and the action taken. The discovery of the thinking behind the action establishes a sense of reasonableness. Upon the discovery, I am under no obligation to agree with the thinking or dismiss the impact of the actions upon me. When I can make the connection between thinking and action, I take a more sympathetic rather than punitive approach to the mistake.

Attribute positive intent. The other person may be well intended but unaware of making a mistake. I have found it helpful to think to myself, "She is clueless as to the impact of her actions upon me" as an alternative to "She is making my life hell." Her action had an unintended impact.

Acknowledge impact and contribution. In most situations, there is a good chance that I might have said or done something to contribute to the problem. Rather than thinking linearly, "It's your fault," I take a systematic approach, seeking to understand how all parties interacted together to create a result no one intended or desired.

Everyone, including myself, has a right to make mistakes as long as we take responsibility to learn from them. Mistakes are not crimes to be punished or covered up, but puzzles to sort out.

By seeing our mistakes in this way, we can exercise a different option than taking the defensive reaction of fight or flight. We can take a learning stance. When someone zings us with an over-the-top attribution or makes a whopping inference about our actions, we can come back with an inquiry rather than a counterattack by asking, "What did you see me do or say that would bring you to that thought?" There is an opportunity to learn. There is a chance to expand beyond the limits of our awareness and discover how our actions had an impact on others. There is a chance to recoup.

Recoup

Before my first paying job as a facilitator, I got nervous. I called my friend Diana Smith and related my fear of completely screwing up. Her response was quick: "You will screw up." I thought to myself, "Thanks for the support," but said instead, "You are using that reverse psychology on me." "No, I'm not," she said. "You will screw up, but the difference between them and you is that you will know how to recoup." She was right. I did screw up in the meeting, and I have learned how to recover from my errors ever since. I always manage to fail better the next time.

Bracket the Defensive Response

I have come to expect my defensive reactions. They are immediate and very visceral. Over time, I have become attuned to the physical cues that signal defensiveness. I notice that I begin to hold my breath slightly. There is tightness in my throat. My teeth are literally set on edge. I formulate a response in my head and ready myself to pounce on the other person's next thought.

Once while I was facilitating a public forum, a gentleman stood up at the end of the meeting and yelled out loud, "How much do they pay you?" It was a shot across the bow. I felt my stomach tighten. The thought that immediately jumped into my head was "None of your business." I recognized that my defenses had been activated. Due to my training and practice with Argyris's theories, I took a momentary pause. I bracketed my defensive reaction long enough to get curious. I asked the man, "What did I say or do during the meeting that might have led you to question my value?" The man paused and looked at me with a stare, then said, "I want to see your resume." Now, my curiosity was piqued. I asked him a second question: "How would seeing my resume help you establish my value?" This time, he was quick with a response. "I want to show it to someone." Fearing that I was close to interrogating him, I said, "One last question: who would you show it to?" His face reddened a bit, and he said, "I didn't want to tell you this, but my mother." My heart immediately melted, and I felt my emotions softening.

He went on to explain that he was a simple laborer and had never heard of a professional facilitator before. His mother was a good judge of character, and he trusted her instincts. I sent his mother my resume, and at the next meeting, he approached me and said, "My mother thinks you are okay."

If you can increase your awareness of when your buttons get pushed or when you have become emotionally hijacked, you can interrupt your response. This is, in a sense, the age-old advice of "counting to ten." Taking a pause before reacting allows you a chance to think about what is going on. Sometimes not taking action is wise because the emotions are so volatile.

After the situation has passed, vent your emotions at an appropriate time and with a trusted colleague. Venting the emotions lets some of the steam out, but it is not an end in itself. Once you have had a chance to vent, try to get curious. Ask your colleague to help you reflect on what in you got triggered. Try to focus your attention on yourself and not on how the other person was the problem.

Quell the Inner Critic

Dwelling on an error creates a disproportionate emphasis on the mistake. No matter what good I might have done, it is eclipsed by the single error. Continually beating myself up neither advances me toward learning from my mistakes nor serves a constructive purpose. The inner critic needs to be stopped. It is a voice that pays no attention to reason and will always find a counterargument to bring the focus back on how terrible the mistake was.

Stopping the inner critic needs a physical analogue because no amount of mental convincing can shut it up. There is a gestalt therapy technique that I found very useful for quelling the inner critic. Years ago, when I was in a gestalt group therapy session, I had a verbal fistfight with myself. The therapist handed me a foam mallet and asked me to stop talking and start hitting myself in the head with the mallet. He shifted the topic of the conversation to someone else and left me to my own devices. After a few minutes of smashing the mallet against my head, I said, "Can I stop now?" His response was simply, "You can stop any time you want to. It is you that is doing it to yourself." Since then, whenever I start beating myself to a pulp mentally, I think of that foam mallet hitting my head and I stop. The continual hammering on how I failed or made a mistake is not productive. If I want to learn from my mistakes, I need to do the work of seeking mutual accountability.

Seek Mutual Accountability

We want to learn from our mistakes so that we don't repeat the same ones over and over again. A preventive measure against repeat performance is a commitment to mutual accountability. Although no one disputes the value of accountability, blaming people for mistakes is what usually happens when things go wrong in the workplace. A corporate executive reflecting on his company's culture said, "The unfortunate result of our culture is that it is a place where people need to place blame on each other, but no one is interested in taking the blame. There is a lack of trust to be able to share the burden of accountability." Sharing the burden of accountability involves a refusal to assign blame and a humble acknowledgment of our own contributions.

I tried my best to explain the meaning of accountability to my son, who heard the word used on the radio one day while we were driving together. When he asked, "What does accountability mean?" I thought to myself, "Great, if I can explain it to a ten-year-old boy, I might get clear on the meaning myself." Yet I found myself fumbling for words.

After some effort, I finally said something like, "It means someone has a lot of explaining to do for what they had done." In a way that only a ten-year-old boy could, he simply responded, "I don't get it, Dad." At that point, I could have responded, "When you do something wrong and you have to pay for it." I could have relied on the blame game and moved on, but accountability isn't that simple. So I struggled on.

The English word *accountability* means "to reckon," which in turn has a rich variety of meanings: "to estimate or compute," "to take into consideration," and "to accept something as certain, as in reliance in your promise to help." All three meanings come into play when we seek mutual accountability.

Accountability involves computing, and the count is always more than one. Accountability inhabits the arena of interpersonal relationships. "Accountability" is spoken in the same breath with the word "mutual." The focus is on contribution. How does each and every single one of us contribute to the situation at hand? It is the corny old line, "When you point the finger at someone, there are three fingers pointing back at you." When one understands one's own contribution, then the process of seeking accountability takes the next step of "taking into consideration."

The past is usually what is taken into consideration. We try to reconstruct what happened. We tell a story, and we try to tell it in a way that includes as many angles as possible. We want to take into consideration the complexity, roles, responsibility, and standards involved in the human action. Our consideration cannot rest on one single factor. There is always more to discover in our effort to tell the whole story. The goal is to find contribution and, through contribution, understanding.

Understanding is the basis for taking accountability. Once understanding is established, then all parties can commit to new action with the certainty that each has the others' promise of help. The promise of help hearkens back to the third meaning of accountability, "to accept something as certain, as in reliance in your promise to help." Seeking mutual accountability carries with it a confidence that all have learned from their mistakes and will not repeat them. All parties communicate with each other by having ongoing conversations and clear contracting. Help comes by way of multiple views, a commitment to tackle the tough issues, and reliance on the human desire to do better.

Mutual accountability embodies one of those endearing features of our humanity: all our actions have consequences, and all our actions involve one another.

Guidelines for Seeing Mistakes as Puzzles

When you are considering a mistake by an individual, team, department, or organization, follow these guidelines for discussing it.

1. Resist jumping to quick solutions.

2. Articulate a neutral description of the problem. Check to see if others have additional information that adds or modifies existing data.

3. Reduce blame by investigating what others might have been up against that led them to think and act in the way they did.

4. See how all parties interacted together to create an unintended or undesirable consequence.

5. Summarize the learning.

6. Mutually design ways to avoid making the same mistake again.

NOTE

Argyris, Chris. *Knowledge for Action: A Guide to Overcoming Barriers to Organizational Change.* San Francisco: Jossey-Bass, 1993, p. 3.

Helping Those Who Teach, Learn

Early on in my career conducting workshops, I would introduce myself by including a few words about my other profession as a hospice counselor. When people would respond, "That must be difficult," I'd always say, "No, death I can handle. It is unambiguous and certain. It is this work I find more difficult." After one workshop, someone approached me and said, "You know, after what you said about this work being more difficult than death, I thought that you were saying that I was in for an experience worse than death." I have since stopped introducing myself in that manner, but I still maintain a healthy respect for the degree of difficulty this work requires and the amount of skill needed to do it well.

In my experience of teaching, people find Argyris's concepts straightforward, easy to understand, and good common sense. The difficulty comes in putting them into practice. I am always relieved when I hear participants say after a workshop, "This is harder than it looks." I take that to mean that they are trying out a new skill. Any new skill requires practice, practice, and more practice.

The reduction of defensive routines in any organization cannot depend on the skills of a solo practitioner, regardless of his or her ability. At some point, members of the organization must put the concepts and skill set to use themselves. For that to happen, the practitioner must teach the concepts of the LHC and the

Ladder of Inference and help transfer the skill set of quality advocacy and inquiry to those other people. This task presents a series of formidable challenges for the practitioner, including developing a well-designed pedagogy and ensuring that the practitioner's cognitive competence and ability to model the skills are at a level where effective and consistent teaching is possible. In the following sections, I will discuss the competencies needed to teach the material and also the common pitfalls, mistakes, and hazards that practitioners can expect to face.

COGNITIVE COMPETENCE AND ABILITY TO MODEL THE SKILLS

Teaching Argyris's material requires the practitioner to possess sufficient cognitive competence and an adequate ability to model the skills. Cognitive competence is reflected by the practitioner's ability to clearly articulate the basic concepts using concrete demonstrations, stories, and examples. Because the order in which he or she presents the concepts has implications and impacts on learning, the practitioner needs to be versatile in his or her pedagogical approach. Related to cognitive competence are the practitioner's public speaking skills. Stage presence and good speaking skills are necessities, and the practitioner must be able to present the concepts to diverse audiences and apply them holistically with "live" industry-specific examples or in well-designed exercises.

The demonstration of high quality advocacy and inquiry is a baseline competency. The practitioner must model the skills during the instructional exercises and also in the real-time interactions with the participants. Fielding questions and comments and responding appropriately to participants are baseline opportunities for modeling the skills. When possible, the practitioner helps make the learning concrete by illustrating the Ladder of Inference or the LHC using an example of a participant's interaction with the practitioner or with another participant. Ultimately, the practitioner's ability to model the skills productively is the single most effective teaching tool for transferring actionable knowledge to the participants.

Modeling the Skills

The transfer of skill is essential to learning. Skill transfer occurs through modeling and experimentation. The practitioner is the primary source for modeling the skills. It is essential that he or she be able to produce the actions of the Mutual Learning Model in real-time situations or in response to the designed instructional exercises. I have seen practitioners with excellent platform skills make very convincing and attractive presentations, but falter when they deviate from the designed script usually found in a train-the-trainer manual.

Regardless of the nature of the skill, its transfer begins with the beginner watching others do it well. At first, he or she is not as proficient as those who are more skilled, but by mirroring their behavior, the beginner gets off to a good start. Even if the beginner uses formulaic recipes, he or she is producing the behaviors consistent with the Mutual Learning Model. As the beginner's skill improves, there is less need to stay bound to scripts and recipes, and a greater integration occurs between the actions of the Mutual Learning Model and the beginner's own natural style of communication.

Rather than doling out abstract advice like "Make a high quality inquiry," the practitioner models what to do in an actual conversation. The goal for the participants is to do the same—produce the actual behavior that is consistent with the Mutual Learning Model. When the practitioner asks participants, "What would you do?" the response is often a problem-solving strategy or an abstract piece of advice. A lot of time gets burned trying to work the problem or counsel others on their approach to the problem. The request to produce actual behavior is counterintuitive to the problem solvers in the group.

I find it necessary to signal to the group what my intentions are when I ask them to produce what they would actually say. If I don't, I create a negative impact. People begin to wonder what I am after and why I don't like their response. I will say something like, "I am going to ask you to produce what you would actually say in the situation. Your actual words are a demonstration of skill. You can experiment and see what impact a new way of acting has and verify its effectiveness." I get a fair to moderate level of agreement, but it never lasts. Very quickly, the discussion of a case study, exercise, or example reverts back to problem solving and the giving of abstract advice. This is more commonly found in beginner groups, and there are many ways to get them back into the swing of practicing the skills.

Role Playing

When abstract advice or problem-solving discussions occur, I like going into role playing. I may construct a role play or spontaneously jump into the antagonist's role in the case study and say, " I am X, and I just said to you . . . ; what are you going to say back?" Role playing is a simulation, but it puts everyone into action. In the role-playing action, people tend to act the way they would in real situations. Their emotions are engaged, and they get stuck in the frames of mind that prevent them from acting productively. The role-playing session provides an excellent artifact to reflect on later, especially if it is audio- or video-recorded.

Role-playing sessions are also a critical opportunity for the practitioner to model the skills. After each demonstration, it is important for the practitioner to check with role players to see if what he or she produced was helpful. I ask, "Can you see yourself saying something like that? If not, what makes it difficult?" I am looking to see if what I created can be replicated. Replication is not simply a mimicking back of my words, but an opportunity to test the skill. If the person responds with, "Yes, I can," then I follow up with "Let's hear how you would say it in your own words." The person now has a chance to practice the skill. Although he or she is most likely using a paraphrased version of what I said, the difference is that the person now fits it into his or her own personal style of communication.

If the person instead responds with "No, I can't see myself doing that," then it is time to pause and investigate the phrasing of my intervention or the person's framing of the situation. I still occasionally get the feedback "No one speaks like that." When I do, it is usually because I am speaking in "consultantese" jargon. Other times, the participant's framing of the situation is getting in the way of doing something different. In that case I find it helpful to switch from role playing to an exploration of alternative frames of mind that would help the person create a more effective advocacy or inquiry.

Role playing sessions are a unique laboratory for experimenting with the quality of advocacy and inquiry. After the case writer or group member attempts a high quality advocacy or inquiry, the practitioner can stop the action and check whether or not the statement or question was effective. One way to verify the effectiveness of a high quality advocacy or inquiry is to ask, "Did that move the conversation forward?" By forward I mean, did the inquiry surface new and additional information? Was there a softening of positions, so that a mutual understanding of diverse perspectives occurred? In the presentation of a view, were the steps of the Ladder of Inference visible? If the person producing the action or his or her fellow group members can answer yes to any of these questions, then there is an affirmation of success. From these successes, the participants can build their confidence in using the skill set.

OFF THE SCRIPT AND ON YOUR OWN

The practitioner has plenty of opportunities during a presentation or workshop to model the skills. The first and most obvious is during the designed exercises.

With workshop exercises, the practitioner has the advantage of preparation and rehearsal. A practitioner with good speaking skills can avoid the appearance of a "canned" response and make it sound natural and smooth.

In real-time situations, the action is more unpredictable than a script. On their own, practitioners can find their own defenses triggered and can model the skills poorly. If this occurs regularly, the participants will begin to doubt whether the theory actually works. They may label the practitioner as someone who does not walk the talk.

Although the practitioner wants to remain in the learning stance and maintain a nondefensive orientation, this doesn't always happen. It is unrealistic to expect any practitioner to model the skill set perfectly. He or she will make mistakes. In the best of all possible worlds, the practitioner can demonstrate real-time reflection on his or her own behavior and make corrections. Then there are those times when even the best practitioner gets triggered, stuck, or emotionally hijacked and can't recover. For these special events, the practitioner can only hope that the session is being recorded to allow for later reflection.

I have a record of some of my early mistakes—times when I became so stuck that the more I talked, the worse the situation became. The first two Unlocking Defensive Routines pilot workshops I conducted were videotaped. I anticipated that I would discover a few design "bugs." My design certainly did not include any live demonstrations of defensiveness by me as the lead facilitator, nor any intentioned misunderstandings, muddled instructions, or getting lost in the details, but they all happened.

The following transcriptions from the videotaped pilots are episodes in which I got stuck, made mistakes, or was completely out to lunch. These are not my best moments, but by sharing them, I hope that you can learn from my mistakes. These mistakes are not uncommon in the practice of teaching concepts and transferring skill. Although each person's specific errors may be different, any practitioner can get defensive when challenged, muddle the instructions, and fail to listen well.

Case: I Thought We Were Home Free!

Note: I am indebted to Phil McArthur for his insights and suggestions with this case.

In this situation, I gave the workshop participants a textbook example of defensiveness when one of them made a comment that set me off. I had spent a day and a half presenting the features of defensive routines. I was careful to model good inquiry skills when engaging the participants and during the exercises. During the morning of the second day, I covered the emotional hot buttons that trigger our defensive reactions. Returning after the lunch break, I was ready to coast to the conclusion of a successful workshop. I sat in the back of the room while my co-trainer facilitated a reflection on the morning activity. He asked the question, "What kind of reactions are you having to what was covered this morning?" After a few responses, a woman spoke up:

What I thought and felt, but didn't say	What was actually said
What in the hell does that mean. No rebuttal?	**Wendy:** This is a reflection, so I am assuming there will be no rebuttal. (laughter from the group)
Got that right!	**Co-Trainer:** This is my opinion, and I am not interested in anyone else's. (more laughter from the group)
	Wendy: I feel the value of emotions has been highly discounted. I have difficulty with that. The second thing I experienced was the inquiry process, what we seem to have engaged in the morning is, "Let me make sure I didn't evoke defensive response from another person." I felt like I was walking on eggs. I don't like the idea of using a technique on someone versus coming from a deeper place where I have conversations.
Where has she been? If anything, that is all that I have been trying to stress. Emotions are very much in play when it comes to organizational defensive routines. Discount	**Bill:** I'm in a bit of a bind. Because on one hand, you say you don't want a response, that this is your reflection, so what I want to know

my ass. This is a lovely interpretation she is stating as fact.

What in the hell is she talking about? A technique versus coming from a deeper place. She is so judgmental and I am not supposed to respond to this[expletive]. What a slam. She is not going to get away with this.

I'm pissed. The hell you aren't.

I am attacking you. What did you lay out to start with, lady? This is a fine mess. I am bailing out of this one. Ready to move on.

is, how can you discover whether your view of that is wrong, that you might have misheard?

Wendy: I am not speaking to you.

Bill: My question is, how you can discover whether you might have misheard what took place this morning, the way I was trying to explain how one conducts inquiry?

Wendy: I want to go back to my understanding of what reflection is, OK? For me to answer the question would be naming the issue in contention. The reflection process, as I understand it, is to be honored as it is, not to be attacked. This is how I experience you.

Bill: We are going into the weeds. Here's a chance I could take to see what kind of learning takes place. I want to serve it up, not in the sense, your experience of me attacking you. My intentions were to challenge the thinking. Now I have to be sensitive to what I might have said that might have triggered some defensiveness on your part that may be shutting down your ability to learn right now. I want to pay attention to that, just as much as you then begin saying to yourself, "Mmm, what might I have missed? How might I have misheard her?

No problem, honey.

Wendy: I request you honor my request.

Bill: I will honor that. I don't want to go there. Who had their hand up next?

I had fallen off the deep end. It is difficult to model productive advocacy and inquiry skills with an LHC like mine. My poor attempt to describe the bind I felt she had put me in came off as, "How can you find out how wrong you are without me telling you how wrong you are?"

I missed her meaning of reflection right from the start by focusing only on the phrase, "there will be no rebuttal." Judging from the group's reaction of laughter and my co-trainer's response, I felt confirmed in my belief that this was going to be a setup. I became defensive on hearing her multilayered assertion that emotions had been discounted and that inquiry was a technique to avoid creating defensiveness in other people.

When I think someone has misunderstood my intentions and words, I internally scream out "That's unfair. I didn't say what you think I said." I was too far gone to figure out what I might have said to contribute to her understanding. I made a feeble attempt to acknowledge my contribution, but even then, it was with the end purpose of getting her to see how badly she had messed up. I was using the language of the Mutual Learning Model to achieve the goals and aims of the Unilateral Control Model.

If I were to share it publicly "as is," my LHC would be the kind of rebuttal she feared would happen; there would be little chance of a productive conversation taking place. Understandably, she would want protection from the attack I launched inside my head. Her view of "reflection" offered her protection, but she did not make explicit its purpose or ground rules. Without knowing them, I was not certain how to "honor" her reflection, nor did I know how I could learn from it.

Doing it differently, I would have investigated her understanding of the purpose and ground rules of the reflection process. I could have said, "I am unfamiliar with a reflective process that does not allow for a rebuttal. I would like to understand how you and others see the purpose of reflection and its ground rules." Is reflection simply a "sharing" with no response? If a response or discussion is not allowed, then I would want to investigate why not. What would be her concern? If "honoring" someone's comments means listening and acknowledging them, would that preclude questions that seek clarification and a deeper understanding? In my mind, an "honoring" that does not allow for clarification would limit learning. Conversely, allowing questions might prevent me from arriving at the conclusion that she is wrong and launching a rebuttal.

I did find myself in a bind, but did not express it in a way that enabled us to learn or to have a meaningful dialogue. A different approach would have been to say something like, "What I have heard raises a concern in my mind that I did not communicate as clearly or as well as I had intended. I would like to correct that, but my bind is that I don't understand what I said or did that might have communicated the message that emotions were discounted." This statement goes to my understanding of reflection's purpose—to learn from and correct error. If a rule for reflection is not to ask questions, then my ability to learn will be limited. Needless to say, without a discussion of the purpose of reflection and its ground rules, the entire group, including Wendy and me, will run afoul with different, yet undisclosed, views on reflection every time.

If I were to choose not to engage the meaning of reflection, I could have simply acknowledged her statement about discounting emotions and the appearance of inquiry as a technique that caused her to feel that she was "walking on eggs." I might have said, "Wendy raised some important issues about the role of emotions, evoking defensiveness in others, and the appearance of inquiry as a technique rather than as an authentic line of questioning." The risk here is that she could still hear my response as engaging in a discussion and therefore off-limits. I would avoid this risk by first making explicit the ground rules for reflection and checking with her and others to see whether my statement was consistent with their understanding.

If my acknowledgment "honored" her reflection, I might have proceeded to broaden the learning by asking the group, "To what degree do others here share the same concerns?" If there were similar concerns, I could have taken the opportunity to learn what I had said that had contributed to this impression and then frame these concerns within the context of learning this material for the first time. Going forward, I could also ask the group, "If something like this happens again, what I would find helpful to my learning is for you to raise any concerns about what I am saying or to test your understanding of my words in the moment."

Since the time of this interaction, I have heard similar reactions about the role of emotions. I now understand them and Wendy's concerns about technique within the context of a beginner's experience with learning a new skill. Within that context, I have learned to pay more attention to achieving a shared understanding of the purpose and ground rules for reflection.

During the course of any presentation, there is a good chance that others will hear the material differently than the practitioner intends. Misunderstandings do occur, but punishing the participant for it, as I did, is not a recommended course of action. The challenge is that each participant will have a unique reaction to the material. Each reaction reflects the participant's own interpretation and frame of mind. Although time constraints do not allow the practitioner to address every reaction in a large group, it is possible to address participants' initial concerns about the practice of new skills.

Case: I've Been Zinged

It always seems that when I get stuck in the muck with someone, it is right before an overdue and much-needed break. Everyone has been sitting for a long time. Someone raises his or her hand and launches the group down a path that tests the patience and bladders of everyone present.

In one workshop, I made the mistake of taking one more question:

Bill: I'll take one more question from Jim, then I'd like to take a break. I am going to advocate strongly that we take a break.

Jim: Bill, are you teaching us, facilitating us, or manipulating us? The concern I have is that most of the language you are using are leading questions. You know where you want to take this course. You have already written on the flip charts the titles and headings. You are asking us to give answers that fall into these categories, like giving you specific examples of when we assign negative intentions. If the answer is not going in the way you want, you probe deeper to get an answer you want. I don't know how many others feel the same way, but I am a little turned off.

Bill: Okay, to answer your question. Yes, I am teaching. Yes, I am facilitating, and yes, I do have design in mind as to where to go, and because of that, there is a tendency for me to fall back on my own strategy of leading questions. It is very important that you raise that with me. It is not my intention to manipulate, but I can understand how you experience it that way. So I will keep checking at different points to see if this is true to your experience or something different. If you find me saying, "Wait a minute, you should be . . . ," then please continue to raise that. Let me test: Do others have the same experience as Jim?

Frank: I don't have the same experience. I recognize that you have a model. I'd like to understand that model. I am not taken aback by the technique you are using. You are using a lot of air time to get something to fly. My irritation level on that is beginning to come up. I'd prefer to deal with the content more and then we can debrief at the end of the day. That is what is going on inside of me. These are useful things; it is a well-developed model. You can accept them; you can reject them. I'd like to get your explanations first.

Bill: Okay, good.

I made several errors in this interaction. First, I didn't hold to my guns and manage the time properly. It was time for a break, and I could have easily said, "We are taking a break. Those with their hands up, please talk to me during the break, and we can negotiate what to raise with the group after we return." Instead, I opened a can of worms.

My intentions were to acknowledge how the use of my rhetorical questions could be experienced as manipulative and to check to see if the impact was on a single individual or on a larger group. If it was the latter, then I needed to make adjustments. Instead, I defended myself and extended the conversation beyond the tolerable limits for a break. As the group approached the break, I ended up with not one, but two publicly made attributions about my teaching style.

It did not escape me that Jim initiated his feedback to me with a leading question. He did explicitly state his view, but opened with "Are you teaching us, facilitating us, or manipulating us?" Rather than going on the defense, I could have mirrored back how his leading question had the same impact on me as mine had on him. When he finished speaking, I could have responded, "Jim, I know how you feel. You just did to me what you say I did to you. Although you did state your view, I found myself reacting first to your opening leading question, 'Are you teaching us, facilitating us, or manipulating us?' I thought to myself, 'What is he trying to do?' which I suspect was the same reaction you had to what I was trying to do in this morning's exercise." This live exchange could have been a positive exploration of how we use leading questions to ease into our positions.

The easing-in strategy is an occupational hazard for teachers. Too often a teacher defends the use of questions as following the Socratic method. In the Socratic method, questions are meant to draw out the student's knowledge. The difference between Socrates and a teacher in my position is that Socrates asked questions from a place of ignorance, whereas I know the material and want the class to arrive at a predetermined correct answer.

There are potential downsides to the approach of using questions to get to the predetermined correct answer. If the class doesn't answer correctly, the teacher keeps asking questions like, "No, that is not it exactly. What other things can you think of?" The students or participants hit a point of frustration where there is finally a collective call to "just tell us the answer."

This pattern is not dissimilar to the bind in which people in a position of authority find themselves. They have a view of how things should go, but want their team to "own" the direction and take the initiative. The person in authority holds back his view or asks a series of leading questions. The team is left to guess what is in the leader's mind. The remedy is for the leader to follow the basic rule of thumb that if you have a view, state it and balance it with inquiry to see if people agree or have different views.

When teaching now, I use fewer rhetorical questions and rely more on directly stating the concept and asking students for examples that make the material concrete. A case in point: when running the unfreezing the LHC exercise, I used to ask students to characterize the type of thinking they found in the LHCs of the case studies. Often, their answers would be very abstract or filled with various psychological interpretations. Instead of responding with "Not exactly; what else could it be?" I now provide a list of common types of thinking found in people's LHCs and ask participants to match the types with examples found in their case studies. If there are examples in the cases that don't match the provided list, then we have a discussion about the distinctive characteristics of the examples. The exercise runs more smoothly because the instructions are easier to follow and the objective is clearer.

Case: To Go Broad or to Stay in the Details; That Is the Question

One of the more difficult decisions for the practitioner is choosing whether to drill down on the specifics or to stay with a broad overview. This issue usually comes up in the diagnosis of a case study or live action. The discussion can get into the minute details of what was said, how it was said, what kind of multiple impacts it had on others, and what could have been said differently. By drilling deeper into an interpersonal interaction, the practitioner can make accommodations for multiple views and create opportunities for experimentation. Although the exchange can be rich for some participants, others get lost or bored. A broad approach, though more fast paced, runs the risk of becoming too abstract and of creating only minimal shared understanding.

At a debrief during one of my earlier workshops, a participant provided a couple of metaphors to describe this dilemma:

A: One thing I saw is that we got very detailed about some very subtle points. I don't really need to know the subtleties. I need to know the broad overview.

Bill: Could you give me an example?

A: An example, a metaphor would be that I didn't come here to learn how to build a watch. I just came here to learn how to tell time.

Bill: Still not helpful to me. Give me an example of when we got too much into the detail.

A: Unfortunately, I can't remember exactly what we were discussing yesterday. It was something yesterday afternoon. The conversation wound up taking about thirty minutes. I can't remember the specific example, but we were talking about minor details. It could be this, it could be that. We were analyzing each sentence to a very, very high degree, as opposed to taking a broad view. It is like anything else: you don't need to understand the fine subtleties to understand that this is an elephant and this is a horse. Unfortunately, I can't remember the example yesterday.

Bill: This illustrates again the difficulty about doing this kind of work. While the specifics are very hard to retrieve, the downside of not having them is that it is difficult for me to learn because I don't know what instance he is referring to.

Because I didn't get an example, I inadvertently invalidated his concern. His metaphors sufficiently communicated a generic concern: a deep drill-down for some is valuable, whereas for others it is beating a dead horse. There are always risks and trade-offs to going deep or staying broad in the learning. It is a difficult decision for a practitioner to make when teaching this material, but it is a decision that should not be made by the practitioner alone.

Learning is a mutual agreement between the practitioner and the group. Early on in any program or workshop, I contract with the group for a learning agreement to manage the pace and depth of learning. I for one tend to engage the live action that is immediate and that draws my attention. I can get carried away, so I need the group's help in determining the value of the discussion.

In contracting with any group, then, I now find it helpful to say something like "I will be relying on you to help gauge the depth and pace of our discussions. If we are going too slow or too fast, I want you to raise the issue. This doesn't mean that we will automatically go with your assessment, but it will give us an opportunity to check and see to what degree your view is shared by others." When it comes to drilling down or going broad, I use a simple contracting clause. If we are in the middle of a long discussion, I will stop and ask, "Is this discussion still providing us with learning, or is it time to move on? What are people's views?" In both cases, the group's response gives me a good indication of whether we should move on to something else or continue the same thread of discussion.

Although usually no one dissents from the learning contract, people don't always abide by it. After the fact, I will still get comments like the one I presented earlier. If I have contracted with the group beforehand, I am at least able to ask the question, "What made it difficult for you to raise your concern knowing you had permission to do so?" The response and ensuing exchange becomes an excellent occasion for exploring the frames of mind and social restrictions around interrupting, the role of the learner, and the value of the current discussion.

Case: Muddled Instructions

Because I know how an exercise should run, my instructions are clear to me. After running an exercise a number of times, I have come to expect a certain range of appropriate responses from the group. When I get a response which indicates that the person did the exercise differently than expected, I immediately go to the default thought that he or she didn't follow the instructions. I have found that this is not always the case, as in this example, where I missed how the person interpreted my multiple instructions.

In one workshop's paraphrasing exercise, the participants had already paraphrased how they as Mark hear Brenda's concerns. So in the second part of the exercise, I gave the following instructions:

"Once you have successfully paraphrased someone's thinking, you need to do something with it, i.e., identify a gap in reasoning or an underlying concern, and make an inquiry. Take a few seconds. Using your paraphrased statement of Brenda's concerns, what kind of inquiry would you make? *(pause)* Give the paraphrase and then share the inquiry you would follow up with."

After a few responses, Mike raised his hand, and we had the following exchange:

> **Mike:** My concern is I see the risks of delaying the exchanger replacement, a possible unplanned shutdown, environmental impacts, budget blown, and possible injury to my people from a reaction to an emergency. How is it that you share in that risk?
>
> **Bill:** I'm a little lost. Who are you speaking as?
>
> **Mike:** I was speaking as the operations manager, Mark.
>
> **Bill:** So, as Mark, he just paraphrased what risks she sees him taking?
>
> **Mike:** My understanding of the exercise is we were to add the second piece after the paraphrase.

Bill: I got lost. I couldn't tell whose voice you were speaking as.

Mike: I'm Mark, so I just said to her I'm hearing you say that taking risks and trying to meet the customer's needs are important for success in a competitive market. You are asking me to share the risks with you. My concern is that I see the risks of delaying the exchanger replacement, a possible unplanned shutdown, environmental impacts, budget blown, and possible injury to my people from a reaction to an emergency. How is it that you share in that risk?

Bill: You did something different with that. I see some nodding of the heads. What would you describe him doing differently? What did he do?

Another Participant: He added the risk that Mark believes he is bearing.

Bill: He added an advocacy. Rather than going immediately to inquiry, you added an advocacy that said this is the risk I am taking, listed them, and then said, "Tell me how you are going to share this with me."

Mike: Now, wait a minute. You said in the instructions to identify a gap in reasoning or an underlying concern. My underlying concern was—

Bill: Let me do a quick check. I had a disconnect with Mike, then he read back what the data was. How he heard the instructions. It made sense, so now I can understand the direction he took in it as opposed to what I was more focused on—the inquiry into Brenda's thinking, rather than your approach of raising the concern and asking how are you going to address this concern.

My response to Mike was vague, confusing, and unclear. I did not demonstrate a clear understanding of how Mike and I differed on the directions for the exercise. I expected Mike to use the original paraphrase he wrote from part one of the exercise—Mark's paraphrase of Brenda's concern. In part two, he was to add to the paraphrase an inquiry into Brenda's concern, asking a question that would surface more information from her point of view.

His answer reflected his understanding of the instructions as "identify the gap in meaning or underlying concern and make an inquiry." This stand-alone direction instructed him to construct an advocacy and balance it with an inquiry. Speaking on behalf of Mark, his advocacy stated Mark's risk and asked how Brenda was going to share in his risk.

My instructions were unclear and layered with three separate directions. The first communicated a meaning that after paraphrasing someone's thinking, you move on to a second distinct step—identifying a gap in reasoning or an underlying concern and making an inquiry. With this understanding, a participant would think that the request is to write an advocacy, different from the paraphrase, and balance it with an inquiry. Mike followed these instructions. In his second attempt to identify whose voice he represents, Mike is clearly able to reproduce his original paraphrase of Brenda's concern, and he then expresses an underlying concern of Mark's followed with an inquiry.

The second set of directions instructs the participants to use the previously constructed paraphrased statement of Brenda's concerns and to make an inquiry. I give no indication to the purpose of the inquiry when I do this. In my mind, it is obvious: it is an inquiry into Brenda's underlying concern. My third direction repeats the instructions at a high level of abstraction: "Give the paraphrase and then share the inquiry you would follow up with." This final direction can be applied to either the first or second set of instructions.

I interpreted Mike's response as "adding an advocacy," thus creating a disconnect in my mind because I was expecting an inquiry. Understandably, my response baffled Mike because he saw himself as following the instructions. Because of my default frame of "he didn't follow the instructions correctly," I failed to inquire into how he understood them or how my delivery of the instructions contributed to his understanding.

Instead, I looked for confirmation from the group that he didn't follow the instructions. I was well on my way to publicly punishing him for not following the instructions, and contributing to a condition of threat and embarrassment. Even my last statement communicates a meaning that he had done something differently than instructed.

An alternative frame would have included the thought, "What did I say that contributed to his understanding of the instructions?" I could have said, "Your answer caught me off guard. It was not what I expected. I may not have been clear in my instructions. What did you hear me say that communicated the directions to state Mark's concerns and add an inquiry?" Most likely he would have repeated what he said to me later in the conversation: "You said in the instructions to identify a gap in reasoning or underlying concern. My underlying concern was—" Rather than cutting him off, I could have picked up on the part of my multilayered instructions he selected, and admitted to having provided confusing directions.

Through the painful experiences of making multiple mistakes, I have discovered that less is more when giving instructions. The more I repeat myself and offer variations of what I am saying, the more confusion I create. Over the years, I have become more conscious of providing instructions that are clear, simple, and concrete.

I could have been clearer with Mike and others if I had said something like, "In part two of our exercise, start with the same paraphrase you created in part one—Mark's paraphrase of Brenda's concerns. Now add an inquiry. Ask a question that allows Mark to discover more about Brenda's concern." The opening set of instructions is what participants hear first and consider the most important, just as Mike obviously had done. Because the exercises help participants practice the skill set, clear instructions are critical to helping them have a successful experience.

On the Lookout for Unintended Impacts

I am on alert for what impact I might have on students, clients, or workshop participants. You never know when something you did or said has set off a firestorm in someone else. I learned this clearly when I was facilitating an intervention for public managers who had received an unequivocal message that their rank and file were not happy with management. They needed a communication course, pronto. I was hired to provide a one-day workshop on improving the quality of their communication.

I concluded my session with them by asking my usual ending question: "Here is your chance to give me feedback on my services. What did I do that helped, and what didn't help?" One manager raised his hand and shouted out, "Yeah, you attacked me all meeting." I was clueless as to what he was talking about. There was nothing I could remember about having a conversation with him or noticing any nonverbal signs of his being upset.

I asked him, "Really, I wasn't aware I was doing so. Tell me, what did I say or do that you experienced as an attack?" He looked at me and started to shake his finger at me violently. "You kept pointing your finger at me the whole time you were talking. I felt you were singling me out." I responded, "I had no idea. Were others aware of that?" A few hands went up.

Others said they had noticed that I talked with my hands a lot, but that it didn't bother them. I received no confirmation that others heard me singling out the one manager. I turn my attention back to the manager and said, "There appears to be different interpretations of my behavior here. What is your reaction to what you heard?" As we continued our discussion a little longer, he modified his position a bit, but still remained suspicious of my role.

For myself, I went home and asked my wife whether I shake my finger in the air when I talk. She said, "Yes, you do. It is the teacher in you." Since then, I have begun folding my arms or keeping my hands in my pockets while delivering a talk.

BECOMING PROFICIENT IN THE SKILLS

In this concluding section, I'll share a few final thoughts on how to become more proficient in the skills and on the continuing challenges a practitioner faces when practicing them.

Learning from Those Who Do It Better

For years, I was fortunate enough to attend the Action Design Institute as an associate faculty member. The role of the associated faculty was to assist with the logistics of the institute, but primarily to observe the senior faculty. From the luxury box of the observer, I was able to watch Chris Argyris, Diana Smith, Phil McArthur, and Bob Putnam practice their craft. Each time, my cognitive understanding deepened. It never hurt to hear a presentation on the Ladder of Inference again. I would write down phrases that I could use later. I saw the senior faculty get stuck as well as make brilliant moves that helped bring clarity to what would originally have been considered a mess.

On a limited basis, the associated faculty was allowed to make comments during the case study sessions or exercises. This opportunity posed a challenge. From the perspective of the beginner, you are under the watchful eye of a more experienced practitioner. You are bound to make mistakes or practice the skills poorly.

The stakes are higher because you think that if you do poorly, the experienced practitioner will judge you as inadequate and ultimately not recommend you to any clients. Under this assumption, any mistake becomes an occasion for embarrassment or threat.

Facing this perceived threat, I and others as beginners adopted the strategy of withdrawing and not saying much. We would figure out what to do privately and get back to our mentors later with a polished advocacy or inquiry. Unfortunately, this strategy bypassed an opportunity to practice our skills. It created a real obstacle to learning. The more you withdraw, the less you are able to demonstrate value. Not demonstrating value means that your mentor is less likely to recommend you for work. At the same time, if you put yourself out there and make loads of mistakes, you run the risk of being evaluated as inadequate. This is a Catch-22. If you don't do anything, you demonstrate no value. If you do something in error, you demonstrate no value. In either case, your fear is that the label "no good, no value" will be assigned to your name. Of course, as in the case of defensive reasoning, these assumptions and attributions are not tested publicly with the more experienced mentor.

I didn't see the fallacy in this reasoning until I became a mentor to those who were just a few degrees less skilled and familiar with the concepts than I was. On occasion, a student would say, "I am afraid to practice the skills around you because you will see how poorly I do them." I didn't see these students as inadequate, stupid, or providing no value. They were simply inexperienced at the skill. The way to learn is to step out there and do it. Making mistakes is the way to learn how to practice the skills better. If you don't try, you don't learn. I would have saved myself a lot of grief and anxiety if I had taken this advice earlier in my career.

Using the Theory

Early in the practice of these skills, I made the unfortunate error of trying them out on my wife in the middle of a marital spat. With the best intentions (I really did want to understand her perspective), I said, "What is the data that leads you to that conclusion?" She looked at me with a hard stare and said, "Don't give me that theory [expletive]!" She was right. I was using the theory. What she didn't know was that I continued to use it. I said, "How do you know that I am using the theory [expletive]?" She shot back, "You paused, your brow furrowed, and then what came out of your mouth wasn't you. I felt manipulated." She was right again. No normal human being says things like "What is the data that leads you to that conclusion." The phrase is a recipe to help beginners get started practicing the skills. It doesn't play in real life.

Reliance on recipes is common during the early stages of practice and will result in an initial period of awkwardness (see the reference to Bob Putnam's article at the end of the chapter). Although it is more apparent that one is making a concentrated, conscious use of the theory in the beginning, the accusation "You are using the theory on me" continues to be leveled against even more seasoned practitioners. An easy response is to say, "Yes, I am. In fact, we all have a theory we use to instruct us how to act. I am just being more explicit with mine." I could go further and explain that effectiveness is what is at issue. Is your theory effective in achieving your desired results? That's the question, but it is usually not what the other person wants to discuss. When someone says to me, "You are using the theory on me," it is a good tip-off that one of several things could be happening.

For example, in many situations, I understand the phrase as a way of saying that the other person believes I have the upper hand. I am in control of the conversation. He or she is under the microscope of my observation. I ask the penetrating questions, and the other person must answer them with a gulp of humility. In those times, I have to remember when the shoe was on the other foot. I can still recall the sensation of embarrassment and the rise of defensiveness within me when I was "getting help" discovering my error. I'd go along for a while trying to be a good learner, but soon the heat of constant focus on my thinking and behavior got to be too much. Particularly if the subject of the investigation was a recent interaction with the person helping me practice these skills, I wanted to know "What about you? Where is your part?" It felt as though we were spending a lot of time focusing on how I screwed up. In those instances, it is easy to think that the other person is using the theory to protect himself or herself and keep the attention on me.

When I am told that I am using the theory on someone, I need to pause and review how I have entered the conversation. There are several things that I could have done to contribute to the other's experience of feeling manipulated by the theory. The most common is that I haven't contracted with another person for reflective learning. Launching into a query of the thinking behind action without having an explicit contract to do so can send the message of "What were you thinking?" The unsuspecting conscripted learner will either shut down completely or tell you to mind your own business.

The majority of the time, I have been hired to help others reflect on their thinking and actions, so there is an explicit contract for learning. The most common format is a case study group. Even with enrolled learners, however, I do not always avoid the hazards of "using the theory." First of all, the setting is ripe for inducing the conditions of threat and embarrassment. Just because people willingly write a case study about their most difficult conversation doesn't mean that the degree of exposure among peers decreases. The threat level can be even higher with the presence of the "expert." Group members tend to see the expert as having an uncanny ability to see their errors and gaps in thinking. Further, the perception of "You do it better than me" adds a factor of intimidation. As the "expert," I am not always aware of how these perceptions others have of me are influencing their behavior. What I do know is how I make matters worse when I *don't* use the theory.

I'm certainly not using the theory when I slip into the Unilateral Control Model yet use the language of the Mutual Learning Model. I step into this particular pitfall whenever I explicitly ask participants to raise any difficulties they might have with either my interventions or instructional design. When I then hear from the sidelines, "People have been talking during the break, and they are saying . . . ," I get pissed. I immediately drop into the Unilateral Control Model. They didn't take me at my word that I truly wanted to know. What comes out of my mouth is "What prevented you from raising your concerns?" What I am really saying is "You didn't raise your concerns, and you should have." They get punished for not doing what I wanted them to do. I take this route and then can't figure out why they get defensive. An alternate route is to sincerely explore what made it difficult for them to raise issues publicly, as is often the case.

Another interesting observation that people have of me that reinforces their perception that I am using the theory is my outwardly calm demeanor while receiving critical feedback. I get comments like, "Wow, he really went after you, and you took it very well" or "You have such a calm way about you under fire." These comments don't always have a ring of admiration about them. They also come with an implied assumption of "Why aren't you as upset as I am? You should be." A calm exterior appearance can add to the perception that I am in control, above the fray, and therefore invulnerable. What others usually don't realize is that this is not the first time I have gotten critical feedback; it has happened plenty of times. In fact, I invite it. I have had practice receiving critical feedback with the hopes of learning from it. Because I have gotten used to it, I take it "more calmly." This is not to say that I don't get upset or defensive. That may very well be going on be-hind my calm exterior. In those times, I have to remember to be more vulnerable and share what is going on with me. When I do so, I get the feedback that I am now more human.

Being human is what it is all about.

NOTE

Putnam, Robert. "Recipes and Reflective Learning: What Would Prevent You From Saying It That Way?" In Donald Schön (ed.), *The Reflective Turn.* New York: Teachers College Press, 1991.

CONCLUSION

One of my favorite quotations that circulates around the Action Design community is from Jim Culter, CEO of Lattice Partners, a Monitor Group Company. In referring to his experience with Argyris's materials, he said, "Before I got into this work, there were a lot of jerks in this world. Now that I have gotten into this work, there are fewer." He didn't say "none," just "fewer." The population of jerks didn't actually decrease. It was Jim Culter's perspective that changed. Mine has too. A change of thinking has created a different way for me to encounter my world.

In my years of applying Argyris's theories, I have had many positive results. Resolutions come quicker and car-wreck conversations happen less frequently. Conversations take on a cleaner and clearer quality. I am less attached to my default way of thinking, and that is a good thing. I live easier within my own human limits. My blindness and my "dangerous neighborhood" mind keep me in check. I am now more familiar with failure when it happens. I still prefer that it wouldn't come for a visit, but when it does, I make room for what it teaches me. The skill set has become easier to practice. Improvement came about through trial and error, experimenting, and repeated use. I am a hybrid of the Unilateral Control and Mutual Learning Models. I am okay with being a hybrid because at least I know I have a choice.

I come in contact with plenty of defensive routines, but I participate in them less often. When I do, though, I am a textbook case of defensiveness. Fortunately my recovery time has shortened, and that is a relief. I continue to make mistakes and still don't like it when I do. But my choice to take a learning stance in the midst of discovering error continues to bear fruit. I have changed and improved. My personal belief is that I am a better person today because of my efforts to practice the skills of the Mutual Learning Model. Anything that helps us become better people in this world has alchemical value in the enterprise of our human spirit.

In every organization I visit, I witness defensive routines. I have come to think of them as weeds in the garden of modern organizations. Weeds exist in every garden. They grow right alongside the good stuff. Their presence deprives healthy, productive plants of needed nutrients. Because weeds are never as pretty as the plants consciously chosen to be in the garden, our immediate and first reaction is to get rid of them.

The only sure way to get rid of all weeds is to sterilize the soil with strong herbicides. If zero growth is the desired result, then a sterile environment with no beauty, value, or produce is what we get. The alternative is to apply herbicide selectively alongside the nutritional produce and plants of aesthetic beauty growing in the garden. Too little will prove ineffective; too much will damage the vegetation and those consuming it.

But if nothing is done with the weeds, the garden can be overrun with them very quickly. They always seem to grow faster than any other plant in the garden.

Personally, I keep on eye on the weeds throughout the growing season. I use herbicides in areas where I want absolutely to stop all growth. I accept a tolerable amount of weeds. When they threaten to take over the garden, I have to roll up my sleeves and get to work. They won't go away by themselves. I think of organizational defensive routines in the same way. Although we can work to minimize their negative impact on an organization's productivity, they will always exist. The work is not a mechanical fix, but a personal "roll up your sleeves" commitment to get your hands dirty.

I have respect for the tenacity of organizational defensive routines. There is always a risk when engaging them publicly. A sincere willingness to talk about the elephant in the room doesn't translate into knowing how to do it. Prudence dictates developing the skill to engage a defensive routine before carelessly venturing into a discussion of the undiscussables in one's organization.

The work to reduce the negative impact of defensive routines in organizations is slow. I live with no illusions of complete eradication. What I do hope is that each individual in an organization will take up the commitment for self-reflection, worry less about the "other guy," and embark on an inner discovery of self.

APPENDIX A:
MAPPING TEMPLATES

The process of mapping defensive routines demands a lot of skill and preparation on the part of the practitioner, but the technique is worth mastering. Conversations among participants involved in the defensive routines can move forward much more smoothly and productively if the practitioner is able to prepare a clear, relatively simple map that demonstrates the pattern of unproductive thinking and behavior.

This appendix describes three mapping templates from Action Design used to map a particular type of encounter and the process that accompanies each template. Mapping can be used to illuminate conversations between two people, teams, or differing factions of an entire organization. The descriptions are more fully explored with examples of each approach.

MAPPING INTERPERSONAL DEFENSIVE ROUTINES
WITH A THINKING-ACTION TEMPLATE

The first and best choice for mapping an interpersonal defensive routine is a Thinking-Action template. This template requires two willing participants (A and B) to provide the private thinking (LHC) that occurred when they became stuck in a defensive routine with one another. When each person reports his or her thinking on the LHC, we can see how person A selectively hears what person B says and how A assigns meanings, censors thoughts, and determines his or her course of action. We can also see how person B hears person A and responds accordingly.

What person A says becomes the stimulus for person B's reaction. Person B's reaction includes both a private thought response and the consequential action.

In turn, B's action is the stimulus for A's reaction. A single loop occurs for every verbal exchange: he thought, then said; she thought, then said.

Preparation

The optimal situation for constructing a map of an interpersonal defensive routine is to have a recorded conversation so that there is no dispute about what was said. In lieu of using a recording, the two people write up the dialogue (RHC) as best they can, then exchange the dialogues and make modifications if there are any discrepancies. As with all case studies, the participants don't need to recall the entire conversation. A critical incident in the conversation is sufficient. Once the RHC dialogue has been transcribed, both people take a copy and write in their LHC comments. They give their copies to the facilitator, who merges both documents in one case study. The final version of the case study includes the actual dialogue and both participants' LHC comments.

Construction of Map

The facilitator can chose either to construct the map independently of the two people and present it to them or to work through the process with them. If the facilitator chooses the former approach, he or she must be prepared to modify the map if the participants make different interpretations of their actions and thoughts.

When mapping two people's thinking and behavior around a defensive loop, the practitioner must avoid any appearance of taking sides. If the facilitator's words betray any bias, they can inadvertently trigger concerns about favoritism. The practitioner's focus needs to be on how both people contribute to the cycle of defensive routines through their actions and thinking. This focus is aided by the practitioner's use of neutral terms and low-level inferences that stay close to the conversational data.

Neutral Terms and Low-Level Inferences

The use of neutral terms to describe the action reduces any interference from the facilitator's own conclusions. For participants familiar with Argyris's concepts, there is a common vocabulary of neutral terms, such as "advocating position at high level of abstraction," "minimal inquiry," and "stating conclusions as factual." The Ladder of Inference also provides an assortment of useful terms, such as "selects the phrase x and de-emphasizes y" and "adds meaning to . . ." These terms help concretize the concepts and illustrate how they can be put into practice. Neutral terms also level the playing field. When both people see the map describing their actions as "asserting view abstractly," they can see that each of them is acting in a similar way.

The practitioner's skillful use of paraphrasing keeps the descriptions of the thinking and action at low levels of inference. Paraphrasing highlights the key meanings and trigger words that account for the stimulus-reaction movement around the loop, such as, "Jane heard 'We aren't going to meet our targets' as a veiled threat to lay off people." The skill of paraphrasing and the use of neutral terms are especially useful for crafting brief and precise statements that are entered into the map's thinking and action boxes. Short, simple statements that communicate the thinking and action are better than longer sentences that clutter up a map and create confusion. The learning objective is for the participants to see quickly and easily how their thinking and actions work together to create the result that no one desires or intends.

Presentation

When the facilitator hands the case study back to the two case writers, they will be reading each other's LHC comments. Reading someone's private thoughts about you can be disconcerting. The first time I read another person's LHC thoughts about me, I had been warned in advance. With the assurance that both of us were adopting a learning stance, I took the comment "If he goes there, I will knock his brains out and feed them to my dog" with a chuckle.

In these situations where people in the same case study are privy to each other's private thoughts, there is always a chance that the case writers have cleaned up the more toxic elements of their LHCs. That is not a bad thing to do. What is important is that each person can see how his or her actions impacted the other's thinking.

Example

A common defensive routine occurs when a person is trying to provide "critical" feedback to his or her boss, peer, or report. In this case, Mary and John are two trainers who have conducted a workshop together. John holds an unfavorable evaluation of Mary's performance.

Read the case study from left to right, starting with John's thoughts on what he should do.

LHC

John: I have had this nagging feeling about Mary's performance for a while, and today I got feedback from others that Mary was too slow and a little boring. I better tell her about it.

Mary: How can you say it was too long? The subject matter is difficult to understand, and I want to do exercises to make it clearer.

John: What do you mean by "often got it very well"? You are used to participants that are patient, but not this crowd. I have told you this several times. Letting the whole presentation unfold is your way of saying, "Don't disturb my process. I am not going to change." I need to let her know how serious the situation is.

Mary: Who are these participants? No one even hinted at not liking my style. Instead, all the feedback came out "glowing" well. John is just pandering to a few. I doubt whether he checked to see if it was a majority vote.

RHC

John: I think the second day was a bit long, and some of the explanations were not very well conveyed, and there were many "answer-the-question-by-yourself" ways of asking questions. I found that's not very effective.

Mary: Well, I have my reason to put those explanations in there. Yes, there is awkwardness at the beginning, but after listening to the whole presentation, they often get it very well. Would it be okay to let the whole presentation unfold? Would that make sense to you?

John: Well, yes, I know you have your rationale for doing that, but Minin participants are very different than those you deal with at Maxims, as I have already told you. Some of the participants also gave me similar feedback.

Mary: But what I have found was that they are quite attentive, and it seems to me that they liked it, so I can't connect with what you mean by "not effective." Please give me an example or some data.

John: How could she be so unaware of this obvious feedback? I better tell her what kind of data she is missing. She is asking me for observable data.

Mary: Wow, this is so unnerving. People find ways to speak behind my back. Maybe they do this because they think they are showing respect to authority.

John: Yes, I know. I found it irritating too. I asked them to speak directly to her, but they refused. It sounds like I made it up and exaggerated the whole thing. Okay, to be fair to her, let's go back to the data. We won't get very far by looking at the data. She will still deny the obvious.

John: People came to me and didn't want to give feedback directly to you.

Mary: I find that irritating that people have something to say, but they are not coming to me directly, but comment behind my back. I really need data before I can make sense of this.

John: Okay, the presentation was taped; I would like to go through the tape with you.

What's Going On? The First Loop

In the first loop, the thinking-action sequence is an exchange of statements at a very high level of abstraction. No one makes any inquiries. Instead each person hears a phrase or two from the other and makes a private negative assessment of what he or she heard. John has had a negative evaluation of Mary's performance for a while. Participants' feedback has confirmed in his mind that what he sees is an accurate assessment. He states his view at a high level of abstraction and as a fact. She was a bit long, and her ideas were not well conveyed. He ends with an evaluation that her use of rhetorical questions was not effective.

Mary selects the phrase "too long" and questions its meaning. She privately defends to herself the validity of the time spent due to the difficulty of the subject matter. She doesn't inquire into John's view of her presentation's being "too long."

Her response minimizes John's evaluation as "initial awkwardness" and states her view of the day at a very abstract level by saying "in the end they often get it well." She concludes with two leading questions looking for agreement that the process should "unfold."

Interpreting the Second Loop

The second loop is a repeat of the same sequence found in the first loop. The repeated pattern of selective meaning, censored thinking, and assertion of abstract views as facts adds intensity to the interaction. John selects Mary's words "often got it well" and believes she is referring to her experience with the client audience with which she is most comfortable. He interprets "unfold" as meaning she doesn't want to change, but doesn't test this understanding with her. John pushes his view while illustrating what the differences are between participants. He defers to "some of the participants gave me similar feedback."

Mary picks up on the phrase "some of the participants" and makes a causal explanation that John is pandering to a select minority. She doesn't make this explanation public, but defends her evaluation of her performance by saying they were attentive and liked it. She returns to John's earlier reference to her being "not effective" and asks for supporting information.

Filters and Assumptions: The Third Loop

Mary makes a productive move by asking for information that supports John's assertions. Her inquiry registers as a legitimate question in John's mind, but is filtered through the frame of "she is not seeing the obvious." There is an assumption that even though she may be using different data, she is missing the obvious and most important data—his. John only reasserts his view that his information comes from others' feedback. His response leads to a feeling of being "unnerved" in Mary. She comes up with a causal explanation about culture and authority, but doesn't share it with John. She does state her irritation about the indirectness of others and again requests supporting data. John defers to a later time when they can observe the tape, but privately concedes that it won't do much good because she will deny the obvious.

Exhibit A.1 is the map that would be presented to John and Mary. Start from the left and read point 1 in the John's Thinking box. Follow the arrow across to point 1 of John's Actions and then down to the first point in the box Mary's Thinking. Move from there to point 1 in Mary's Actions, then return to John's Thinking, point 2, and go around the loop again.

When John and Mary review the map, they are able to see how certain words they said triggered thoughts in the other person. Both were selective in what they heard, and neither of them tested or made explicit their understanding of what the other was saying. As a map often does, it allows John and Mary to see how similar they were acting toward each other and serves as basis for further inquiry into each other's thinking.

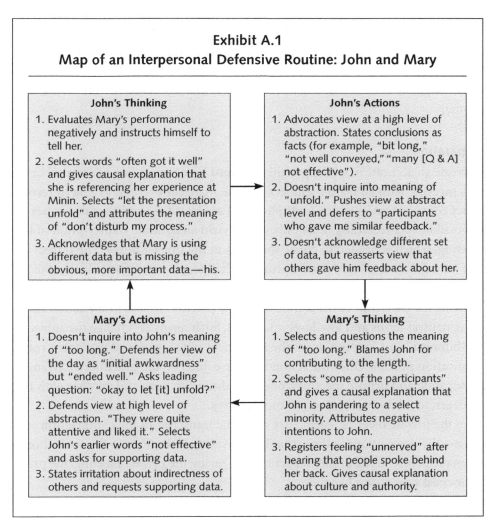

Exhibit A.1
Map of an Interpersonal Defensive Routine: John and Mary

John's Thinking
1. Evaluates Mary's performance negatively and instructs himself to tell her.
2. Selects words "often got it well" and gives causal explanation that she is referencing her experience at Minin. Selects "let the presentation unfold" and attributes the meaning of "don't disturb my process."
3. Acknowledges that Mary is using different data but is missing the obvious, more important data—his.

John's Actions
1. Advocates view at a high level of abstraction. States conclusions as facts (for example, "bit long," "not well conveyed," "many [Q & A] not effective").
2. Doesn't inquire into meaning of "unfold." Pushes view at abstract level and defers to "participants who gave me similar feedback."
3. Doesn't acknowledge different set of data, but reasserts view that others gave him feedback about her.

Mary's Actions
1. Doesn't inquire into John's meaning of "too long." Defends her view of the day as "initial awkwardness" but "ended well." Asks leading question: "okay to let [it] unfold?"
2. Defends view at high level of abstraction. "They were quite attentive and liked it." Selects John's earlier words "not effective" and asks for supporting data.
3. States irritation about indirectness of others and requests supporting data.

Mary's Thinking
1. Selects and questions the meaning of "too long." Blames John for contributing to the length.
2. Selects "some of the participants" and gives a causal explanation that John is pandering to a select minority. Attributes negative intentions to John.
3. Registers feeling "unnerved" after hearing that people spoke behind her back. Gives causal explanation about culture and authority.

MAPPING A MANAGER-TEAM INTERACTION

When mapping a manager-team defensive routine, it is logistically difficult to record all the private thoughts of each group member and place them within the structure of a Thinking-Action template. An Action-Impact template is the preferred method for capturing the dynamic between a manager and his or her team. The action boxes are filled in exactly like the Thinking-Action template. The difference is that the actions are attributed to the group rather than to one individual. The impact boxes register the effect the actions of the team had on the manager and that of the manager's actions upon the team. The descriptions in the action boxes are taken from a team meeting, and the items in the impact boxes are created by the manager and the team in separate private sessions shortly after the meeting. Once the practitioner constructs a complete Action-Impact map, he or she arranges a facilitated dialogue between the manager and the team to discuss the map.

Preparation

To create an accurate map, the practitioner must have a recording of a typical business meeting with all team members and the manager present. Trying to reconstruct conversation in which multiple voices are heard around the table is nearly impossible, so a recording is the only way to yield an accurate transcription of the meeting, which is needed to create the items in the impact boxes. The transcription later serves as a "hard data" document that people can refer to during the facilitated learning dialogue between the team and manager.

Using the transcript of the conversation, the practitioner fills in the action boxes using neutral terms and low-level inferences. Such terms as "change the subject," "withdrawal," and "oppose" track the movement of the team and manager's communication process. Once the action boxes are filled in, the practitioner arranges for separate and private meetings, one with the entire team and another with the manager, to fill in their respective impact boxes.

In the private meeting, each party reads the transcript of the conversation and reviews the descriptions in the action boxes. Any modifications to the action boxes are made before filling in the impact boxes. During the private meeting, the practitioner asks questions like these:

"When the boss [team member] said x, what was your reaction?"

"What were you thinking or feeling at the time, but didn't say?"

"What interpretation did you give to his [her] words?"

After hearing responses to the questions and discussing the information with the team or manager, the practitioner paraphrases the impact and tests its wording with them. The agreed-on wording of the impact should help everyone see the connection between impact and the consequential action taken in response to the impact. For example, if the impact of the manager's actions was "to shut the conversation down," then the team's silence or change in topic is their action in response to the impact. The team fills in only the impact box that describes how the manager's actions impacted them, and the manager fills in only the impact box for how the team's action impacted him or her.

As a wrap-up to their respective private meetings, the practitioner can ask, "What impact do you think your actions had on the team [manager]?" This gives both parties a chance to reflect on the impact of their own actions. Any response that raises the level of self-awareness prior to the facilitated meeting will help smooth the way for a productive dialogue and curtail any blaming activity.

Presentation: Facilitated Dialogue

Similar to the first time you read another person's private thoughts about you, reading how your actions impacted another person can cause a mild shock. The phrase "I didn't mean to" is usually the first response in an attempt to protect yourself from any potential embarrassment caused by the unintended impact. This response is expected, but the practitioner must resist the temptation to leave it at that and move on. It is a good teaching opportunity to address our common blindness and lack of awareness around intent and impact. Once that is acknowledged, the focus of the dialogue should return to how the sequence of impact and action locked the team and the manager in a pattern of unproductive behavior.

Example

After a staff meeting that I had not attended, a team member approached me and said, "Boy, the boss sure shut down the conversation." I responded by asking, "What did he say that shut down the conversation?" As often happens, the person couldn't retrieve the actual dialogue. Fortunately, the meeting was videotaped. I had it transcribed, and constructed an Action-Impact map of the defensive routine that occurred during the meeting.

The Meeting

This is a small division of internal consultants who serve a larger organization. The discussion centered on the limits of the internal consultants' expertise and when it is appropriate to rely on external resources. Whether the expertise comes from internal or external sources, the team needed to determine how to transfer the knowledge gained from their own training and expertise in ways that were helpful to their clients.

The Actual Dialogue

Alice: If I'm going to do an in-depth consulting project where I'm working with senior leaders in the area of strategy, I don't have enough expertise to do that right now. I could give a workshop on strategy that is predominately prescriptive. That is what we have been doing, providing programs. I don't think our customers would accept that level of programmatic offering. If we are going to provide holistic consulting that gets into more rigorous technical areas, we will need an external consultant or a full-time internal person.

Manager: Well, why would you try?

Alice: I would try in the areas where we can rely on external consultants.

David: That would create a bottleneck for our capability. We would have to rely on two or three externals through which to channel our true expertise. But I also appreciate your point. I don't feel that we can achieve expertise in all the areas.

Phil: We should have focused dialogue on what is our role as consultants. As a consulting firm, I see this group as being the partners, meaning the people who are managing the client relationship and then coordinating the external consultants who come in and do the detail work.

Sally: You bring up a number of issues and if we're uncertain of our roles, it behooves us to clarify what is our strategy right now. How would we implement our strategy? What is it going to look like beyond delivering programs?

Alice: We have to stop in thirty-five minutes. I know this is a rich conversation, and I'm also aware that another ten minutes isn't going to bring resolution. This topic requires further conversation. So what would we like to do?

Manager: I guess we could pose some questions to ponder. We spent the better part of the year trying to define and clarify roles. If we are not clear on those, we need to revisit it, but we're not going to spend a year doing it. We've invested a year on doing that and letting people shape how we were going to create it. We need to invest time if you're unclear about your role. But we have no luxury of turning inward from the customer for a year and doing that again. It seems we have done this for a whole year. But we are not there obviously by the comments, so I would pose the question for the people who are not clear on your role. You need to articulate somehow what that is and we can find a practice forum for discussing that.

Mike: One of the questions that were asked before you came in was in this particular context, what more people feel we are at on this particular topic, and I think we may have strayed a little from that question that Alice originally posed. There is a bigger issue, by the way. There is also a question of how do we address these Post-it stickies that we have put up there on the wall. I don't know if we really addressed those particular questions very much.

Map: The Action Boxes

The first description of the group's action is based on the number of advocacies and inquiries and their quality. In the quoted transcript, the exchanges are all advocacies, and there are only four questions. The one question from the manager is leading: "Why would you try?" Two questions are rhetorical and get no response. The last question asks for a direction on what to do next. In sum, there were a few poor-quality inquiries. "Engage in minimal inquiry" is a general, neutral term that can be entered into the Team's Actions box.

The expressed views consist of poor-quality advocacies insofar as they were vague, general, or abstract.

Alice evaluates her skills as not sufficient for providing their clients a service beyond prescriptive programs. She is uncertain as to whether or not clients want them anymore. She provides no information or examples to support her assertions. She restates her position following the manager's leading question by suggesting that "a more holistic counseling" model would mean partnering with an external consultant who could provide technical expertise.

David names any reliance on external consultants as a "bottleneck for our capacity." He does not make his concern explicit. Instead, he makes a brief acknowledgment of Alice's point by citing the claim that the consulting team can't achieve expertise in all areas.

Phil shifts the conversation to another topic by making a proposal to have a "focused dialogue." He does not stop for a reaction, but continues with a general definition of the consulting team's role and responsibility.

Sally interprets the discussion as a possible uncertainty around the team's strategy. She advocates a course of action that if they are uncertain, then they should get clear. She gives two examples of questions they should be asking themselves.

Alice raises the time constraints and proposes a recommendation to talk further on the subject.

Mike shifts the subject away from the manager's statement and alludes to an original question and bigger issues on the sticky notes, but does not make them explicit.

Five of the nine members of the team spoke up. Four remained silent.

All of these advocacies on the part of the team can be summed up as follows:

Assert views in vague and general terms

Propose action

Change subject

Remain silent

Besides the one leading question, the manager only spoke up once to express his view. He delegated the task to his team to get clear on their roles. He repeated his request three times with the warning not to take another year to do it.

Map: The Impact Boxes
In the private meetings, the manager described the impact the team discussion had on him as hearing a distinct message that they were "unclear about their roles." He

saw himself as providing guidance to the team. When they made no response to his direction to get clear on roles, he interpreted it as an acceptance of what he said, and he would expect compliance from them. In contrast, the team saw themselves as having a "rich conversation" and felt that the manager had "shut down" the conversation by what he said. Many members wondered if he was talking about them. In the staff meeting, no one had expressed his or her fears or private assessments, so the action "Cover up fears and private assessments" was added to the Team's Actions box.

Using the agreed-on action boxes and the information from the private meetings, I drew a map to be used during the facilitated dialogue, as shown in Exhibit A.2.

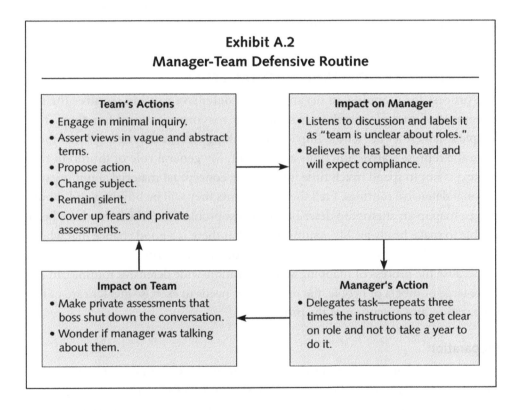

Exhibit A.2
Manager-Team Defensive Routine

Team's Actions
- Engage in minimal inquiry.
- Assert views in vague and abstract terms.
- Propose action.
- Change subject.
- Remain silent.
- Cover up fears and private assessments.

Impact on Manager
- Listens to discussion and labels it as "team is unclear about roles."
- Believes he has been heard and will expect compliance.

Impact on Team
- Make private assessments that boss shut down the conversation.
- Wonder if manager was talking about them.

Manager's Action
- Delegates task—repeats three times the instructions to get clear on role and not to take a year to do it.

The Facilitated Dialogue

In the facilitated dialogue session, the map served as a dramatic visual aid for seeing how the quality of their interactions led the manager and his team to walk away with two completely different understandings of what took place in the meeting.

The team members were able to see how their manager's response to them was reasonable given their high-level, abstract discussion about roles. The manager realized how he had made several conclusions about what was going on in the meeting and assumed everyone else shared them. Because the team and manager had not secured a mutual understanding of the issue, what the manager thought of as providing guidance turned out to be "shutting down the conversation" from the team's point of view. He resolved to publicly test both his understanding of what he heard them discuss and how they heard his requests for action. The team acknowledged their defensive role and the pattern of covering up their fears and concerns about the manager. They, like the manager, resolved to test their understanding of his words with him.

MAPPING AT THE ORGANIZATIONAL LEVEL

The process for mapping an organizational defensive routine requires the involvement of multiple members from teams across organizational functions. The template can either be Action-Impact or Thinking-Action as long as all members from the representative functions are present. My general rule of thumb in this context is not to spend much time introducing conceptual material about organizational defensive routines. I tell the participants they will be building and modifying a map in an attempt to describe a business problem on which they have been unable to make headway. My assumption is that there is a good chance that where they are stuck, there exists an organizational defensive routine.

Because the process of mapping an organization-wide defensive routine can involve large numbers of people, the practitioner needs to exercise greater care in the preparation and execution of the process.

Preparation

Prior to the meeting, set out flip-chart pages or poster-size sticky notes and create a template that looks like Exhibit A.3. Each page or note represents one of the boxes shown in Exhibit A.3. Write each box's respective title on top of the paper. If possible, create arrow cutouts and place them in their appropriate positions between the boxes. You will have to create separate templates if dealing with multiple groups who choose different business problems to map. If only one business problem is the focus of the entire group, a single template is sufficient. On another flip-chart page or sticky note, write the title: Business Problem.

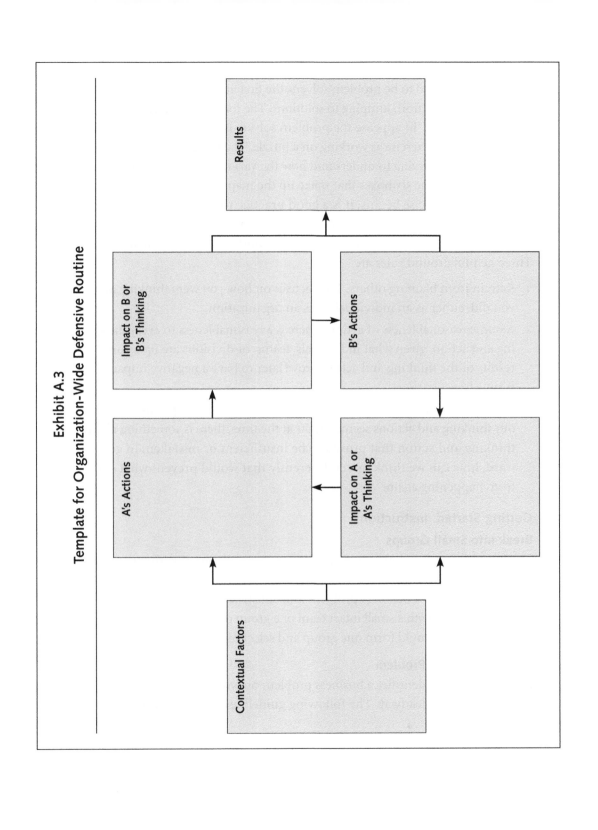

Exhibit A.3
Template for Organization-Wide Defensive Routine

Ground Rules

Because people tend to be problem solvers, the first and most important rule is for everyone to refrain from jumping to solutions. The focus is on describing the problem, not solving it. To appease the problem solvers in the group, the practitioner can introduce the exercise as working on a puzzle. The image of a puzzle shifts participants' focus to trying to understand how the various parts interlock. The pieces of the puzzle are the six boxes that make up the map.

Before the exercise begins, it is a good practice to review a few basic ground rules. Ground rules help establish a desired tone for dialogue. Rather than grounds for punishment, any violation can serve as a point of investigation and learning. Three helpful ground rules are

1. Refrain from blaming others. The focus is on how you were thinking and what you did, either as an individual or as an organization.

2. Assume reasonableness of action. There is a reasonableness to everyone's thinking and action, given what individuals, teams, or divisions are up against. If the results of the thinking and action prove later to have a negative impact, then it is time to get curious.

3. Get curious. Learn from the mistakes, errors, or false assumptions. Even though our thinking and actions seemed right at the time, there is something about the thinking and action that proved to be insufficient or mistaken. In going forward, how can we think or act differently that would prevent what occurred from happening again?

Getting Started: Instructions

Break into Small Groups

The first step is to break the participants up into small groups with representatives from interdependent divisions or departments. When following this process, each group will identify a business problem and construct a map different from other groups. If dealing with a small intact team or a group of fewer than eight to ten people, participants should form one group and select one business problem to map.

Identify Business Problem

Each small group identifies a business problem on which members have been unable to make any headway. The following guidelines can help the group select a business problem:

- Brainstorm a number of problems. Try to think of at least three business problems. List them on the flip chart.

- Refrain from jumping to solutions. There are no quick fixes. The purpose of the exercise is to address how the organization deals with problems and errors.

- Select one business problem that the group will map. The problem should be

    General enough to apply to a variety of situations

    Representative of the departments in the group

    Moderately difficult—difficult enough to pose a challenge, but not so difficult that its complexity would doom any chance of creating a clear, compelling map

- Write a one- or two-line statement of the business problem on the flip-chart page or sticky note titled Business Problem.

Predict Results or Unintended Consequences

The small group discussion begins by identifying results. Each group answers the following question:

What results does this problem generate now? If it continues, what you do predict will occur?

The group writes its responses in the Results box. Before the group fills in the thinking and action boxes, the next step takes the group discussion to the other side of the map and identifies the contextual factors.

Identify Contextual Factors

Contextual factors provide some insight into what people might have been up against that led them to think and act the way they did. The small groups identify the specific factors that influenced the understanding of the business problem and the course of action taken. A list of the demands and constraints imposed by external factors (business environment, organizational structure or tasks) can also be included.

Once the contextual factors have been identified, the group is ready to proceed to the part of the map that represents the interlocking patterns of thinking and acting. If members from all relevant teams or departments are present, then use the Thinking-Action template. If they are not present, then use the Action-Impact template. Participants will have to imagine what kind of impact their team's actions might have had on the other group or groups.

At this stage, let curiosity take over. How did members or departments think and act together to create results no one originally intended or desired? Instead of focusing on the "other guy," each member of the small group seeks to understand how his or her team's thoughts and actions contributed to the problem.

Actions of A

One team or department represented in the small group selects A and puts its name under each A box title. It does not make a huge difference who starts first. Whoever goes first starts with the A's Actions box. They discuss and respond to the following question:

> What action(s) did you or your team take (or not take) to deal with the problem in the light of the contextual factors you faced?

> Group A lists its actions in the A's Actions box.

Impact on B

The group designated as B puts its name in the B boxes and fills in the box labeled either B's Thinking or Impact on B. If groups are using the Impact on B box, they respond to the question,

> What was the impact of A's actions on you?

> If groups are using the B's Thinking box, they respond to the question,
> What did you think in response to A's action?

Actions of B

Depending on what group B wrote in its Impact on B or B's Thinking box, the group members now move to the B's Actions box. They answer the following question:

> On the basis of what is written in the Impact on B [B's Thinking] box, what action(s) did you take?

> Group B writes its action(s) in the box, and the loop comes full circle. B's actions have an impact on A.

Impact on A

Group A fills in its Impact on A (or A's Thinking) box with its reaction to B's action.

The small group can continue and create another loop if the impact of B's actions on A set in motion another sequence of action on A's part.

Example

This example takes place in a processing plant where two different organizational departments are at odds with each other over their roles and responsibilities for maintaining plant reliability and technical integrity. Engineering is responsible for quality assurance; it provides technical guidance to Plant Maintenance, which is responsible for quality control. For the plant to operate at its optimal level of capacity, its equipment must remain in a state of high reliability. Equipment failure and unexpected shutdowns negatively impact production, which translates directly to lost revenue.

The Engineering staff consists of highly trained engineers with advanced degrees in their field. They provide Maintenance with the codes and procedures needed to maintain the highest level of equipment reliability. They publish schedules for regular inspection and maintenance. If there is an equipment failure, they are called in to analyze the problem and design a solution.

Maintenance carries out the daily operational functions of the plant. Maintenance personnel consist of various operational functions. The operators have a certification level of education, but pride themselves on possessing long-time practical experience gained from being on the job and being responsible for different equipment, such as pumps, compressors, and heat exchangers. They carry out preventive maintenance schedules and make sure that the equipment is operating within the design perimeters set by Engineering.

The relationship between the Engineering and Maintenance staffs has had a long history of problems. They gathered together for a meeting to explore how their working relationship affects plant reliability.

Identify Business Problem

After their initial brainstorming session, the group selected the following problem statement: explore the differing perspectives between Engineering and Maintenance as they apply to plant reliability and technical integrity.

Identify Results or Unintended Consequences

The members of both teams had no trouble identifying the results or unintended consequences.

Repetitive failure of equipment

Loss of production due to shutdown

Unsafe operation

Increases in cost of production

Disputes among teams

Increases in workload due to redundant activity

Identify Contextual Factors

Having created the list of results, the group moved on to identify the contextual factors. Their discussion covered a broad range of topics that helped flush out the larger contextual setting:

Varying levels of technical expertise

Personnel turnover

Management's drive for safe production

Actions and Impacts

The Engineering team volunteered to go first and fill in the A's Actions (Engineering Actions) box. They talked about how they write up instructional procedures and generate reports on equipment failure, all of which is sent to Maintenance to implement. The facilitator wrote in the Engineering Actions box, "Sends Maintenance instructional procedures and reports for how to address equipment maintenance or failure."

Turning to the Maintenance team, the facilitator asked, "What kinds of reactions do you have when you receive these reports?" Team members reported a range of reactions. Some acknowledged that they didn't understand the reports or instructions, but never asked Engineering for clarification. Others questioned the reports' recommendations, but did not raise their concerns with Engineering. When asked what their response was to Engineering, many simply said, "I tell them it is okay and that I'll do it." The facilitator summarized their responses in the Impact on B (Impact on Maintenance) box by writing, "Reads reports or instructions and doesn't understand them, or completely disagrees with recommendations."

The facilitator asked the Maintenance group what they typically do to respond to the reports or instructional procedures. Their responses were straightforward. The facilitator recorded them in the B's Actions (Maintenance Actions) box:

Tells Engineering that the reports are okay.

Covers up disagreement or the embarrassment of not understanding.

Does not follow up on recommendations

Acts on experience, not instructions.

When Engineering staff hear from Maintenance that their reports and recommendations are accepted, but don't see them followed or done correctly, then there is a negative impact on how Engineering views Maintenance. The Engineering group filled in its Impact on A (Impact on Engineering) box accordingly: "Sees Maintenance as incompetent and inadequately trained."

The facilitator began the second loop by asking Engineering staff how they responded to Maintenance when something went wrong. They talked about the different strategies they used to get Maintenance to comply with the necessary rules and procedures. Their increased pressure for compliance was experienced by Maintenance as blaming and punishing. Maintenance began to see Engineering as an internal police force ready to point out any and all mistakes. In return, Maintenance blamed Engineering for "low" quality work. They started to avoid the Engineering staff. The avoidance behavior was interpreted by Engineering as a lack of support for their expertise and value in the organization. They responded by pressuring the level of authority above Maintenance. Their efforts only served to reinforce the Maintenance staff's perception that Engineering was a police force.

The facilitator recorded their responses and completed the map as illustrated in Exhibit A.4.

The end result of the mapping exercise was that the members of each department saw that they were making similar claims of incompetence about the other and devaluing the role of the other in the organization.

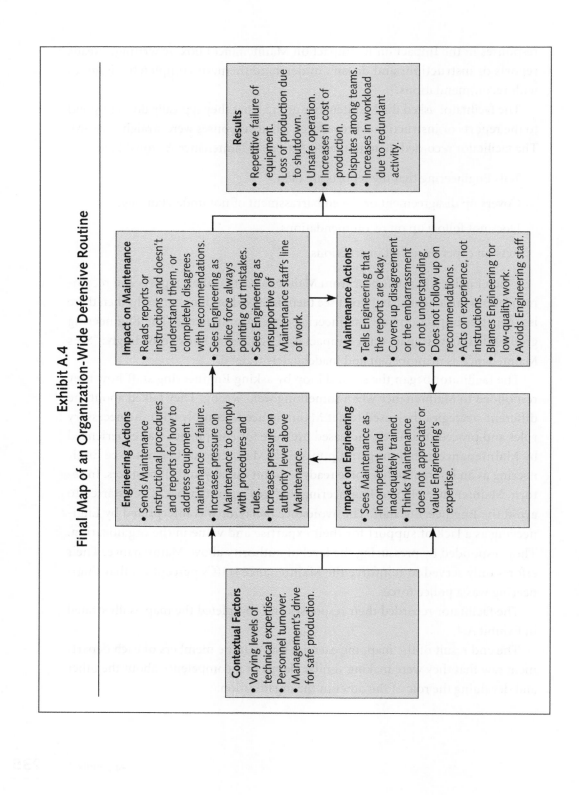

Exhibit A.4

Final Map of an Organization-Wide Defensive Routine

Contextual Factors
- Varying levels of technical expertise.
- Personnel turnover.
- Management's drive for safe production.

Engineering Actions
- Sends Maintenance instructional procedures and reports for how to address equipment maintenance or failure.
- Increases pressure on Maintenance to comply with procedures and rules.
- Increases pressure on authority level above Maintenance.

Impact on Maintenance
- Reads reports or instructions and doesn't understand them, or completely disagrees with recommendations.
- Sees Engineering as police force always pointing out mistakes.
- Sees Engineering as unsupportive of Maintenance staff's line of work.

Impact on Engineering
- Sees Maintenance as incompetent and inadequately trained.
- Thinks Maintenance does not appreciate or value Engineering's expertise.

Maintenance Actions
- Tells Engineering that the reports are okay.
- Covers up disagreement or the embarrassment of not understanding.
- Does not follow up on recommendations.
- Acts on experience, not instructions.
- Blames Engineering for low-quality work.
- Avoids Engineering staff.

Results
- Repetitive failure of equipment.
- Loss of production due to shutdown.
- Unsafe operation.
- Increases in cost of production.
- Disputes among teams.
- Increases in workload due to redundant activity.

Exercise

Going Forward

As a follow-up to the construction and discussion of maps, the following questions bring closure to the session and help participants think about the future.

1. Given the contextual factors and how A and B interacted, do you see how the impact and actions created results no one intended or desired? If you don't see how they created them, how do you see it?

2. How could you think differently in the future that might prevent what occurred?

3. What could you have done differently that might have prevented what occurred?

4. How do you see your role and responsibility differently now?

5. How do you see others' role and responsibility differently now?

⌇

The logistics for constructing the maps are fairly simple and follow a predictable method. In and of themselves, maps will not eliminate the existence of defensive routines. Maps of interpersonal, team, and organization-wide defensive routines serve as a starting point for conversation. Conversations about defensive routines aren't always simple or easy, but when conducted in the spirit of the Mutual Learning Model, they stand a better change of success.

For additional information on mapping, go to the Action Design website: www.actiondesign.com. More important, take the opportunity to increase your skill by attending the Action Design Institute.

APPENDIX B:
STRATEGIES FOR CASE STUDY GROUPS

The key to a successful application of any skill set is practice, practice, and more practice. Practice is best conducted in a group setting where participants can experiment with new behaviors, exercise their skills, and receive productive feedback in an environment of trust, safety, and learning. The object and focus of a study group is the LHC-RHC case study. The following are guidelines for setting up case study groups and structuring the sessions.

GROUP STRUCTURE AND PROCESS

Ideally, case study groups should consist of six to seven participants. An hour and a half is a comfortable time period to discuss a case. One person comes prepared with a case and a copy for everyone in the group. The case writer uses the LHC-RHC format and picks a recent conversation in which he or she got stuck or didn't achieve his or her desired results.

The group begins by reading the case study. Once everyone has read the case study, the case writer answers the question, "What kind of help would you like?" The case writer's answer serves to focus the help the group will offer. The group can also ask the case writer any questions about the business context or conversation. There is always a temptation to ask for a lot of contextual information, but loading up on contextual information can burn up a lot of time and often causes participants to slip into problem solving. The group will probably never have enough information or expertise to solve the problem, so it is important to limit the amount of time discussing the context. The goal of a study group is not to solve the business problem but to practice the skills. The group should limit questions about context to those that would help the group or case writer practice the skills. Often groups find they can move more efficiently through the case without knowing a lot about the context.

The following are a few helpful facilitation hints and general guidelines for study groups:

- When people appear off track from the case study, ask "What are the implications for the case study given what you are saying?"

- When people start pitching in to "help" the case writer and the case writer doesn't respond to the suggestions or repeatedly says "I've tried that," it is time to switch the focus off the group and ask the case writer, "What is going on in your LHC?" or "What is it about the group's comments that is not helpful?"

- When group members start talking about themselves and how they would act, ask them, "Where do you see the case writer doing that?" Ask people to model what they would actually say if they were the case writer. As a general rule, participants should always try to role-play exactly what they would say, rather than describe an abstract strategy or approach.

The case writer closes the study group session by reflecting on such questions as the following:

What are the key things you learned from the discussion that you'd like to go forward with?

What did you find helpful from the group, and what was not as helpful?

Is this what you had in mind when you requested a focus on the case?

Even though the focus of the study group is on the case writer, group interactions are potential opportunities for reflection. If it is possible to do so, tape-recording the group sessions is extremely useful, for two reasons. First, the case writer owns the tape. He or she is relieved of taking notes, but can refer to the tape later. Second, and more important, the tape recorder captures live, hard conversational data. If the group gets stuck in its own interactions, there is an undisputed recording of the data that provides a valuable opportunity for reflection. The recording can either be played back during the session or be transcribed so that the group can later reflect on its own practice of the skills.

STRATEGIES FOR CASE REFLECTION

There are several different ways to reflect on a case; we look at four strategies in this section. Each approach addresses a different skill set, concept, or diagnostic ability. Using different approaches helps keep the group fresh and engaged in learning. Regardless of which strategy you use, the session starts with a diagnosis of the case.

Diagnosing the Case Study

The following diagram illustrates a simple process to use for case diagnosis:

Results

Start by describing the results of the conversation. Results can be described, for example, as "Failed to communicate my view fully" or "Stalemate; agreed to disagree." If group members volunteer results, be sure to check back with the case writer to see if he or she accepts their suggested result or wants to modify it.

Action

Although the results were neither desired nor intended, they came about through a series of interactions between the case writer and the opposing character in the case study. Along with the group, the case writer reflects on what was said or done and what was not said, but was felt and thought privately. This stage is primarily diagnostic; it is not prescriptive, and the group does not engage in problem solving.

The group describes the case writer's actions. The group can practice good advocacy skills by avoiding any of its own high-level, abstract assertions, such as "You shut the person down." A simple, good start is to go through each line of dialogue and identify all questions as inquiries (I) and all statements as advocacies (A). Next, review the quality of each inquiry or advocacy. Low-quality advocacies are general, vague, and abstract, whereas high quality advocacies make explicit the person's reasoning, or steps on the Ladder of Inference.

Low-quality inquiries are usually leading questions, or they elicit abstract information, whereas high quality inquiries yield information low on the Ladder of Inference.

After a review, the group discusses the following question: To what extent does the quality of the advocacy or inquiry help us explain the result?" This question can be applied to the overall quality of advocacies and inquiries in the case study or the specific ones that mark a critical incident in the conversation.

Thinking

The case writer's thinking is recorded in the LHC of the case study. By reviewing his or her thinking, the group will be able to make the connection between the Thinking box and the Action box. The connection should demonstrate an internal reasonableness to the case writer's actions, given how he or she was thinking.

After the initial diagnosis, the group is ready to help the case writer practice using the skills to see if he or she can create different results.

Strategy 1

This strategy helps group members practice their advocacy and inquiry skills. The case writer can experiment with multiple approaches to the conversation by sampling the group's interventions and testing to see if they generate different results.

1. After the group has diagnosed the case, the case writer selects a point in the conversation where he or she would like to do something different. Everyone in the group writes down what he or she would say differently using high quality advocacies or inquiries. Group members must write down the actual words that would be said, rather than an abstract strategy, such as "offer a compromise."

2. Break the group into pairs or trios and share with each other their attempts to practice the skills. Each pair or trio then selects what it thinks is the best representation of the skills and transcribes it on a flip chart. The chosen version can be an exact replication of one person's attempt or a modification based on the subgroup's discussion.

3. Once the pairs or trios have written their modifications on the flip charts, the whole group reviews each pair or trio's work (the quality of the inquiries and advocacies) and tries to predict the results. Ask the case writer what he or she likes the best and why.

Strategy 2

This second strategy uses the Ladder of Inference as a reflective and action tool.

1. After the group has diagnosed the case, the case writer selects one abstract conclusion from his or her LHC or RHC. On a flip chart, draw the pool of data and a Ladder of Inference with a space for each step: select data, add meaning and interpret data, and draw conclusion. The group asks the case writer questions that help him or her down the Ladder of Inference. Record the case writer's responses in the spaces for each appropriate step on the ladder. The group can go through this process to chart more than one Ladder of Inference, as it is likely there are multiple Ladders of Inference in the case study. *Caution:* the group can construct the Ladder of Inference only for the case writer. The opposing character in the case study is unlikely to be available to answer questions, so it is difficult to construct a Ladder of Inference for the other character. The exception is if the conversation is a transcription of the actual conversation and there is sufficient information on the RHC of the opposing character to fill in all the rungs on the ladder.

2. Once the group has charted one or more Ladders of Inference, members split up into small groups. Each small group works with one of the ladders and writes a high quality advocacy statement using the steps in the Ladder of Inference. A high quality advocacy is one in which the steps of the ladder are visible. Each subgroup writes the high quality advocacy statements on a flip chart.

3. The large group reviews the quality of the advocacy statements by asking the following questions:

> What is the data in this advocacy? How could it be verified independently of the person's conclusion?
>
> Is the advocacy illustrated with examples?
>
> Are the steps in the ladder visible?
>
> If this advocacy was said, what could you predict as possible results?
>
> If you were on the receiving end of this advocacy, what might be in your LHC?

Strategy 3

This third approach focuses on the case writer's LHC. With the help of the group, the case writer works on how he or she can reframe his and her thinking in order to act differently.

1. After diagnosing the case, look at the case writer's LHC for examples that would answer the following kinds of questions:

   What are the case writer's concerns about the other person?

   What are the key ways the case writer is evaluating the other person?

   What kind of information remains in the LHC and is not expressed? For example: "She is in the way." "She doesn't get our new relationship." "She can be manipulative." "She is blaming me unfairly."

2. Make a list of how the case writer sees himself or herself, the other person, and the task. For example:

   Self: I am right

       I am looking out for the good of the company.

   Other: He is wrong.

       He is only out for his own self-interest.

   Task: Convince him.

       Block his efforts to get his own way.

   When discussing the case writer's LHC, the participants need to watch out for how they make their own inferences about what is in the case writer's LHC. A good practice is to always ground comments in the "data" of the case—that is, what is actually written in the case study LHC. Someone making an inference should claim it as his or her own and check with the case writer to see if he or she would agree with or modify the inference.

3. Reframe how the case writer sees himself or herself, the other person, and the task. For example:

   Self: I could be right, but also missing something.

   Other: He might be seeing something I don't. He has positive intentions.

   Task: Ask him a question to learn more.

   Try to come up with as many reframes as possible.

4. The case writer starts at the place in the conversation where he or she wants to insert a new frame of thinking. The case writer selects another group member to play the "other" in the case study and starts a role play. The role play runs until the case writer gets stuck or arrives at a satisfying result.

5. If the case writer slips back into the old frame, stop the action and reflect on what is going on in the conversation. If the conversation takes a new direction, reflect on what actions (what the case writer said or did) created different results.

Role playing allows the group to experiment with alternative ways of acting. This is a critical phase in skill building. The group needs to resist the temptation to either problem-solve or give abstract advice like "Make a high quality inquiry" or "You should be less political." Members should encourage each other to role-play different approaches as much as possible, so that the case writer and members of the group practice what they would actually say or do.

Strategy 4

1. After diagnosing the case by evaluating the quality of the advocacies and inquiries, go immediately into a role play.

2. In this approach, the case writer plays the other person in the case, and one of the group members volunteers to play the case writer's role. Before conducting the role play, the group member interviews the case writer about how he or she typically responds to the other person in the case and how he or she tends to act under stress or in a disagreement.

3. Pick up the dialogue in the case study at the beginning. Read the first few lines, but then drop the case study and improvise the conversation. If at any point the group member playing the case writer deviates too far from the case writer's character, the case writer can break the role play and give instructions on how he or she would typically respond. Resume the role play and stop after a few minutes or if the conversation gets stuck. Ask the case writer any of the following questions:

   What was in your LHC as you experienced yourself being played by another person?

   What impacts did the person playing you have on you?

   Is it likely that those impacts may have been similar to the actual impacts you had on the other person in the case study?

Another approach is to ask the group to take on the role of the other person and share the likely impact of the case writer's actions upon them. In other words, what might have been on their LHC after reading what the case writer had done or said?

4. After discussing the likely impacts, return to the dialogue and discuss how what was said could have had those kinds of impacts. Again, it is helpful to the case writer to be specific and to ground comments in the data of the case study. For example, it is not helpful for a group member to say, "If I was the other person, I would have withdrawn because you were just plain rude." A more helpful, grounded comment would be something like "When you said, 'Look, it is obvious that this is the only way to go with this project,' I could imagine someone having a difficult time disagreeing, and if so, he or she might appear stupid in your eyes for not seeing the obvious."

5. Locate a critical incident in the case and ask the case writer to state what his or her intentions were in saying what he or she did, and restart the conversation. In the second role play, have the case writer play himself or herself and try new behavior that uses the skills of the Mutual Learning Model.

BIBLIOGRAPHY

Arend, J. Ardon. *Leadership and Interventions in Dynamically Complex Change Processes.* Amsterdam: Free University, forthcoming.

Argyris, Chris. *Overcoming Organizational Defenses: Facilitating Organizational Learning.* Upper Saddle River, N.J.: Prentice Hall, 1990.

Argyris, Chris. "Teaching Smart People How to Learn." *Harvard Business Review,* May-June 1991, *69*(3), 99–109.

Argyris, Chris. *Knowledge in Action: A Guide to Overcoming Barriers to Organizational Change.* San Francisco: Jossey-Bass, 1993.

Argyris, Chris. "Good Communication That Blocks Learning." *Harvard Business Review,* July-Aug. 1994, *72*(4), 77–85.

Argyris, Chris. *Flawed Advice and the Management Trap.* New York: Oxford University Press, 2000.

Argyris, Chris. "Double-Loop Learning, Teaching, and Research." *Academy of Management Learning and Education,* 2002, *1*(2), 206–218.

Argyris, Chris. "Reflection and Beyond in Research on Organizational Learning." *Management Learning,* 2004, *35*(4), 507–509.

Argyris, Chris, and Donald Schön. *Theory in Practice: Increasing Professional Effectiveness.* San Francisco: Jossey-Bass, 1978.

Bain, Alastair. "Social Defenses Against Organizational Learning." *Human Relations,* 1998, *51*(3), 413–429.

Barnes, William, Myles Gartland, and Martin Stack. "Old Habits Did Hard: Path Dependency and Behavioral Lock-In." *Journal of Economic Issues,* 2004, *38*(2), 371–377.

Beer, Michael. "Organizational Diagnosis: Its Role in Organizational Learning." *Journal of Counseling and Development,* 1993, *71*(7), 642–650.

Bill, David. "What Are the Socio-Psychological Sources of Information Restriction Within an Organization?" *Centurion Systems.* www.centurionsys.com/rtcl56.html. Aug. 7, 1997.

Bokeno, Michael R. "The Work of Chris Argyris as Critical Organization Practice." *Journal of Organizational Change Management,* 2003, *16*(1), 633–649.

Choo, Chun. "Information Failures and Organizational Disasters." *MIT Sloan Management Review,* 2005, *46*(3), 8–10. http//sloanreview.mit.edu/smr/issue/2005/spring/03/.

Church, Allan H. "From Both Sides Now: Organizational Learning." (Society for Industrial-Organization Psychology). *TIP: Quarterly News,* Oct. 1997. http://siop.org.

Coutts, Rev. Peter. "An Introduction to Organizational Defensive Routines." Paper prepared for St. Andrew's Presbyterian Church, Calgary. www.telusplanet.net/public/pdcoutts/leadership/orgldefenses.htm. July 7, 2000.

Crossan, Mary. "Altering Theories of Learning and Action: An Interview with Chris Argyris." *Academy of Executive Management,* May 2003, *17*(2), 40–46.

Goleman, Daniel. *Emotional Intelligence.* New York: Bantam Books, 1995.

Hargrove, Robert. *Masterful Coaching Fieldbook.* San Francisco: Jossey-Bass, 1999.

Henfridsson, Ola, and Anders Söderholm. "On Organizational Defenses and Vicious Circles in Technological Adaptation." *Accounting, Management and Technological Information Technologies,* 2000, *10,* 33–51.

Isaacs, William N. "Taking Flight: Dialogue, Collective Thinking, and Organizational Learning." *Organizational Dynamics,* 1993, *22*(2), 24–39.

Johnson, Lauren Keller. "Combating Defensive Reasoning." *Harvard Management Update,* Mar. 2005, *10*(3), 3–4.

Kanter, Rosabeth M. "Leaders with Passion, Conviction, and Confidence Can Use Several Techniques to Take Charge of Change Rather Than React to It." *Ivey Business Journal,* May/June 2000, pp. 32–36.

Martin, Roger. "Changing the Mind of the Corporation." *Harvard Business Review,* Nov.-Dec. 1993, *71*(6), 81–94.

Martin, Roger. *The Responsibility Virus.* New York: Basic Books, 2002.

McArthur, Philip, Robert Putnam, and Diana McLain Smith. "Climbing out of the Muck" and "The Muck Stops Here." In Peter M. Senge and others, *The Dance of Change.* New York: Doubleday, 1999. Also available at www.actiondesign.com.

McKenna, Stephen. "The Business Impact of Management Attitudes Towards Dealing with Conflict: A Cross-Cultural Assessment." *Journal of Managerial Psychology,* 1995, *10*(7), 22–27.

Putnam, Robert. "Unlocking Organizational Routines." *The Systems Thinker,* Aug. 1993, *4*(6), 1–4.

Putnam, Robert. "Recipes and Reflective Learning: What Would Prevent You From Saying It That Way?" In Donald Schön (ed.), *The Reflective Turn.* New York: Teachers College Press, 1991.

Rahim, M. Afzaur. "Toward a Theory of Managing Organizational Conflict." *International Journal of Conflict Management,* 2002, *13*(3), 60–90.

Reed, George, Craig Bullis, Ruth Collins, and Christopher Paparone. "Mapping the Route of Leadership Education: Caution Ahead." *Parameters,* Autumn 2004, pp. 46–60. www.carlisle.army.mil/usawc/Parameters/04autumn/reed.htm.

Roberts, Charlotte. "Can We Talk?" *Journal for Quality and Participation,* Jul.-Aug. 1998, *21*(4), 4–8.

Rudolph, Jenny, Steven. S. Taylor, and Erica Foldy. "Collaborative Off-Line Reflection: A Way to Develop Skill in Action Science and Action Inquiry." In P. Reason and H. Bradbury (eds.), *Handbook of Action Research.* Thousand Oaks, Calif.: Sage, 2001.

Schein, Edgar H. "On Dialogue, Culture, and Organizational Learning." *Organizational Dynamics,* Autumn 1993, *22*(2), 40–51.

Schein, Edgar H. *The Corporate Culture Survival Guide: Sense and Nonsense About Culture Change.* San Francisco: Jossey-Bass, 1999.

Schein, Edgar H. "Organization Development and the Study of Organizational Culture." *Organization Development and Change,* Summer 1990. www.aom.pace.edu/odc/newsletters/SUM90.htm#OD>.

Schein, Edgar H. "How Can Organizations Learn Faster?" *Sloan Management Review,* 1993, *34*(2), 85–92.

Senge, Peter M. "Team Learning." *McKinsley Quarterly,* 1991, *2*(2), 82–93.

Senge, Peter M. "Taking Personal Change Seriously: The Impact of Organizational Learning on Management Practice." *Academy of Executive Management,* 2003, *17*(2), 47–51.

Seo, Myeong-Gu. "Overcoming Emotional Barriers, Political Obstacles in the Action-science Approach to Individual and Organizational Learning." *Academy of Executive Management,* 2003, *2*(1), 7–21.

Smith, Diana McLain. "Keeping a Strategic Dialogue Moving." In P. S. Brown and R. Wiig (eds.), *Corporate Communication: A Strategic Approach to Building Reputation.* Oslo, Norway: Gyldendal Norsk Forlag, 2002. Also available at www.actiondesign.com.

Staebler Tardino, Vicki M., Kimberlee A. Einspahr, Dean N. Daniel, and Thomas J. Kramer. "Bridging Organizational Learning Theory and Practice: Case Study of the Action Map Process." *Bridging Theory and Practice,* 2002, pp. 1–31.

Stark, Mallory. "Surfacing Your Underground Organization." *Harvard Business School Working Knowledge,* Nov. 1, 2004. http://hbswk.hbs.edu/item.jhtml?id=4456&t=organizations&nl=y.

Stone, Douglas, Bruce Patton, and Shelia Heen. *Difficult Conversations: How to Discuss What Matters Most.* New York: Viking Penguin, 1999.

Sun, Peter Y-T., and John L. Scott. "An Investigation of Barriers to Knowledge Transfer." *Journal of Knowledge Management,* 2005, *9*(2), 75–90.

Taylor, Steven. "Presentational Form in First Person Research: Off-Line Collaborative Reflection Using Art." *Action Research,* 2004, *2*(1), 71–88.

Wastell, David G. "Learning Dysfunctions in Information Systems Development: Overcoming the Social Defenses with Transitional Objects." *MIS Quarterly,* Dec. 1999, *23*(4), 581–600.

Zell, Deone. "Overcoming Barriers to Work Innovations." *Organizational Dynamics,* 2001, *30*(1), 77–86.

INDEX

A

Ability, direct questioning of, case involving, 49–51

Acceptance, 126

Accountability: issue of, 94–95; meaning of, 187; mutual, 126, 186–187

Action Design, 16, 108, 112, 130, 143, 158, 159, 165, 183, 213, 215, 237

Action Design Institute, 73, 158, 207, 237

Action science, 6, 7

Action-Impact map, 112, *227, 236*

Action-Impact mapping template: for manager-team interaction, 222–228; for the organizational level, 228, *229,* 230–235

Actions: alternative, beginning, with curiosity, 142; capturing our, 133–135; chicken-and-egg type of question involving, 173; committing to new, with the certainty of help from others, 187; corrective, benefits of, 182; describing, for case diagnosis, 241–242; gap between intentions and, 166–167; influence of thinking on, 111; monitoring our, requirement for, 136; new, changes in thinking allowing for, 128, 157, 159; and Newton's third law of motion, 113; pausing and holding off on, 185;

proposing, 143–144, 145; resistance to proposed, addressing, 146; shared, creating, 139; stopping the, 155. *See also* Impact and contribution; Thinking-Action map; Thinking-Action mapping template

Advanced Action Design Institute, 158

Advocacy: described, 29; mapping, 226; purpose of, 18. *See also* High quality advocacy

Advocacy and inquiry: balancing, 33–35, 170, 200, 205; in crafting interventions, exercise involving, 148; described, 29; experimenting with the quality of, 192; as a foundational skill, 16; identifying all forms of, during case diagnostic process, 241–242; mapping, 225; mistakes made in modeling, 196–197; purpose of, 18; skills in, practicing, in case study groups, 242; transferring the skill set of, 190. *See also* Advocacy; Inquiry

Advocacy statement, 150

Alcoholics Anonymous (AA) slogan, 163, 165, 178

Alertness, new state of, 168–169, 171

Alignment, issue of, 139, 168

Animation, loss of, 5

Arabian culture, 71, 90–91

Argyris, C., 3, 4, 5, 6–7, 11, 12, 15, 16, 18, 35, 64, 66, 69, 73, 74, 82, 92, 93, 98, 99, 112, 125, 130, 133, 138, 153, 156, 158, 159, 164, 177, 179, 185, 188, 189, 190, 207, 213

Argyris, D., 158

Arrogance, assumption reflecting, example of, 158–159

Asian cultures, 75

Assuming partiality, *23*, 35, 142, 162–165, 183

Assumptions: alternative, making, 172; about conflict, 137; about drawing conclusions, 228; embedded, 19, 144, 147–148; false, 163, 182, 208, 230; implicit, example of, reflecting arrogance, 158–159; about intentions, 93–94, 130, 166, 172–173; large-scale, ability to change, 119; and mapping interpersonal defensive routines, 220; neutral, making, 173; of the obviousness of our thinking, 165; about roles and responsibilities, 111; and selecting data, 149; unfair, 161

Authority, relationships with, issue of, 71, 75

Avoidance, 68–69

AWARE, 20, 21

Awareness: of differences, 154; human, limits of, 131–132, 167; lack of, addressing, opportunity for, 223; of the Ladder of Inference, 141; of trigger points, 20, 44–45, 59, 169; of the Unilateral Control Model, 74; unlearning something outside our, difficulty of, 133

B

Babson College, 73

Background story, telling the, 106

Bad news, delivering, strategy of, 85

BALANCE, 29, 30

Balancing advocacy and inquiry, 33–35, 170, 200, 205

Behavior: new, learning, through practice, 6–7; unproductive, escalating cycles of, caught up in, 3, 4–5. *See also specific behaviors*

Biondi, M., 133

Blaming: curtailing, in facilitated dialogue, 223; mapping, 235; in organizational culture, 186; reducing tendency toward, 112; refraining from, as a ground rule for mapping, 230; spotting, 130; stopping, result of, 126; when mistakes are made, 181–182

Blindness, 131–132, 167, 168, 172, 213, 223

Bracketing defensive reactions, 184–185

Brainstorming, use of, 231, 233

Brevity, in paraphrasing, 151

Broad overview vs. details, questions of, case involving, 201–203

Business problems, identifying, 230–231, 233

Bypass strategies: and assuming a false humility, 164; common forms of, 82–92; exercise involving, 92; mapping, 113; purpose of, 81–82; reflecting on, 137; reinforcing, 93–99; scenario involving, 79–81; that have backfired, example of, 158; used by change agents, 125–126

C

"Calvin and Hobbes" (cartoon), 153

Case studies: reflecting practitioner mistakes, 193–207; writing, 134–135. *See also* LHC-RHC case studies

Case study groups: strategies for, 241–246; structure of, and process guidelines, 239–240; use of, 134–135

Catch-22, 178, 182, 208

Causal explanations: inventing, 95–96, 144, 220; trading, 145

Certainty, high degree of, holding a, 68

Change: ability to, as requisite for de-escalation, 119; beginning, by taking the initiative to do something different, 127; chicken-and-egg type of question involving, 173; fundamental, of thinking, 183; gradual, of thinking, 159–160; greatest leverage for, 13; in habits of thought, aspects of, 128; incentives for, 129–131; instant, of thinking, 157–159; internal commitment to, 127; long-term and productive, 129; reality of, adapting to, 68

Change agents, criticism of, 125–126

Characters, using, to learn from, 10–11. *See also* "Fix It Now or Fix It Later" scenarios

Chicken-and-egg question, 173

Childlike emotional mode, 58

Chinese social reality, 89

Choices, offering, 74

Christian scriptures, 94

Cognitive competence, 190

Command-and-control management style, 125

Communication: basic dilemma of, 19; poor, escalating error and, 128; quality of our, improving, importance of, 13, 15

Competence, cognitive, required of practitioners, 190

Competency, sense of: eroding our, 180–181; false, hiding a, 181; threatened, understanding, 44, 182. *See also* Threat and embarrassment, conditions of

Conclusions, drawing: and advocacy, 30; and arguing them, 145; in case study

groups, 243; and conflict between them, 28; as inferences, recognizing, 163–164; and the Ladder of Inference, 22, *23*, 24, 25, 26, 27, 28; making assumptions about, 228; variations on, 143–144

Conflict: assumptions about, 137; benefiting from, 137–138; between conclusions, 28; of personality, writing off defensive routines as a, 138

Consideration, taking the past into, 187

Contextual factors, identifying, 231–232, 234, *236*

Contribution to defensive routines. *See* Impact and contribution

Control: default response to being out of, 160; exercise of, by management, problem with, 125; giving false assurances of, 126; vs. influence, 126–127; mechanical, 124

Control, being in: belief about, when using theory, 209, 210; exercise involving, 76; scenario involving, 61–64. *See also* Unilateral Control Model

Conversational data, 31, 106, 110, 170, 216

Conversations: balance in, 34; basic units of, 29; conducted in the spirit of the Mutual Learning Model, 237; ongoing, having, and clear contracting, 187; quality of our, improving, importance of, 13, 15, 213; recalling, 31–32; recording, practice of, 134, 193, 216, 222, 223, 240; starting point for, maps serving as, 237. *See also* Facilitated dialogue; Point-counterpoint conversations

Correction, opportunity for, gaining, 169

Covering up, 82, 92–93, 125–126, 137, 182, 184, 227, 228

Critical feedback: demeanor while receiving, 210–211; LHC-RHC case study involving, 217–219

Critical thinking skills, use of, 127, 128
Cronkite, W., 163
Culter, J., 213
Cultural history, organizational, 117
Cultural meaning, Western, attached to making mistakes, 179
Cultural norms, effect of, 67, 71, 75, 76, 89, 90–91
Cultural precepts, 90
Curiosity: beginning alternative action with, 142; as the driver of discovery, 156; fostering, 164; having, as a ground rule for mapping, 230; shift to, 155, 185; stage for, 232

D

Data: characteristics of, 23, 149; conversational, 31, 106, 110, 170, 216; eliciting, 106–107; grounding comments in the, during case study groups, 244, 246; pool of, 23, 24, 243. *See also* Information; Interpreting data and adding meaning; Selecting data
Data document, use of a, 222
Day-to-day errors, unnoticed, 178–179
Decision making: better, information leading to, 32, 33; delay in, 116, 145; poor, dynamic resulting in, 117, 128; prolonging, 72
De-escalation: change requisite for, 119; commitment needed for, 120; incentives for engaging in, 129–132; and inviting reflection, 132–140; key to, 127; as not about fixing something, 124–127; and the power of reflection, 127–128; realization leading to, 123–124; scenario involving, 121–123
Default state of mind, 66, 160, 213
Defense, just cause for, 58

Defensive routines. *See* Organizational defensive routines
Delivering bad news, strategy of, 85
Denial, 72, 73–74
Details vs. broad overview, question of, case involving, 201–203
Diagnosing case studies, 241–242
Dialogue. *See* Conversations; Facilitated dialogue
Differences in views, as a constant theme, 56–57. *See also* Engaging differences
Dilemmas, managing, 138–140, 201–203
Direct questioning of ability, case involving, 49–51
Disconnection, exact point of, locating, 162
Dishonesty, issue of, 86–87
Double-loop learning, 15–16, 141, 157. *See also* Mutual Learning Model
Doubt, importance of, 163–164
Dueling ladders, 26–27

E

Easing-in strategy, 82–83, 113, 200
Egos, using, as an excuse, 138
Einstein, A., 128
Embarrassment, understanding, 43–44. *See also* Threat and embarrassment, conditions of
Emotional Intelligence (Goleman), 57
Emotional temperature, rising, case involving, 45–48
Emotions: covering up, revealed during mapping, 227, 228; having different, 65; reflection on the role of, mistakes in responding to, case involving, 194–198; role of, 57–58; suppression of, 68–69; surrounding discovery of a mistake, 180; venting, benefit of, 106, 185

Engaging differences: by adopting a learning stance, 153–155; as an alternative action, 141; by beginning with curiosity, 142; four step process for, 155–156; using the advanced version of the Ladder of Inference for, 143–152; willingness for, 137

Entitlement, 89–90

Epicurus, 6

Errors. *See* Mistakes and errors

Escalation, potential, promise of, 75. *See also* De-escalation

Evaluating, 143, 144, 145

Examples, offering, 31, 85

Exit strategy, 178

Expectations: dropping, 161; measuring up to, issue of, 90–91, 92

Experimentation: improvement through, 213; scientific principles of, applying, 164, 172; and skill transfer, 190, 191, 192; using a group setting for, 239, 245

Explaining, 95–96, 143, 144, 145, 220

F

Face, meaning of, 89–90

Face-saving strategy: backfired, 158; cultural norms for, 90–91; described, 88–89; mapping, 113; Western reaction to, 92

Facilitated dialogue: as an intervention strategy, 104, 105; in mapping defensive routines, 222, 223, 227–228, 234–235

Facilitated reflection, mistakes made during, case study involving, 194–198

Facts vs. inferences, 22, 28–29, 114, 125

False assumptions: being "mugged" by, 163; learning from, 182, 230; not testing, 208

False competency, hiding a, 181

False humility, 164

Favoritism, guarding against, 111, 160, 216

Fears, covering up, revealed during mapping, 227, 228

Feedback: demeanor while receiving, 210–211; failure in presenting, 179; initiating, with leading questions, issue with, 200; in interviews, 107; LHC-RHC case study involving, 217–219; using a group setting for receiving, 239; in workshops, asking for, 206–207

Feelings and emotions. *See* Emotions

Fictional narrative, using, to learn from, 9–10. *See also* "Fix It Now or Fix It Later" scenarios

Fifth Discipline Fieldbook, The (Senge), 33

"Fight-or-flight mode," 44, 57, 184

Filters, 220

"Fix It Now or Fix It Later" scenarios: and being in control, 61–64; and bypass tactics, 79–81; and conditions of threat and embarrassment, 39–42; and de-escalation, 121–123; mapping the, 112–119; using, to learn from, 7, 9

Fixing defensive routines, believing in, problem with, 124–127

Fixing metaphor, limits of the, 124–126

Flawed Advice (Argyris), 125

Follett, M. P., 138, 140

Forgiveness: appropriate candidates for, 166; little evidence of, 97; unwilling to extend, 181–182

Foundational skill set. *See* Advocacy and inquiry; Ladder of Inference; Left Hand Column (LHC)

Frame of mind: access to, 107, 108, 113; eliciting a person's, 106, 107–110

Freudian slip, 21–22

G

Gap, spotting the, 130–131, 166–167
Gestalt therapy technique, 186
"Get rid of it" reaction, 72, 74
Godfather, The (movie), 129
Goleman, D., 57–58
Granting legitimacy, 160–162, 183–184
Greek Stoics, 126
Grilled for information, getting, case of, 48–49
Ground rules, 197, 230
Group discussions vs. private interviews, 105–106
Groups, breaking into, for mapping, 230
Groups, study. *See* Case study groups

H

"Hard data" document, use of a, 222
Help from others: enlisting, 135–136, 185; promise of, 187; reliance on, 165; requesting, strategy of, 83–85, 113
Helping practitioners teach others. *See* Practitioners as teachers
Helplessness, 98–99, 124
High quality advocacy: attempting, in role playing, 192; benefits of, 29; crafting, 170; and dealing with bypass strategies, 85, 87; described, 30–32; to engage differences, 141; identifying, during case diagnostic process, 241; meaning behind, 35–36; practicing, in case study groups, 242, 243; and shift in thinking, 162
High quality inquiry: and assuming partiality, 163; attempting, in role playing, 192; benefits of, 29; and dealing with bypass strategies, 85, 87; described, 32–33; to engage differences, 141; 145–146, 153, 154–155; identifying, during case diagnostic process, 242; in interviews, 106, 110; meaning behind,

35–36; practicing, in case study groups, 242; and reflection, 128
History: claiming there's a, 97–98; established, of dysfunctional behavior, and reciprocity, 172
Ho, D. Y., 89, 91, 100
Holding others accountable, 94–95
Home free, coasting, mistaken belief in, case involving, 193–198
Honesty, issue with, 71–72, 86
Humanity, endearing feature of, 187
Humility, virtue of, 164, 168, 186, 209
Hybrid model, 213
Hypotheses, ideas as, 164

I

Impact and contribution: acknowledging our, 167–171, 173, 184, 186, 187; avoiding our own, 181; discussing, in case study groups, 245, 246; meaning of, 168; practitioners staying alert to unintended, importance of, 206–207; reflecting on, when mapping manager-team interaction, 223; registering the, 170, 173; responsibility to talk about another's, 166, 173; seeing each other's, 217. *See also* Action-Impact map; Action-Impact mapping template
Impact, physical, characteristics of, 167–168
Implementation, effective, likelihood of, increasing, 32, 33
Inaction, 98
Incompetence, skilled, 178–179
Inconsistent messages: sending, strategy of, 85–86; types of, 86–88; and using false humility, 164
Inferences, making. *See* Ladder of Inference
Influence vs. control, 126–127
Information: leading to better decision making, 32, 33; organizing, 110–112. *See also* Data; Mapping

Ingenuity, 3

Injustice, confronting, 116

Inner critic: as an obstacle to learning, 180, 186; quelling the, 185–186

Innovation, 3

Inquiry: described, 29; to discover others' Ladder of Inference, 170; exercises using, to engage differences, 147, 148–149, 149–150; genuine, lack of, 125; lack of, 219; and learning from mistakes, 183–184; line of, pursing a, 156; and mapping interpersonal defensive routines, 220; muddled instructions for exercise on using, case of, 203–206; in paraphrasing, 151; purpose of, 18; reasonableness waiting to be discovered through, 165; reflection on the process of, mistakes in responding to, case involving, 194–198. *See also* Advocacy and inquiry; High quality inquiry

Insanity, 178

Instructions, muddled, case of, 203–206

Intentions: categorizing views on, 108; gap between, and actions, 166–167; making assumptions about, 93–94, 130, 166, 172–173; mismatch between results and, occurrence of, 177, 178, 179, 180; positive, attributing, 165–167, 172–173, 184; practitioner, questioning of, mistakes in responding to, cases involving, 193–207; reacting to misinterpretation of, 170; signaling, 154

Intergroup conflict, turning dilemmas into, 138, 139

Interpersonal defensive routines, mapping, 113–116, 215–221, 237

Interpersonal relationships, dynamic motion of, 111

Interpreting data and adding meaning: and the advanced version of the Ladder of Inference, 143; in case study groups, 243; difference in, understanding, 162; discovering others' means of, 170; and the Ladder of Inference, *23*, 24, 25, 26, 27, 28, 30; and mapping interpersonal defensive routines, 220; moving down the ladder to, 146; naming as, 147–149, 156; paraphrasing as, 150–152, 156

Interruptions, as a strategy, 87–88, 153

Interventions, strategic. *See* Interviews; Mapping

Interviews, 104, 105, 105–110

Inventing motives, 93–94

J

Joyce, J., 182

Judgments, making, issue of, 90–91, 114, 125, 127, 130

JUMP, 22, 23

Justice, pursuit of, 6, 161

K

Knots, massaging, 104, 110

Knowledge for Action (Argyris), 177

Knowledge, purpose of, 6

L

Ladder of Inference: in action, 18; advanced version of the, using the, 143–152; and advocacy, 30, 31; awareness of the, 141; as a critical thinking tool, 128; described, 21–29; exercises involving the, 146, 147, 148–149, 149–150, 151–152; as a foundational skill, 16; gaining insights into an individual's, 106; good reminder to return to the, 162; hazards of arguing from atop the, 145–146; interjecting doubt or mistrust of your, importance of, 163–164; low level on the, example of, 150; neutral terms provided by the, 216–217; presentations on the, learning from, 207; as productive, 85; purpose of the, 17; questions to discover others', 170; and a shared reasoning process, 161; and strategies for case study groups, 242, 243; teaching the, 189–190; trading abstract conclusions from atop the, 113; as a tuning device, 142; visibility of the, in role playing, 192

Ladders: dueling, 26–27; multiple, 27–28, 243; rungs on, 24, 27

Lattice Partners, 213

Leadership, senior, participation of, 138

Leading questions: and bypass strategies, 83, 85, 200; case involving, 198–201; and inquiry quality, 242; mapping, 113, 220, 225, 226; that come to mind when others make mistakes, 181

Learning: appetite for, 142; consideration for, 87; continual process of unlearning and, 132, 133; crucibles for, 58–59; double-loop, 15–16, 141, 157; from the dying, 132, 136, 137; environment of, 239; from experienced practitioners, 207–208; explicit contract for, 210; inhibiting, 137; lifelong pursuit of, 173; in the moment, 135–136; as a mutual agreement, 202; mutual, dance of reflection and, first step in the, 168; obstacle to, 72, 208; promoting, technique for, 35; reflective, failure to contract with another person for, effect of, 209; required, limiting, 76; skill transfer essential to, 190; staple of, 133. *See also* Mistakes, learning from; Mutual Learning Model

Learning agreements, 202

Learning stance: adopting a, 153–155, 184, 213, 217; remaining in the, issue of, 193

Left Hand Column (LHC): access to frame of mind in the, 107, 108, 113; and advocacy and inquiry, 29; and being rational and avoiding upset, 69; blurting out comments from the, during an evaluation, inviting, 135; common types of thinking in the, providing a list of, 201; and denial, 73; described, 18–21; focus on the, in case study groups, 243–244; as a foundational skill, 16; gaining insights into an individual's, 106; and holding others accountable, 95; increasing toxicity of the, mapping the, 114; inventing causal explanations in the, 96; organizing the, 108, 109; productive use of the, 141; purpose of the, 17; and requesting help, 84; teaching the, 189; unfreezing the, 130–131. *See also* LHC-RHC case studies

Legitimacy, granting, 160–162, 183–184

Letting go, 126

LHC-RHC case studies: accessing private thinking from, 108, 113; comparing columns in, 131; involving conditions of threat and embarrassment, 45–47, 48–49, 50–51, 52, 53, 54; as the object and focus of study groups, 239, 240; and practitioner mistakes, 194–196; process for writing, 134–135; study groups using, process and strategies for, 239, 240, 241–246; and the Unilateral Control Model, 73; for use in mapping defensive routines, 216, 218–219; writing and reviewing one's own, 92

Lies, telling, strategy involving, 86–87

150–152, 156; exercise on, muddling the instructions for, case involving, 203–206; in mapping, 217, 223; in our own minds, 24; when using thought enablers, 170, 173

Partiality, assuming, *23*, 35, 142, 162–165, 183

"Peanuts" (cartoon), 181

Pedagogical approach, versatility in, importance of, 190

Perpetuating defensive routines, 5, 125

Personal responsibility, distancing ourselves from, 5

Personal triggers. *See* Trigger points

Personality conflicts, writing off defensive routines as, 138

Philosophy, study of, 5–6

Physical cues, being alert to, 171, 184–185

"Pick your battles" recommendation, issue with the, 75

Pilot workshops, cases from, 193–207

Point-counterpoint conversations, 17, 28, 113, 116, 147, 154, 155, 160, 171. *See also* Stalemates

Politeness, misguided, 70

Positive intent, attributing, 165–167, 172–173, 184

Practice: gap between theory and, 130–131; habits of, engaging in, 7, 157, 189, 207–208, 213–214, 239, 240

Practitioners as teachers: challenges facing, overview of, 189–190; competencies and abilities required of, 190–192; experienced, learning from, 207–208; mistakes made by, cases reflecting, 193–207; and moving from the script to modeling the skills, 192–193; tips for, on becoming skill proficient and facing challenges, 207–211

Private assessments, mapping, 219–220, 227, 228

Private interviews vs. group discussions, 105–106

Private thinking. *See* Left Hand Column (LHC)

Problem solving, limited, 145

Productivity, lost, 72, 117

Proposing action, 143–144

Protective strategies, as a constant theme, 57–58, 103. *See also* Bypass strategies; Control, being in

Public speaking skills, importance of, 190, 193

Punishment: and acknowledging impact, 170; for being on top of the ladder, 27; and ground rules, 230; for making mistakes, 177, 180, 181, 182, 183, 184; mapping, 235; for misunderstandings, 198; practitioner use of, as a sign of not using theory, 210

Putnam, R., 16, 207, 209, 211

Puzzles: maps as, 230; mistakes as, 182–188

Q

Questions: rhetorical, using, 199, 200, 219, 225; why, issue of, 33, 49. *See also* Inquiry; Leading questions

Quick thinking, issue with, 22

R

Rather, D., 163

Rational, remaining, 68–69

Reality: of change, adapting to, 68; inaccurate interpretation of, 98–99; of our actions, being subjected to the, 134; outside, inability to acknowledge the difference between our view and, 163; social, Chinese, 89

Real-time help, enlisting, 135–136

Real-time reflection, demonstrating, 193

Real-time situations, ability to model the skills in, importance of, 190

Reasonableness: acknowledgment of, 160, 161, 162; assuming, as a ground rule for mapping, 230; discovering others', 183; listening for, 169; waiting to be discovered, 165

Recall, 31–32, 106

Receiving end, being on the, of others' actions, 169–170

Recipes, reliance on, 209

Reciprocity, 91, 171–172

Recouping ability, 184

Reflection: alternative avenue into, 134–135; artifacts for, 18, 192, 193; in case study groups, 240, 241–246; commitment to, sustaining, 119; dance of, and mutual learning, first step in the, 168; facilitated, mistakes made during, case study involving, 194–198; failure to contract with another person for, effect of, 209; importance of, 120; invitation to, 132–140, 154; journey of, embarking on the, 123–124; lack of, after making mistakes, 178; and the Ladder of Inference, *23*; mirrored, 165; pausing for, 116, 171; power of, 127–128; real-time, demonstrating, 193; reasons for engaging in, 129–132, 214; as requisite, 6; team, 136–138; on trigger points, 185. *See also* Left Hand Column (LHC)

Reframing, 159, 244

Reinforcing defensive routines, 93–99

Repeated patterns, 220

Repetition, 67

Replication, 192

Reputation on the line, case involving, 51–53

Requesting help, strategy of, 83–85, 113

Resignation, 98

Resistance: addressing, 146; understanding, 165

Respecting others' views, issue with, 71, 76

Responsibility: assumptions about, coming to the table with, 111; categorizing views on, 108; issue of, and holding others accountable, 95, 114; to learn from mistakes, 184; mapping, 118, 233; personal, distancing ourselves from, 5; to talk about the impact of another's actions, 166

Results: describing, for case diagnosis, 241; effective, likelihood of, increasing, 33; identifying, 231, 234, *236*; mismatch between intentions and, occurrence of, 177, 178, 179, 180

Rhetorical questions, use of, 199, 200, 219, 225

Riceour, P., 8

Right Hand Column (RHC), 18, 19, 131. *See also* LHC-RHC case studies

Rogers, W., 68

Role playing, 191–192, 240, 244–245, 246

Roles: assumptions about, coming to the table with, 111; categorizing views on, 108; mapping, 118, 233

Romans 7:19, 166

S

Safety, environment of, 239

St. Paul, 166

Saudi Arabia, culture of, 71, 90–91

Saving face. *See* Face-saving strategy

Schön, D., 11, 15, 16, 18, 130

Selecting data: and the advanced version of the Ladder of Inference, 143, 149–150; in case study groups, 243; discovering others' means of, 170; and the Ladder of Inference, *23*, 24, 25, 26, 27, 28, 30; moving down the ladder to, 146

Selective listening, 150, 221

Self category, 108, 109

Self-discovery, journey of, embarking on, 132, 214

Self-fulfilling prophecies, defensive routines becoming, 97–98

Self-referential logic, 97

Self-reflection: beginning the journey toward, reason for, 123; challenge of, 133; full commitment to, aspects of, 132–136; importance of, 120; offering to help others with, 132; reasons for committing to, 129–132, 214. *See also* Reflection

Senge, P. M., 33, 130, 140

Senior leadership, participation of, 138

Shared actions, creating, 139

Shared meaning: creating, 139; making assumptions about, 144, 147–148

Shared reasoning process, 161

Shell Oil Company's Learning and Transformation Services, 7

Silence, 92, 116, 137, 226

Simulation, use of, 191

Skill transfer, 190, 191. *See also* Experimentation; Modeling

Skilled incompetence, 178–179

Smith, D. M., 16, 28, 158, 183, 184, 207

Social face, 90. *See also* Face-saving strategy

Social justice, pursuit of, 6

Social reality, 89, 90

Social virtues, 69–72, 75, 86, 87, 158

Socrates, 120

Socratic method, 200

Stalemates, 28, 145, 241. *See also* Point-counterpoint conversations

STATE and ASK, 35

Statements, making. *See* Advocacy

STEP process, 155–156

Storytelling, use of, 8–9, 96–97

Strategic interventions. *See* Interviews; Mapping

Stravinsky, I., 182

Stress, effect of, 160

Study groups. *See* Case study groups

Subjectivity, 131

Successful organizations, hallmarks of, 3

Supporting others, issue with, 69–70, 76, 158

Systems thinking discipline, 33

T

"Taking Personal Change Seriously" (Senge), 130

Task category, 108, 109

Teachers, helping practitioners be. *See* Practitioners as teachers

Teaching style, being questioned about, mistakes in responding to, case involving, 198–201

Team defensive routines, mapping, 116–117, 222–228, 237

Team efficiency, reduced, 145

Team polarization, 145

Team reflection, 136–138

Tension, escalation of, potential, promise of, 75

Theory: in practice, gap between espoused theory and, 130–131; using, issues with, 208–211

Thinking: agility of, 164; chicken-and-egg type of question involving, 173; critical, use of, 127, 128; different, effect of, 157; fundamental change of, 183; gradual change of, 159–160; influence of, on actions, 111; instant change of, 157–159; limits of our, acknowledging the, *23*, 35, 163–164; obviousness of our, assumption of the, 165; one-sided, 67–68; outside the box, 3; partiality of our, acknowledging, 35,

142, 162–165, 183; quick, 22; recording, for case diagnosis, 242; shifts of, 128, 159, 161–162, 166, 172–173; toxic, 20, 106, 110, 217; win-lose, 66–68, 74–75, 93, 123, 128, 145

Thinking models, 16, 64. *See also* Mutual Learning Model; Unilateral Control Model

Thinking privately. *See* Left Hand Column (LHC)

Thinking-Action map, 112, *115, 117, 119, 221, 236*

Thinking-Action mapping template: for interpersonal defensive routines, 215–221; issue of using, for mapping manager-team interaction, 222; for the organizational level, 228, *229,* 230–235

Third party, use of a, 104, 105. *See also* Facilitated dialogue; Interviews; Mapping

Thomas Aquinas, 7

Thought enablers: acknowledging impact and contribution as, 167–171, 184; assuming partiality as, 162–165, 183; attributing positive intent as, 165–167, 184; drawing on, to learn from mistakes, 183–184; exercise involving use of, 172–173; gradually changing thinking with use of, 159–160; granting legitimacy as, 160–162, 183–184; instantly changing thinking without use of, 157–159; need for, 157; working with, 171–173

Threat and embarrassment, conditions of: activating, by talking about undiscussables, 112; and admitting one's impact and contribution, 168; and being in control, 64, 65, 69, 74; breeding grounds for, 68, 182; and bypass

strategies, 81, 86, 89, 91, 92, 125, 137, 158; case studies of, 45–55; changing the default response to, 160; constant themes featured in, 55–58; as crucibles for learning, 58–59; denial leading to, 73; difficulty identifying errors and mistakes in, 177; exercises involving, 59; faced by beginning practitioners, 207–208; in facilitated dialogue, addressing, 223; first level of protection against, 181; and "getting help" discovering mistakes, 209; as just cause for defense, 58; potential, features of, 43–45; presence of the "expert" inducing, 210; reaction to, 3, 4, 103, 182; scenario involving, 39–42; ubiquity of, 129

Threats, understanding, 44

Time constraints, 198

Time management, importance of, in conducting workshops, 199

Time period, for case study group discussion, 239

Toxic thinking, 20, 106, 110, 217

Toxic work environment, 5, 98

Trigger points: awareness of, 20, 44–45, 59, 169; having different, 65; identifying, 107, 113; mapping the, *115,* 221; reflecting on, 185; respective actions serving as, realization of, 123; and talking about mistakes, 182

Trust, environment of, 239

Twain, M., 27

U

Understanding: advocating for, 150; asking for, 145–146; assuming mutual, 228; as the basis for taking accountability, 187; deeper, fostering, 153, 157; mutual, conversation yielding, 170

SYSTEM REQUIREMENTS

PC with Microsoft Windows 98SE or later
Mac with Apple OS version 8.6 or later

USING THE DVD

To view the items on the DVD, follow these steps:

1. Insert the DVD into your computer's CD-ROM drive or into your DVD player.

2. If you do not have autorun enabled on your computer, or if the autorun window does not appear, follow these steps to access the DVD:

   - Click Start→Run.

   - In the dialog box that appears, type d:\start.exe, where d is the letter of your CD-ROM drive. This brings up the autorun window described in the preceding set of steps.

   - Choose the desired option from the menu.

IN CASE OF TROUBLE

If you experience difficulty using the DVD, please follow these steps:

1. Make sure your hardware and systems configurations conform to the systems requirements noted under "System Requirements" above.

2. Review the installation procedure for your type of hardware and operating system. It is possible to reinstall the software if necessary.

To speak with someone in Product Technical Support, call 800-762-2974 or 317-572-3994 Monday through Friday from 8:30 A.M. to 5:00 P.M. EST. You can also contact Product Technical Support and get support information through our website at www.wiley.com/techsupport.

Before calling or writing, please have the following information available:

- Type of computer and operating system.
- Any error messages displayed.
- Complete description of the problem.

It is best if you are sitting at your computer when making the call.

Printed and bound by CPI Group (UK) Ltd, Croydon, CR0 4YY

23/04/2025

14660933-0001